THE CRIMMIGRANT OTHER

Western societies are immersed in debates about immigration and illegality. This book examines these processes and outlines how the figure of the "crimmigrant other" has emerged not only as a central object of media and political discourse, but also as a distinct penal subject connecting migration and the logic of criminalisation and insecurity. Illegality defines not only a quality of certain acts, but becomes an existential condition, which shapes the daily lives of large groups within the society. Drawing on rich empirical material from national and international contexts, Katja Franko outlines the social production of the crimmigrant other as a multi-layered phenomenon that is deeply rooted in the intricate connections between law, scientific knowledge, bureaucratic practices, politics, and popular discourse.

Katja Franko is Professor of Criminology at University of Oslo, Norway. She has published widely on issues of globalisation, border control, criminalisation of migration, and surveillance of everyday life. She is among others the author of *Globalization and Crime* (Sage Publications) and *The Borders of Punishment* (co-edited with M. Bosworth, Oxford University Press).

KEY IDEAS IN CRIMINOLOGY

Key Ideas in Criminology explores the major concepts, issues, debates and controversies in criminology. The series aims to provide authoritative essays on central topics within the broader area of criminology. Each book adopts a strong individual 'line', constituting original essays rather than literature surveys, and offer lively and agenda setting treatments of their subject matter.

These books will appeal to students, teachers and researchers in criminology, sociology, social policy, cultural studies, law and political science.

Series Editor

Tim Newburn is Professor of Criminology and Social Policy, Director of the Mannheim Centre for Criminology, London School of Economics and President of the British Society of Criminology. He has written and researched widely on issues of crime and justice.

Other titles in the series:

John Pratt: Penal Populism
Tony Ward & Shadd Maruna: Rehabilitation
Lucia Zedner: Security
Benjamin Goold: Surveillance
Claire Renzetti: Feminist Criminology
Ian Loader and Richard Sparks: Public Criminology?
Michael Kempa and Clifford Shearing: Policing
Alex Alvarez: Genocidal Crimes
Walter S. DeKeseredy: Contemporary Critical Criminology
Katja Franko: The Crimmigrant Other

THE CRIMMIGRANT OTHER

Migration and Penal Power

Katja Franko

Routledge
Taylor & Francis Group

LONDON AND NEW YORK

First published 2020
by Routledge
2 Park Square, Milton Park, Abingdon, Oxon OX14 4RN

and by Routledge
52 Vanderbilt Avenue, New York, NY 10017

Routledge is an imprint of the Taylor & Francis Group, an informa business

British Library Cataloguing-in-Publication Data
A catalogue record for this book is available from the British Library

Library of Congress Cataloging-in-Publication Data
A catalog record has been requested for this book

ISBN: 978-1-138-54596-0 (hbk)
ISBN: 978-1-138-54597-7 (pbk)
ISBN: 978-1-351-00144-1 (ebk)

Typeset in Bembo
by Taylor & Francis Books

To my parents

You who are so-called illegal aliens must know that no human being is illegal. That is a contradiction in terms. Human beings can be beautiful or more beautiful, they can be fat or skinny, they can be right or wrong, but illegal? How can a human being be illegal?

Ellie Wiesel (writer, Nobel Peace Prize winner, and Holocaust survivor)

And isn't that the kind of thing that we fear strangers will do? Disturb. Betray. Prove they are not like us? That is why it is so hard to know what to do with them.

Toni Morrison (2017: 34)

CONTENTS

ILLUSTRATIONS

Figures

Tables

ACKNOWLEDGMENTS

Writing this book has been a long process. Perhaps its origins can be even traced back to the time of my first encounters as an immigrant with a host state. Perhaps it was the memory of sitting in a police station in Oslo and reflecting on the difference between the bright room with a waterfall dedicated to Norwegian passport applicants and the dark corridor in which I was waiting for hours for my residence permit that awoke my initial curiosity. My fascination with these yearly bureaucratic rituals was such that I continued performing them for several years even after I could have obtained a permanent residence permit. The friendly, but inquisitive police officers who interviewed my husband and myself on suspicion of pro forma marriage probably added to this sociological curiosity.

In practical terms, this book would not have been possible without a research project, generously funded by the European Research Council. Its grant gave me not only the luxury of dedicating myself to a topic over a long period of time, but also the possibility to work with a unique team of colleagues: Helene O. I. Gundhus, Thomas Ugelvik, Sigmund Book Mohn, Nicolay B. Johansen, Anette Vestby, Synnøve Jahnsen, Kristin K. Slettvåg, Kjersti Strømnes, Linda Gulli, Elisabeth Mork, Jenny Maria Lundgaard, Marit Fosse, and Julie Estdahl Stuestøl. The book is therefore a result of collective work, not only in a practical sense, but above all intellectually. Our weekly lunches and conversations have been an enormous source of inspiration.

More recently, I have been fortunate to be a part of another inspiring research project, Nordhost, where conversations with Trygve Wyller, Vanessa Barker, Maartje van Der Woude, Thomas Hylland Eriksen, Arne Johan Vetlesen, Dorina Damsa, Cathrine Thorleifsson, Synnøve Bendixen, Kaja Rønsdal, and others, have greatly expanded my understanding of the (in)hospitality towards migrants in Nordic societies. A big thank you is also owed to Mary Bosworth at the Centre for Criminology in Oxford for her intellectual companionship and wide-ranging conversations on this project. The Department of Criminology and Sociology of Law at the University of Oslo has been my institutional home for almost a quarter of a century. I am enormously grateful to my PhD supervisor, Nils Christie, whose work has in several ways inspired this book (even though he might have disagreed with its conclusions). My sincere thanks go especially to my colleagues Per Jørgen Ystehede, Heidi Mork Lomell, Erlend Paasche, May-Len Skilbrei, Lill Scherdin, and, above all, to Helene Gundhus, who heroically commented on the last draft during her holidays.

The findings of this book have been presented at numerous academic events and lectures, as well as seminars and talks given to police and immigration authorities in Norway. The book has greatly benefited from their critical feedback. A huge thank you is also owed to the men and women who have agreed to talk to us during this project. Without them the book would not have been possible.

Several ideas presented in this book have been previously published. Short segments from Chapter 1 have been published in two papers: "The Body Does Not Lie", in *Crime, Media, Culture* (2(2): 143–158), and "The Bordered and the Ordered Society", in *The Borders of Punishment: Migration, Citizenship, and Social Exclusion* (co-edited with Mary Bosworth and published in 2013 by Oxford University Press). Parts of Chapter 3 and Chapter 5 are based on ideas developed in an article, 'Bordered Penality; Precarious membership and abnormal justice', published in *Punishment & Society* 16(5): 520–541, while ideas presented in Chapter 4 developed from a joint essay written with Helene O.I. Gundhus (published in the *British Journal of Criminology,* 55(1):1–18). I am grateful for permission to reprint copyright material.

A huge thank you is also owed to Thomas Sutton at Routledge for his enormous patience and his belief in this project; Daphne Day for her expedient editing; and Lise Martens for her wise advice.

Most of all I am grateful to my family; to Øyvind Næss for always being there, for his wonderful cooking, humour, and intellectual critique; and to Eva, Maria, and Mona for bringing so much joy into our lives. The writing of this book has been marked by many painful absences – most of all Barbro's – and by the death of my grandparents, Vida and Iztok. The book is dedicated to my parents, Danica and Janez.

Oslo, August 2019

INTRODUCTION

In early September 2015, the death of a three-year-old Syrian boy, Alan Kurdi, made headlines worldwide and seemed to stir the conscience of the public and politicians in Europe. The boy's body was washed onto the Turkish coast after the small overcrowded boat, in which he and his family were trying to reach Europe, capsized shortly after it set off. The moving image of Kurdi's death symbolised the plight of Syrian refugees and the brutal death toll of their dangerous journeys to Europe. For a short moment it created an impression that European responses to sea-crossing asylum seekers would be based on humanity and compassion. The British Prime Minister, David Cameron, declared that he was deeply moved by the image and that Britain was a moral nation and would "fulfil its moral responsibilities".[1] Similarly, French President François Hollande made an impassioned statement:

> Is there anybody on the planet who could not be moved by what they saw in the papers – anybody with a sense of humanity – who saw the body of a young boy washed up on a beach like driftwood. This is a human catastrophe.[2]

However, today, both the image and the political promises it prompted seem all but forgotten. Kurdi's tragic death has been overshadowed by other more potent narratives about migration. The terrorist attacks in Paris in November the same year, the outrage provoked by sexual assaults during New Year's Eve celebrations in Cologne, and numerous other events, have been catalysts shifting the tone of political and media discourse. Rather than being perceived as people who are need protection and who should appeal to our humanitarian and moral sensibilities, migrants are increasingly associated with notions of fear, chaos, anger, danger and a need for control. Unwanted migration thus elicits coercive responses involving the use not only of penal but also of military power. For example, in July 2017, the Austrian defence minister announced that four armoured personnel carriers had been sent to his country's border with Italy to prevent the arrival of North African migrants and that 750 troops were on standby.[3] Such measures no longer raise eyebrows or attract much attention in the current political climate. As one of the responses to the 2015 refugee crisis, NATO naval vessels began to patrol the Mediterranean. Symbolic and real measures to close and militarise the border have become routine in European politics. And, although the tragic death toll in the Mediterranean continues, in fact, rose dramatically in the years following Kurdi's death,[4] Europe has responded with ever more stringent border closures and by outsourcing its migration burdens to neighbouring countries.

International migration presents us with one of the most challenging political and ethical dilemmas of our time. It is the area in which rhetorical battles are lost and won. These battles are, on both sides, fought by invoking images of suffering and appealing to moral sentiments, protection, identity, and justice. This book is an attempt to understand this battlefield. More precisely, it is an attempt to examine a puzzle: why is Europe, despite its acute awareness of its humanitarian ideals and moral responsibilities, nevertheless consistently opting for border closure? How does this leap from humanitarian ideals to border closure come about? No doubt there are several answers to the puzzle, which can and have been found in the realms of ethics and political philosophy (see, inter alia, Honig, 2001; Carens, 2015; Miller, 2016), sociological analysis (Anderson, 2013; Collier, 2013; Barker, 2018), and law (Dauvergne, 2008; Dembour, 2015). This book, however, suggests that an essential element for solving the puzzle is to understand the notion of immigrant criminality; this is vital if one is to understand the perceived legitimacy of social exclusion in societies, and in a continent, with a vivid humanitarian self-perception.

The meeting of European countries and large migration flows is essentially mediated through a discourse of insecurity, criminality and criminalisation. As Paul d'Auchamp, Office of the High Commissioner for Human Rights observed: "Within the EU policy context, irregular migration remains largely viewed as a security concern that must be stopped. This is fundamentally at odds with the human rights approach."[5] Instead of adopting the discourse of rights, humanitarian principles, and the rule of law, on which it based much of its postwar identity, Europe has ultimately chosen to set these aside and focus on issues of crime and insecurity. In the past two decades, stricter border controls, and reliance on penal measures such as detention, policing, and deportation, have thus become defining features of Europe's responses to migration. Such measures often, explicitly or implicitly, invoke the notion of immigrant criminality. Immigrants are no longer people in need of protection, or a potential source of labour; they have been turned into to rule-breakers and criminal offenders, or what can be termed "crimmigrant others". Their presence is associated with illegality and crime. This book documents how this change has come about. It charts a profound cultural reconfiguration of inclusionary and exclusionary rationalities, practices, and sentiments, and how questions of crime and punishment contribute to these processes. It outlines how the figure of the crimmigrant other has emerged as a central object of media and political discourse and state intervention. The book analyses the social processes which support, on a daily basis, the perpetual "production" of immigrant criminality.

It is important to note, though, that such processes are not only political, and do not provide support for a simplistic understanding, whereby the work of othering can be laid at the door of right-wing groups and populist political leaders such as Donald Trump and Hungary's Victor Orban, or other politicians of similar colours. The production of othering and immigrant criminality is a much more complex process, which has a long history, and has become deeply ingrained in the minutiae of state bureaucratic procedures. It does not occur only on social media platforms, in national political debates, or through international media outlets. This book shows that the "production" of the crimmigrant other is a multi-layered phenomenon, deeply rooted in the intricate connections between the law, scientific knowledge, bureaucratic practices, politics, media, and popular discourse. As a result, social exclusion and border closure become a seemingly natural response: the use of force and punishment is an obvious solution. The book's main argument is that the association between migration and crime serves as a central means to justify such exclusionary measures and, ultimately, their human costs. Through the myriad connections and associations between migration, criminality, and illegality, and through the construction of the crimmigrant other, policing, detention, deportation, and other penal measures, as well as military action, such as that taken by Austria and NATO, become normalised as means to control national borders and the boundaries of membership.

The crimmigrant other

One of defining features of the crimmigrant other is that he or she is unwanted, and unwanted not only by the proponents of restrictive border control measures. Liberal advocates of more humane border policies are also wary of the figure, which represents a challenge, since it taints the picture of migrants as innocent victims in need of help and deserving of hospitality. The notion of the criminal immigrant has therefore largely been avoided in academic discourse, rather than addressed head-on. This book is written in the belief that this omission should be corrected.

Giorgio Agamben's figure of the "homo sacer" (1998) has long been a point of reference for those trying to capture the condition of migrants' social marginality and exclusion from the sovereign state's sphere of bio-political protection. Images of Alan Kurdi and the thousands of other casualties of Western border policies (Weber and Pickering, 2011) are thus often seen as exemplifying the bare life described by Agamben. However, despite the power of its narrative, the homo sacer captures only one part of the story. It does not help us to account for the fervour with which the French president, François Hollande, and other Western leaders spoke of humanity. NGOs, human rights advocates, and other civil society actors have seen a remarkable growth of, and engagement in, welfare provision for migrants. Migration, like so many other issues, is enmeshed with humanitarian concerns and emotional displays of sympathy and humanity (Ticktin, 2011; Fassin, 2012). The banishment of migrants to the sphere of bare life is, therefore, by no means simple, but involves a complex set of rationalities which are full of moral judgments, ideology, appeals to a shared identity, and emotions. These issues are not fully addressed by the concept of the homo sacer, which in fact does little to help us understand the strength of feelings involved and the power of stories of othering.

The main premise of this book is that the exclusion of the immigrant is built on a complex set of divisions between insiders and outsiders, good and bad, deserving and undeserving, in which the notion of immigrant criminality does important discursive work. Today, the border is a site of a clash of moralities, with fights over conflicting notions of membership, identity, and what is right and good. The notion of the crimmigrant other is, therefore, central in justifying the use of increasingly coercive border control measures and in reversing Europe's tradition of strong commitment to human rights and humanitarian principles. Like such classic criminological and sociological figures as Georg Simmel's stranger (1964), Howard Becker's outsider (1963), Christie and Bruun's suitable enemy (1985) and Stan Cohen's folk devil (1972/2002), the crimmigrant other exemplifies how stories can be created about those who are considered different and as not fitting in the societies they inhabit. These stories translate challenging issues of social change into narratives about threat, danger, and moral decay. As a criminologist, I see the emotional debates raised by migration as reminiscent of past discussions about crime problems, such as those about illegal drugs. They are characterised by a similar sense of danger, and concern to reinstate the social order and protect a value system which is threatened by those who do not fit in. The state's coercive apparatus is then made use of to preserve the damaged fabric of social life.

The notion of the crimmigrant other helps us to understand better why, in such a social climate, migration and state penal power begin to come together. Increasingly, penal measures, police agencies and criminal justice institutions are employed to control unwanted migrants. This is the case throughout most of the Western world. Such developments are receiving growing academic attention (see, inter alia, Anderson, 2013;

Aas and Bosworth, 2013; Weber, 2013; Bosworth, 2014; Aliverti, 2013; Kaufman, 2015; Melossi, 2015; Mitsilegas, 2015; Barker, 2018). The book's primary aim is to capture the figure who is inspiring these developments.

Although writing about the crimmigrant other may be a way of approaching migration by starting from what Cohen (1972/2002) describes as "the layman's picture of the world", it should also be frankly acknowledged that the *crimmigrant other* is by no means an attractive term. Far from it – it is what Nils Christie (2009) might term a dangerous word. It has the potential to preclude a deeper understanding and prevent dialogue. It may well be misused in the overheated political climate. Notions of migrants as "criminal aliens", "bogus asylum seekers", and the like permeate political and (social) media discourse. The notion of the crimmigrant other is already present there. Its power to stereotype and misunderstand animates anti-immigration sentiment in numerous countries. For that very reason, rather than avoiding it, because it leaves a nasty taste in the mouth, this books aims to look into its "nastiness" and examine how this is created.

By proposing to examine the notion of the crimmigrant other, this book does not simply argue for a critical approach to the labelling of migrants as criminal offenders (the crim- part of the crimmigrant other). Instead, it aims to examine certain ontological assumptions that underpin the positioning of migrants as penal subjects. In her study of strangers and their embodiment in a community, Sarah Ahmed (2000: 3) challenges "the assumption that we can have an ontology of strangers". She argues that "an investment in strangerhood as an ontological condition" (ibid.: 5) marks both the fearful discourses of "stranger danger" and community safety, as well as discourses celebrating the love of the stranger as a basis for an ethics of alterity. Similarly, it could be argued that the investment in the category of the migrant as a distinct subject marks both nation-state definitions as well as a growing spectrum of humanitarian industries and other enterprises (Fassin, 2012; Fassin, 2014).

As a particular construction of the subject, the migrant is, as Basaran and Guild (2017: 272) point out, "anchored in statist imaginaries, and tied to particular spaces, movements and legal constructions". This book aims to examine these assumptions and shows how the figure of the migrant in itself is intimately connected to illegality. Such an approach aims to dig deeper than the most obvious aspects of association of migrants with illegality, such as the use of criminal law or stereotyping in the media discourse. It turns attention to the concepts of "illegality" and "crime" as well as the global structural conditions that divide global mobility into distinct categories of migrants and various categories of bona fide travellers, such as tourists, students, and business travellers (Aas, 2011). In this context of pervasive global inequality, the label migrant is, as Basaran and Guild (2017: 273) suggest, "reserved for those associated with particular origins and geographies. Embedded in colonial politics and sustained in post-colonial imaginaries".

Punishment and global society: crimmigration control and bordered penality.

According to several observers, the spheres of immigration control and crime control have traditionally been quite distinct (García Hernández, 2015). How the state addressed the question of crime was quite different to how it dealt with migration issues. In recent decades, however, the two have gradually been brought closer together by the growing use of penal measures for the purpose of border control, and vice versa. Juliet Stumpf (2006) was influential in describing the trend as a development of crimmigration law. This book will offer empirical material which illustrates many of these trends. It is a result of a five-year research project which sought to examine the use of penal power in Europe at national and supranational levels.

The story of the crimmigrant other is, then, a story of the growing intertwining of migration and punishment, and the changing meaning of punishment. Criminal law and immigration law share, as Stumpf (2006) observes, the social function of being the gatekeepers of membership. They have a crucial role in creating and enforcing the "us" and "them" division. According to Stumpf (ibid.: 38), the state's expression of moral condemnation is the same in immigration law as in criminal law and is now used, jointly, to reassure the public of its commitment to controlling crime. In the United States, while mass imprisonment disproportionately targets African Americans, 94 per cent of those deported for criminal violations are Latinos, who have become the paradigmatic "criminal alien" (Vazquez, 2012). The topic has been of growing interest to criminologists and students of punishment and society, as well as to a wide range of migration scholars. However, interdisciplinary conversations – like the coupling of migration and crime itself – are often uncomfortable. Crimmigration control is a process of intertwining and merging fields and entities which may not naturally fit together. While nation states across the Western world possess rhetorical power and self-assurance, and increasingly exercise their sovereign prerogative to control borders through the use of penal measures, we do not yet have an adequate vocabulary to interrogate these processes. This book aims to examine the apparent reasonableness of state-imposed categories and how and why they come about. Crimmigration may seem like a high-octane political tornado, which is fundamentally reshaping states' use of coercive measures, such as policing and imprisonment, but we seldom address the concept which is situated in the eye of the storm – quietly reposing in its very centre: the concept of immigrant criminality.

"We are being treated like criminals", "We are not terrorists", and "No human being is illegal" are complaints and slogans frequently heard at migrant rallies. They are at the heart of the book's subject matter. Such statements are sometimes mirrored by complaints by police officers who, rather than doing border control, would prefer to use their resources to catch "proper criminals" (Mohn, forthcoming). Also EU and UN bodies have consistently expressed unease with using the term "illegal migrant" (Council of Europe, 2006).[6] Taken together, they all suggest a sense of discomfort, a feeling that there is something not right about migrants being subjected to penal measures and treated "like criminals". So, then, the main questions posed in this book are: What is immigrant criminality? How is it made? Who are the actors involved in its production, and what are the social forces animating these processes? What kind of "work" does the crimmigrant other do in contemporary societies?

By asking these questions, the book builds on one of the central tenets of studies of the role of punishment in society, namely that the use of penal power is relatively autonomous of crime (Garland, 2013a: 24). As David Garland (ibid.) observes, from Durkheim onwards, most theoretical perspectives on punishment have been built on the axiom that

> [P]unishment's forms, functions and transformations are to be understood not (just) as an instrumental response to crime but as a constitutive aspect of larger social processes. … It is not "crime" that dictates penal laws, penal sentences, and penal policy decisions but rather the ways in which crime is socially perceived and problematized, together with the political and administrative decisions to which these reactions give rise.

The figure of the criminal immigrant has, undoubtedly, deep historical and cultural roots. One need only think of the entrenched perceptions of Jewish criminality that existed before the Second World War (Knepper, 2010). Similarly, in early 20th-century Chicago, "[f]oreigners were often depicted as possessing powerful criminal tendencies. For instance, fighting was seen as the national habit of the Irish, to the extent that bricks were popularly known as 'Irish confetti'" (Valier, 2003: 2; see also Melossi, 2003, 2015). Today, as in previous times, popular perceptions of and state responses to the problem are shaped by very specific social forces and developments, rather than the objective nature of immigrant criminality. They are deeply connected to issues of social solidarity, political economy, cultural norms, and perceptions of punitiveness and wrongdoing, as well as to everyday bureaucratic rationalities.

The subject of immigrant criminality demands critical examination of the law and its definitional powers. Contrary to popular belief, which sees the migrant as a figure inhabiting a space outside or beyond the scope of law – a state of exception – this book shows how the notion of immigrant criminality is painstakingly and systematically crafted through a myriad of rules and regulations. The crimmigrant other is illegalised and criminalised through the sustained and targeted use of the state's legal apparatus. Yet, although having an acute lack of rights, and being excluded from established notions of membership and justice (Dembour and Kelly, 2011; Dembour, 2015), the crimmigrant other's position cannot be simply described as extra-legal, since it is deeply involved with the contemporary transformations and functioning of the law.

Drawing on critical legal studies (Dauvergne, 2008), the book situates the notion of immigrant illegality within the context of global inequality where, through the definitional power of the law, large groups of non-western citizens are condemned to almost permanent illegality and subjected to a particular type of penal power, described as bordered penality (Aas, 2014). Such use of penal power is shaped by entrenched divisions between the global North and South. By coercively controlling mobility, affluent societies protect their membership as one of the most precious privileges still possessed by their citizens. Penal power is therefore used not only to protect access to welfare in affluent societies (Barker, 2018), but also to reassure those whose welfare rights have been eroded by the ravages of neoliberal policies that they still have their privileged position.

A defining feature of the crimmigrant other is, therefore, that he or she is not a member, or that his/her claim to membership is tenuous and can be revoked through the use of penal power. This type of penality, which is geared towards banishment and exclusion from the nation, represents a significant break from the ways in which penal power was used in the past. This is the case, even though (as pointed out above) the connection of punishment to wrongdoing has often been tenuous. Traditionally, its purpose has been either to redress harm, isolate the offender from society, or reform him/her – or all of these. Today the traditional purposes of punishment are increasingly being overshadowed by another objective: border control (Aas, 2014). The book shows how controlling unwanted mobility has become a driving force behind traditional penal strategies, such as imprisonment, as well as a driver of penal innovation (Bosworth, 2017).

The book is therefore also a story of how the role and nature of punishment is changing under conditions of globalisation and mass mobility. Penal power directed at crimmigrant others is fundamentally defined by the fact that those subjected to it, in formal (and often informal) terms, are perceived as non-members and that the mere fact of their subjection to it can destroy their aspirations to membership. The figure of the crimmigrant other, therefore, reveals a great deal about a number of fundamental social processes; the most notable of these is how lines are drawn between members and non-members and how limits are set to social solidarity. Although at first sight this book may appear to be about punishment, the law and social constructions of criminality, it is above all a book about social inequality and the contested nature of membership in contemporary societies.

The divided continent: penal power in contemporary Europe

It is important to bear in mind, however, that the processes described above do not only shape the meeting of the global North and South on the external borders of Europe. As we shall see, the crimmigrant other also reflects Europe's difficult relationship with its own diversity and its internal others (Barker, 2017). The book shows how the crimmigrant other has become a vehicle for managing the conflicted relationship between the West and the East (Neumann, 1999). Penal control of criminal immigrants becomes a means to achieve social control and exclusion in a continent seemingly committed to integration, unity, and internal freedom of movement, yet deeply at odds with certain populations within its own territory.

The mechanisms used to control the crimmigrant other thus reveal a great deal, not only about the deep divisions between the global North and South, but also about the fault lines which run across Europe. They reveal a divided continent where the Western half imprisons remarkably high numbers of foreign citizens, many of whom are Eastern European. In most countries the percentage of foreign prisoners does not exceed 5 per cent of the total prison population, but the figure in most Western European countries is well above 20 per cent, reaching 71.5 per cent in Switzerland, 54.7 per cent in Austria, and 52.7 per cent in Greece.[7]

For the purpose of this book, such figures serve as an illustration of the growing diversity of imprisoned populations and of the changing nature of the state-sanctioned use of force. Every day police forces in Scandinavia (Aas, 2014; Sausdal, 2018), the Netherlands (van der Woude and Brouwer, 2017), the UK, and numerous other countries, are preoccupied with catching, punishing, and deporting unwanted mobility from the East. This is, therefore, also a story about how the West controls the East through the deployment of penal power, and how the perceived criminogenic nature of the East serves as a way of creating boundaries within Europe and a rift in European identity.

Penal power is a form of state-sanctioned social exclusion. Its use is essentially connected to issues of morality and reveals the limits to solidarity in a given society. Drawing on Durkheim's classic work,

David Garland (2013a: 23) points out that "punishment must be understood as a *moral* institution, shaped by collective values and social relationships rather than an *instrumental* one shaped by the demands of crime control". This book aims to understand how notions of morality, social solidarity, and membership shape Western European responses to certain groups of Eastern European migrants. These classical themes in sociological accounts of the use of penal power thus become particularly salient when it comes to understanding contemporary Europe.

The story told in this book is thus quite different from the established criminological narratives about Europe, which stress its progressive commitment to human rights (Van Zyl Smit and Snacken, 2009) and penal welfarism (Smith and Ugelvik, 2017), together with its difference from the US and its punitive approach. This book, by contrast, describes a continent where the use of penal power is marked by the constant pushing of boundaries, and often a blatant disregard of human rights (Dembour, 2015). Instead of being a counter-pole to the US penal system, which has condemned racialised others to social exclusion on a massive scale, Europe, when it comes to migration, seems to display many similarities to America (Melossi, 2013b). In Europe of penal power over those deemed non-members is closely connected with social inequality, and driven by openly exclusionary rather than welfare rationalities. In order to protect their own welfare and affluence, European states use penal power at the border (Barker, 2018). The contrast is particularly striking when it comes to the Scandinavian countries, which have traditionally been seen as the champions of welfare-oriented penality, but which now display markedly different penal rationalities regarding those considered non-members (Aas, 2014; Todd-Kvam, 2018). Europe is a globally prosperous continent surrounded by war, dramatic population growth, and great social need. It is a Northern state – marked both by affluence and a willingness to protect this affluence by any means at its disposal, including drawing on its colonial legacies (Bosworth, 2017).

Today, Europe is a divided continent which stands at the crossroads in terms of how it lives up to its ideals and founding principles of free movement, and commitment to human rights and the rule of law. While it may seem that the discourses surrounding the crimmigrant other, exemplified by Brexit and resurgent nationalism and xenophobia

(Thorleifsson, 2019), are tearing the continent apart, this book suggests that this figure also has important constitutive qualities. It serves as a catalyst for a series of processes of constitution, which do not – as one might expect – relate only to the constitution of ideal and prototypical national identities. The control of the crimmigrant other also provides an impetus for further integration and strengthening of EU agencies such as Frontex, the recently revamped European Border and Coast Guard Agency. The book, therefore, seeks to understand how the crimmigrant other functions as a constitutive other (Neumann, 1999) in relation to various processes of integration identity building in contemporary Europe.

From old to new poor laws

The processes described in this book are by no means a historical novelty. The crimmigrant other has a number of predecessors and penal power has, in previous times too, been used to control mobility, particularly of poor populations. The prison itself came about as an institution aiming to control mobility of the poor (Melossi, 2013a). In the early days of the United States, Kristin O'Brasill-Kulfan (2019) shows how mobile poor migrants, such as work-seekers and escaped slaves, broke settlement laws and welfare policies and were subjected to punishment by the authorities. Also, in pre-industrial England, as Weber and Bowling (2008) point out, "masterless men" and "valiant beggars" were subjected to harsh measures designed to curtail their mobility. The Vagabonds and Beggars Act of 1494, for example, stated that:

> Vagabonds, idle and suspected persons shall be set in the stocks for three days and three nights and have none other sustenance but bread and water and then shall be put out of Town. Every beggar suitable to work shall resort to the Hundred where he last dwelled, is best known, or was born and there remain upon the pain aforesaid.

The poor laws functioned, as historian Gertrude Himmelfarb (1991) shows, as a system for controlling the poor and poor relief before the emergence of the welfare state. And, while this book describes a particular regime of sovereignty whereby modern states "return" unwanted bodies to their "proper sovereigns" (Walters, 2010), the system bears considerable similarity to those employed by parishes in pre-modern England and Norway, which returned unwanted paupers to their original parish. The historic archives of the Poor Authorities (Fattigvesenet) in the Norwegian capital Kristiania show how interviews and investigations were systematically conducted to "establish the home place" of the poor who were considered in the care of the state (Bergkvist, 2008). Such practices resemble contemporary state identification efforts described in this book.

The practice of driving the unwanted poor back to their place of origin, after first inflicting pain on them, is thus far from being an invention of contemporary states. Quite the opposite. States have always aimed to order people according to their prescribed identities. As James C. Scott (1998: 65) shows, the creation of legible people – "of fixing an individual's identity and linking him or her to a kin group" – has been a necessary precondition of modern statecraft (see also Caplan and Torpey, 2001). In line with these tendencies, contemporary states in the global North are developing an apparatus of growing sophistication for the purpose of the management and surveillance of movement across their borders. For this reason, instead of simply connecting the production of the crimmigrant other to the recent resurgence of nationalism, popular punitiveness and exclusionary sentiments towards migrants, the book describes how such processes are an inherent part of state bureaucratic rationalities, and fundamentally connected with the nature of state sovereignty.

The crimmigrant other does not represent a problem just for the state authorities attempting to control the unwanted movement of the poor from the global South and from poorer European countries. The phenomenon is also a conundrum for scholars attempting to understand the complex layers of othering involved in its production. He or she clearly belongs to the unwanted mobile populations which are perceived in legal and cultural terms as non-members of the societies they enter. However, another crucial aspect of their existence is that they have a number of other distinctive features: they are poor, racialised, and gendered. Historically, these features have shaped some of the techniques that can be seen as the precursors of contemporary crimmigration control. Penal transportation, for example, was a vital technology of punishment in England in the 17th and 18th centuries

(Feeley, 2002). This form of penal power, which exported Britain's social problems first to the North American colonies and then to Australia, has several things in common with contemporary forms of bordered penality (Bosworth et al., 2018). Like deportation today, transportation was a product of an unequal global order, and was shaped by the forces of colonialism (Anderson, 2016), which allow powerful states to co-opt less powerful states to help them address challenging social issues.

The processes of production of the crimmigrant other support Marxist accounts of penal power which focus on exploring the material foundations of life and explaining how economic forces and struggles against inequality generate and shape forms of penality (Calavita, 2005; Giorgi, 2013; Melossi, 2013a; Melossi et al., 2017). Processes of criminalisation are fundamentally connected to issues of class, economy, and welfare. Acknowledging the great importance of such perspectives, the book is based on the assumption that the conundrum of the crimmigrant other demands a multifaceted approach, which takes into account the materialities of global inequality and economic exploitation, the bureaucratic mentalities of the state, and more emotive aspects to do with issues of social solidarity and Europe's conflicted relationship with its own diversity. The story of the crimmigrant other is therefore not simply a story of the intertwining of immigration law and crime control. More importantly, it is a story about Europe's responses to global suffering and inequality, the exclusionary nature of its welfare states, and about internal European divisions between East and West. The book attempts to address the various forms of otherness embodied in the notion of the crimmigrant other. It also reflects on the conflicting relationship between the crimmigrant other and emerging humanitarian rationalities and forms of governance. Here, too, the conflict between the desire to help and the urge to control has several historic parallels in workhouses and other forms of relief, particularly those directed at children and minors (Himmelfarb, 1991).

Methods and structure of the book

The book is based on the findings of a six-year empirical project conducted between 2011 and 2017. The project consisted of several interrelated sub-projects which have been published separately and can offer a more in-depth understanding of the issues described in this book. The projects systematically examined various aspects of bordered penality, including imprisonment and detention (Ugelvik, 2012, 2013; Arentzen, 2013), policing (Aas and Gundhus, 2015; Gundhus, 2016; Gundhus and Franko, 2016 Mohn, forthcoming), deportation (Strømnes, 2013; Franko and Mohn, 2015), social exclusion (Johansen, 2013), punishment (Slettvåg, 2016), and penal culture (Johansen et al., 2013; Aas, 2014). The empirical findings presented in Chapter 3 and Chapter 4 draw on document analysis, observations, and interviews (conducted with Helene O.I. Gundhus, Anette Vestby, and Synnøve Jahnsen) with police officers, lawyers, and practitioners working in the field of border control in Norway, as well as in the European Border and Coast Guard Agency (Frontex).[8]

The book consists of five chapters and a conclusion. Chapter 1 has five subsections ("The crimmigrant body", "Illegality", "Deportability", "The spectacle", and "Knowledge"), and sets out the main traits and conditions which define the crimmigrant other as a distinctive penal subject. The crimmigrant body is marked and controlled by a series of technologies, such as fingerprinting, dental and skeletal identification, as well as by traditional policing and profiling technologies focused on race and ethnicity. His/her existence is, moreover, shaped by crime statistics and other types of knowledge practices and forms of expertise, as well as by heated media discourses about migration, crime, and terrorism. The chapter addresses the concept of "illegal migration" as the background for understanding immigrant illegality, and the centrality of immigration law in shaping the living conditions of non-citizens. In addition to illegality, deportability is the defining feature which shapes state coercive responses to migrants. Deportability is achieved through a series of state strategies and interventions, which include cooperating with third countries and enlisting private actors. It is also resisted through several counter-strategies, which will be addressed in the chapter.

Chapter 2 provides an overview of various facets of bordered penality and situates them within the novel penal rationalities that are geared towards territorial exclusion and cancellation of membership. The sovereign powers to punish and to banish thus become inextricably linked. The chapter consists of subsections ("Bordered penality", "Criminalisation", "Policing", "Imprisonment", "Deportation", "Penal alienage", and "Racialised otherness"), each representing an aspect of bordered penality. The concept of penal alienage is introduced to define the condition which results from the use of penal power for the purpose of questioning and, ultimately, for cancellation of membership. The chapter debates the crimmigration thesis, outlines the main points at which immigration law and criminal justice come together, and discusses the implications of these developments for our understanding of punishment and penal power. While this chapter presents the main theoretical contours of bordered penality, the chapter that follows it reveals how the crimmigrant other emerges as a result of penal interventions at the level of practice.

Chapter 3 offers an empirical analysis of bordered penality in Norway. At its peak in 2016, Norway deported over 8,000 people and can also in comparative terms be described as one of European "leaders" in the effectiveness of its deportation policies (Van Houte and Leerkes, 2019). The chapter outlines the political and bureaucratic processes which have in the past ten years led to the development of this efficient "deportation machine" (Mohn, forthcoming). With the right-wing Progress Party in government since 2013, high deportation numbers, and an opening of a prison exclusively for foreign nationals, the country is in many ways at the forefront of European developments in crimmigration control. The chapter analyses how these developments impact on policing practices, the courts, and institutional innovations, and provides detailed insight into the views of practitioners working in the system about their experience of transition from welfare to bordered penality. It illuminates the construction of the crimmigrant other at the national level, while the following chapter addresses the issue from a supranational perspective.

Chapter 4 thus maps the plethora of border control measures and technologies, such as the Schengen system, and suggests that, contrary to popular opinion of migration as tearing apart the EU, migration control has been an important driving force for European integration, particularly in the field of criminal justice. The chapter also outlines the extraterritorial aspects of the EU's border control regime that are to be seen in its policy towards neighbouring countries, most notably Turkey and Libya, and in its deportation regimes, which are haunted by the ghosts of colonialism. The analysis demonstrates the complexities of exercising penal power on Europe's frontiers, where its commitment to human rights is profoundly challenged by realpolitik. These tensions are particularly visible in the activities of Frontex (European Border and Coast Guard Agency). This controversial body (dubbed by the Human Rights Watch "the EU's dirty hands") reveals not only the inescapable challenges of European policing and integration, but also the steady transformation of border policing into a crime control and security matter, one indication of this being the intensified efforts to fight criminal smuggling networks. The chapter suggests that the crimmigrant other is a central element in a circular rationale where criminalisation is justified by the presence of deviance produced by the system itself.

However, while they are excluded from the traditional discourse of rights and solidarity, particularly visible in the tragic numbers of border deaths, migrants are included in the humanitarian discourse, which is based on notions of compassion, care and protection (Fassin, 2012). Drawing on E.P. Thompson's (1971) seminal work on moral economy, the book argues that contemporary systems of border control are in central ways shaped by layers of judgments about right and wrong, good and evil. Illustrated by detailed empirical material, the book outlines the practical and discursive strategies employed by practitioners in outsourcing moral responsibility for the measures taken. The deep moral discomfort experienced by those working on the ground challenges the legitimacy of the system. The crimmigrant other should be thus understood as a symbolic mechanism for the externalisation of discomfort and blame and an important justification for the continued use of coercive force.

The final chapter (Chapter 5) addresses the normative and ethical issues related to the use of penal power at the border. It outlines how contemporary criminal justice has been transformed from "normal" justice (envisioned primarily as a relation between citizens) to a deeply globalised "abnormal" justice, which struggles to accommodate the claims of non-members. The crimmigrant other is subjected to a hybrid system of control where he or she encounters measures belonging to the sphere of penal power, but where the language of justice has not yet caught up with developments. Adjustment to the new realities would entail not only acknowledging the penal nature of immigration measures such as detention and deportation, but also giving non-citizens due process rights which are, as a rule, given to "ordinary" offenders. The chapter frames the discussion in terms of the morality of nationalism and the nature of ethical frameworks that support the exclusion of those deemed non-members. The chapter discusses the role of penal power in shaping the nature of membership and belonging, and for guarding the boundaries of citizenship. These boundaries which are being guarded today are increasingly contentious, due to the privileged status of Western citizenship and residence rights in a deeply unequal global order. The book's main contribution is to show how the social production of the crimmigrant other serves to turn issues of global privilege into issues of morality and the maintenance of the moral order. He or she emerges as a symbolic representation of justified social exclusion.

Notes

1 www.independent.co.uk/news/uk/politics/aylan-kurdi-david-cameron-says -he-felt-deeply-moved-by-images-of-dead-syrian-boy-but-gives-no-104846 41.html
2 www.washingtonpost.com/news/worldviews/wp/2015/09/03/image-of- drowned-syrian-toddler-aylan-kurdi-jolts-world-leaders/?utm_term=.bcec7e 2d78cb
3 www.theguardian.com/world/2017/jul/04/austrian-troops-to-stop-migrants -crossing-border-with-italy
4 According to the data provided by the IOM (2017: 6), there were 5,143 migrant deaths and disappearances in 2016, the highest number recorded since the year 2000. The Mediterranean, in fact, accounts for the vast majority of migrant deaths recorded globally (ibid.).
5 www.ohchr.org/EN/NewsEvents/Pages/ProtectingRightsOfMigrants.aspx
6 The 2018 UN Compact for Safe, Orderly and Regular Migration, for example, does not have any mention of 'illegal' migration and consistently uses the term 'irregular'. Source: www.un.org/pga/72/wp-content/uploads/ sites/51/2018/07/migration.pdf
7 Source: www.prisonstudies.org/map/europe (viewed on 3 July 2019).
8 In total, 78 interviews were conducted between 2012 and 2016. The interviews can be categorized into eight different cases related to policing of borders. The European Border and Coast Guard agency (Frontex) and the Norwegian public police are the main sources of data. The Norwegian agencies included in the study are the National Criminal Investigation Service (KRIPOS), Police Directorate, International Section and Immigration/ Foreigner project, Norwegian National Police Immigration Service, Ministry of Justice and Public Security, Frontex National Expert Pool, and Frontex personnel in Warsaw. Our data also include three cases in the Oslo Police

District focusing on cooperation with Romania (conducted by Annette Vestby), West African networks, deportation (conducted by Synnøve Jahnsen), as well as the Norwegian Police University College, training and education.

Of the 78 interviewees, 36 were or had been Frontex employees or had participated in Frontex-related activities. One third (12) of the 36 were or are members of the so-called Frontex National Expert Pool in Norway (and participated in international Frontex operations part-time, while having a regular job at home), while five are employed full-time at the Frontex headquarters in Warsaw, and have different European nationalities (see also Aas and Gundhus, 2015). Other informants held various positions within the Norwegian police force.

Most of the interviewed were police officers by training, while the rest were legal professionals, analysts, and social scientists. In addition to the interviews, the data consist of an analysis of relevant policy and official documents. In addition, we participated in relevant professional events both in Norway and in Warsaw, such as seminars directed at police professionals working on migration issues, a training seminar for Frontex national pool experts before their deployment on joint operations. We visited the National Coordination Centre for Eurosur in Norway, as well as seminars organised by Frontex in Warsaw, where we also visited Frontex headquarters. The interviews were semi-structured, lasting between one and two hours, and typically took place at the informants' office or in a meeting room. Over the past years, the findings of this book have presented at various police professional events and have greatly benefited from the feedback received.

1

(DE)CONSTRUCTING THE CRIMMIGRANT OTHER

The crimmigrant body

An image associated with one of the first meetings between an asylum seeker and a European state is that of a dark-skinned hand being fingerprinted by a white-gloved police officer. The scene may take place in a refugee reception centre in Greece or Italy, in a police station in a European city, or on a rescue boat in the Mediterranean. At registration and identification centres termed "hot spots", swift and more efficient fingerprinting procedures were one of the EU's immediate responses to the so-called migration crisis in 2015. As the European Commission wrote in its characteristic style:[1]

> As part of the immediate action to assist frontline Member States which are facing disproportionate migratory pressures at the EU's external borders, in the European Agenda on Migration presented in May, the European Commission proposed to develop a new Hotspot approach. The European Asylum Support Office (EASO), EU Border Agency (Frontex) EU Police Cooperation Agency (Europol) and EU Judicial Cooperation Agency (Eurojust) will work on the ground with the authorities of the frontline Member

State to help to fulfil their obligations under EU law and swiftly identify, register and fingerprint incoming migrants.

Since 2000, fingerprinting has been the core element of the EU's response to asylum, by means of the Eurodac database and the Dublin Agreement, which established that, as a principle, the first country someone arrives in is responsible for processing that person's asylum claim. Eurodac authorises the fingerprinting of all individuals aged over 14 who apply for asylum in an EU country, or who are found illegally present on EU borders or in EU territory. A "positive hit" may thus result in the removal of an asylum seeker from a country solely on the basis of fingerprint identification.

It is important to note that the EU's ambition to "identify, screen and filter" the migratory flows on its borders, and to achieve a "100% identification rate", has been bound up with the use of force. Migrants often resist fingerprinting, since the Dublin Agreement essentially forces onto the southern states – which have the greatest migratory burdens and the fewest resources – the responsibility for the majority of asylum claims. Many migrants wish to move to wealthier countries further north. The EU Commission therefore suggested in May 2015 that, if migrants do not cooperate, "Member States should make use of specific and limited use of detention, and use coercion as a last resort."[2] The suggestion drew criticism from actors such as the EU's Agency for Fundamental Rights (FRA), which found it "difficult to imagine a situation where the use of physical or psychological force to obtain fingerprints for Eurodac would be justified". The Civil Liberties, Justice and Home Affairs Committee (LIBE) also said that "coercive methods for securing fingerprinting raise serious legal, practical, and ethical concerns". The proposal was, nevertheless, implemented and effectively lowered the threshold for the use of force and detention for identification purposes in a number of European countries. A year later, Amnesty International suggested that migrants attempting to pass through Italy without being identified were often exposed to "coercive methods used by the Italian police to obtain fingerprints, including alleged beatings, electric shocks and sexual humiliation".[3]

However, the use of force and detention for the purpose of fingerprinting and identification is not new. Several European states have used such means to identify foreign citizens living in their territories. The Norwegian authorities (Politidirektiratet, 2010), for example, provide the following template to police officers for imprisoning persons whose identity is unknown:[4]

According to Immigration Act §37 sixth section, cf. §37c third section, cf. Criminal Procedure Act §170a, we determine apprehension of:
Name:
Citizen of:
Born:
Address:

- since there exist reasonable grounds to suspect that the person in question has provided false identity.

We point to the fact that he cannot provide any form of identity documents that confirm his stated identity and that his fingertips have been buffed, which makes fingerprinting difficult.
An imposition of a notification requirement or staying at a specific address seems based on the nature of the case and circumstances obviously inadequate cf. Immigration Act §37 sixth section.
The individual in question was apprehended
* This decision was orally conveyed (date and time)*
Decision applies until

The template reveals not only migrants' strategies of resistance, but also how the establishment of their identity is fundamentally connected to the use of various forms of state-sanctioned force. One might ask why identifying them is so important to the state, and why it justifies the use of the most intrusive forms of state penal power, such as imprisonment. Furthermore, why are European states willing to prioritise the identification of migrants over their human rights record? The answers to these questions lie in the ways identity, penal power, and the body intersect with one another, and this can also help us to understand the creation of the crimmigrant other as a distinctive penal subject.

Meetings between strangers and societies are, as Sarah Ahmed (2000) points out, embodied meetings. Strangers become of interest to a society once their bodies materialise at its doorstep. The political technologies of the body can, as Michel Foucault powerfully argued, serve as a useful starting point for "read[ing] a common history of power relations and object relations" in a society (1977: 24). The history of punishment and the various uses of penal power should not be read simply in the light of moral ideas and legal structures, but rather against the background of a "history of bodies", or what Foucault termed the political economy of the body (ibid.: 25). The docile body of disciplinary power, described by Foucault (1977), is thus a historical construction, created at an intersection of truth and power. Although the disciplinary logic described by Foucault has largely been superseded (Simon, 2013), the bodies of those who are subject to penal power today are still caught up in a system of knowledge, truth, and control. A closer look at these knowledge practices reveals how immigrants are met by state authorities and what kind of subjectivity this gives rise to. By "following the body" (Simon, 2013), this chapter will begin to uncover the processes involved in constituting the crimmigrant other and the regimes of truth that he or she is inscribed in.

The example of fingerprinting reveals the central importance of biometrics and the body in the so-called management of migration. Migrants' bodies are – like the bodies of convicts in the past – deeply connected to sovereignty and the production of truth. From the first meeting, the state sets out to take hold of the crimmigrant's body and subject it to a series of technologies, such as fingerprinting, and dental and skeleton records, designed to control movement and uncover fraud. In several EU states dental and skeleton records are used to determine the age of asylum applicants, but biometric technologies are used primarily for identification purposes. According to Heinemann et al. (2016: 2), at least 17 European countries have incorporated DNA testing into decision making on family reunification in immigration cases. As we have seen, the Dublin system for assessing asylum claims, with its aim to prevent unwanted movement and so-called "asylum shopping" and "refugees in orbit", has resulted in the mass biometric surveillance of migrant populations that is demonstrated by the growth of the Eurodac database. By the end of 2016, the number of fingerprint datasets stored in its central system exceeded five million, which was a 25 per cent increase on the four million records stored over the previous reporting period.[5] Also, the EU's VIS system for visa applications has experienced a remarkable growth and is now one of the world's largest biometric databases. By September 2017, the VIS database stored over 49 million visa applications and almost 42 million fingerprint sets.[6]

The crimmigrant body is mediated by technology. Today, the exercise of power, including in the penal domain, is essentially technological. Contemporary border control systems aim to create bodies which are fused with technology (Aas, 2006). This is the case for both the privileged and the disadvantaged (Aas, 2011). All travellers are subjected to increasing technological surveillance of their mobility. However, the effects of state surveillance on various social groups are quite different. While for privileged Western citizens technological surveillance can indeed enable faster, more seamless border crossing, for disadvantaged groups such as asylum seekers and irregular travellers such technological systems often mean more intrusive and coercive control.

By the technological coding of bodies which are moving across borders, migrants are inscribed in the state-created production of truth about human movement. The bodies of young asylum seekers thus become the ultimate source of knowledge about their true age and, consequently, determine the rights and protection they will receive. Similarly, the bodies of asylum seekers fingerprinted by the police become a vital source of knowledge about their movements across Europe and, ultimately, may determine which country will process their application and become the designated end point of their journey. In their capacity to reveal the "truth" about migrants' identities and movements, the crimmigrant body represents a point where state power gains a grip over the individual and uses their body for its own purposes – namely, the strengthening of control of mobility. To borrow Giorgio Agamben's (2005) expression, bodies become marked by "biopolitical tattoos", which distinguish between good and bad citizens. The body emerges as a source of instant truth, unlike the crimmigrant, who the authorities always assume to be potentially untruthful. In Foucault's history, bodies are seen as unruly and disorderly, things that have to be trained and disciplined by military procedures and institutional routines. Now, with the help of technology, bodies are seen as a source of unparalleled accuracy and precision. The coded body does not need to be disciplined, because its natural patterns are in themselves a source of order (Aas, 2006).

However, state surveillance of the body does not simply involve finding information about individuals' identities; it also creates identities. As van der Ploeg points out in her analysis of the Eurodac: "rather than determining any preexisting identity, these practices may be better understood as ways to *establish* identity, in the sense that 'identity' becomes that which *results* from these efforts" (1999: 300, emphasis in original). With the help of technology, immigration authorities, faced with immigrants and asylum applicants who possess nothing but their stories, are able to produce an identity "that is independent of that story, and yet undeniably belonging to that person" (1999: 300). Identity, therefore, is not established on the basis of self-knowledge and a biographical narrative that an individual can present about him/herself. Rather, it is non-verbal and implemented through symbols that are completely empty of meaning (Aas, 2006).

It should be pointed out, though, that establishing reliable identification is a central, indispensable task and a perennial challenge for modern states. As James Scott's (1998) seminal work has demonstrated, the creation of a "legible people" has in the past greatly enhanced the state's grasp over its territory – be it for the purpose of taxation, conscription, health, or other purposes – and has become a hallmark of modern statehood. From the imposition and recording of permanent surnames to the eventual development of portable identity documents, states worldwide have devised methods to enhance the legibility of society. These efforts also include "the need to identify and track those who had wandered or traveled beyond the circle in which they were personally known" (Caplan and Torpey, 2001: 2).

Identification efforts directed at cross-border movement today, therefore, belong to a long tradition of state identification for the purpose of controlling mobility where, as John Torpey points out, passports became not only a vital technique for identification and control of mobility, but also a building block in the process of constructing national identity.

> [T]he historical development of passport controls as a way of illu-
> minating the institutionalization of the idea of the "nation-state" as
> a prospectively homogenous ethnocultural unit, a project that

necessarily entailed efforts to regulate people's movements. Yet because nation-states are both territorial and membership organisations, they must erect and sustain boundaries between nationals and non-nationals both at their physical borders and among people within those borders.

(Torpey, 2000: 1)

"Identificatory logic", therefore, plays an especially important role in the construction of national identity (Caplan and Torpey, 2001: 47). Because of their reach over the state's entire territory, identification processes have been a powerful factor in the process of national integration and a central precondition for universal citizenship and equal access to rights. Identity documentation has always had, in varying measures, both emancipatory and repressive aspects, which have been richly documented in scholarly literature (Caplan and Torpey, 2001). It has not only enhanced state power and citizens' access to welfare and other rights but also, for example, enabled the Nazis to use population registers and identification documents to track Jewish populations.

Although the identificatory logic is deeply engrained in the bureaucratic practices of states in the global North, it can by no means be taken for granted. According to the World Bank estimates, 1.5 billion people worldwide lack a government-issued and -recognised document as a proof of their identity.[7] There are deep global inequalities in terms of identification, which make the efforts of contemporary mostly Northern states to identify vast globally mobile populations all the more ambitious (and perhaps futile). During our empirical investigation we visited the Norwegian ID Centre, an administrative body whose purpose is to assist Norwegian authorities in establishing identities of foreign nationals.[8] There we were shown around a room with a large filing system containing samples of passports and ID documents from around the world. While exhibiting historic continuities, such efforts also represent a certain departure, or a leap forward, from the early days of the passport. They are directed not only within the state territory for the purpose of constructing national identity and making legible the state's own citizens, but also outwards, towards citizens of other states. Northern states devote considerable resources to identifying which country a person belongs to, in order to determine their rights of residence and entitlement to protection and, ultimately, so that they can deport them. Through systems such as Eurodac, the Schengen Information System, and VIS, and by the use of national and international policing registers, states in the global North are ascribing individuals to a global system of standardised identification and seeking to create the *global intelligibility* of populations. Ultimately this ascription also enables states to relieve themselves of unwanted populations (Walters, 2010). Unless they establish which sovereign state an individual "belongs to", this goal cannot be achieved.

This rationale indicates why the identification of *other states' citizens* becomes of such vital importance that it is seen as requiring criminal penalties and even imprisonment. As Elspeth Guild (2009: 121) points out, "Ascertaining the correct identity of the individual, and in particular the foreigner, is increasingly accepted as a security issue." Similarly, representatives of the Norwegian police have spoken about the great dangers of "identity-less asylum seekers". As one Norwegian police officers' union representative put it: "Police officers are particularly frustrated by all the identity-less asylum seekers of various ethnic origins, who are totally out of control" (Aas, 2006). Lack of appropriate identification is seen as harbouring possibilities for "double identities" and avoidance of criminal prosecution. Of course, the ideas of identity-less asylum seekers, of identity loss and identity theft, would sound almost absurd to a neutral observer. Describing asylum seekers as "identity-less" means that they do not have the kind of identity required by state bureaucracy: one that is stable, objective, and unambiguous.

Such concerns result in exhaustive searching for documents to pin down the identities of strangers and connect them to their national identities (Weber, 2013; Gundhus, 2016; Van der Woude and Van der Leun, 2017). Identification has always been a vital preoccupation of the modern state, and is exemplified by the rise of the biometric ID card and passport, the "enhanced" driving licence, DNA databases, RFIDs, fingerprinting and iris scans, and related databases all of which are "identification efforts aimed at making citizens more 'legible' within the 'embrace' of the state" (Lyon 2009: 22) – however, such practices should be distinguished according to the citizenship and social status of the populations they aim to make legible. While identification measures may be ubiquitous in the West, creating what some fear to be a climate of general surveillance and raising privacy concerns, their effects on citizens of the global North are markedly different from those felt by citizens of the global South.

In the case of migrants, the lack of "legibility" and of a trustworthy identity is treated as a criminal matter and increasingly intrusive measures ensue (Aliverti, 2013). Several European states have lowered the threshold of evidence for imprisonment in cases of false identity, doubts about identity, or perceived lack of cooperation with the authorities in establishing identity (Kmak, 2015). People can thus be deprived of liberty for not providing documents, or for providing inadequate ones, and the duration of detention may be longer if the person's state of origin is not cooperative. The length of detention (which often exceeds the length of imprisonment given for serious crimes such as property offences and even violence) serves as an indication of how important an objective identification is for the state. These seemingly trivial administrative practices are in fact of central importance to the preservation of the current social order and to the global allocation of resources. They are vital techniques for maintaining the existing divisions between the global North and South, which is why so many migrants resist state identification efforts by destroying or hiding their ID documents or ruining their fingerprints.

Contemporary identification practices belong to a sovereignty regime where the objective is not only to make citizens of the state legible or to uncover fraud but, ultimately, to return "fraudulent" unwanted bodies to their proper sovereigns (Walters, 2010). While limitations of space preclude detailed discussion of this subject, it needs to be pointed out that the kind of knowledge about the individual that is being sought by these techniques is not biopolitical knowledge – an expression of penal or therapeutic power described by Foucault (1977), that seeks to know the offender's soul. Rather, the state wants to gain knowledge about identity in the formal sense of establishing citizenship, to facilitate its ultimate goal – deportation. If a connection between an individual and another state (i.e. citizenship) is established, that person can be placed in the global mobility regime and allocated to their "proper sovereign". The latter is obliged to take back its citizen, and the deporting state is relieved of responsibility. The question for the authorities is therefore not "Where do you feel you belong?" or "Who are you?" in terms of experienced identity, but "Which state are you a citizen of?" Identity is considered to be a binary issue: either you are a citizen or not. It does not involve values or social or national senses of belonging. As we shall see in the following chapters, deportees may be socially integrated, with deep family and community ties. They may have grown up in the deporting state, and feel and act like nationals (Coutin, 2007; Brotherton and Barrios, 2009). Legal citizenship origin is thus elevated over other measures of belonging (Coutin, 2010: 356).

The discussion so far has revealed some central traits of the crimmigrant other and his/her relationship to the Northern state. It shows a constellation of crimmigrant bodies, whose mobility the state wishes to contain by fusing them with technology, and which are surrounded by suspicion and danger. In the eyes of the state, they are, as one police officer put it, the "people we don't know who they are". Although immigrants may feel a sense of belonging to a society, they are – in Simmel's (1964) sense of the word – strangers, whose identity, despite their nearness, is always marked by remoteness and suspicion. In the eyes of the state, their identity needs to be pinned down and becomes a vital concern. However, this is not identity in a lived sense of the term, as experienced by the individuals themselves, but in a formal sense, in terms of citizenship and residence status. As will become even clearer in the following chapters, for crimmigrant others it is not their inner thoughts and motivations, what they have done or the seriousness of their offences, which define them, but rather who they are in terms of citizenship status (Aas, 2013a).

The surveillance practices directed at crimmigrant bodies also demonstrate that the crimmigrant other's identity is strongly marked by distrust and suspicion. Even as a minor, his or her claims about his/her age cannot be trusted and need to be checked by physical examination. As asylum seekers, their stories are overshadowed by suspicions of "asylum shopping" and "fortune hunting" and need to be checked by elaborate biometric databases. Their documents are suspected of being false, because the suspicion directed at crimmigrant others is connected to the perceived untrustworthiness of the state they originate from. Untrustworthy states produce untrustworthy identities. The mobility of certain groups is thus systematically connected to notions of danger and control. Suspicion is intrinsically linked to the crimmigrant other's identity, as is evident from the proliferation of profiling practices, terrorism watch lists, and other forms of systematic surveillance of travel and mobility (Bigo et al., 2013). For example, in 2017, the European Council suggested that "terrorists could exploit irregular migratory movements to enter into the European Union", and highlighted the importance of setting up best practice in terms of security checks on irregular migrants, including using biometric data (Frontex, 2018: 31). In the next section we shall see how the mobility of certain groups is not only securitised, but also illegalised and systematically associated with illegality. We shall see how the state-defined aspects of the crimmigrant other's identity are fundamentally connected to two conditions which are the main planks of crimmigration control: illegality and deportability.

Illegality

In his seminal work on the sociology of deviance, Kai T. Erikson shows that, rather than being "a property *inherent in* any particular kind of behavior", whether something is defined as deviant in a society essentially depends "on the circumstances under which it was performed and the temper of the audience which witnessed it" (1966: 6). This insight – supported by a large body of criminological and sociological studies (Becker, 1963; Christie, 2004) – can serve as a useful starting point for understanding the nature of "immigrant illegality". An illegal immigrant is, as Elspeth Guild suggests (2009: 15), "someone in respect of whose presence on the territory the state has passed a law making mere existence a criminal offence". While the prerogative to decide who has the right of entry into the country is one of the essential features of any sovereign state, it is applied with selectivity. This means that the label of illegality can be removed from large groups of people at a stroke of the pen, as happened, for example, with EU enlargement in 2007, which made legally authorised travel possible for millions of Eastern European citizens (Kubal, 2013). On the other hand, the instability of the category means that immigrant illegality can be redefined and expanded through societal processes.

This chapter will go on to show that, although high-octane media and political discourse about "illegal immigration" and "illegal aliens" may appear to refer to a stable quality, the category of immigrant illegality is by no means clear-cut or transparent. The meaning of the category is historically contingent and has been fiercely contested by immigrants themselves, legal advocates, and civil society organisations (Coutin, 2005). For example, charges of illegal entry and re-entry, unused for decades, now dominate US federal courts. Crimes against immigration law have become the largest category of offences pursued by federal prosecutors in recent years (García Hernández, 2015: 147).

However, rather than focusing on the increasingly punitive reactions against violations and violators of immigration law, we shall first address the main premise of the notion of immigrant illegality and illegal migration, which produces novel forms of criminalisation and state punitiveness. The main premise for the creation of the category of illegal migration and of the crimmigrant other is the interest of certain states – which in this book will be defined as the Northern (penal) states – in controlling unwanted cross-border movement. The patterns of criminalisation are crucially defined by the geopolitical position of the state. Northern states have created an elaborate legal regime that criminalises certain forms of movement, thus rendering a large proportion of the world's population "illegal" (Dauvergne, 2008). While these control regimes are driven by the interests of the Northern (migration importing) states, the people affected by them are primarily citizens of the global South.[9] The "illegality" of migration follows a similar, although not identical, trajectory to other forms of international criminalisation, where new laws and prohibition regimes are not simply a response to a stable category (i.e. crime), but rather depend on the activities of powerful states and actors who are able to redefine certain cross-border activities once considered "normal" and condemn them as "deviant" (Andreas and Nadelmann, 2006: 7; Jakobi, 2013).

As we shall see throughout this book, the various regimes of migration do not consist only of legal regulation, but also include an assemblage of transnational mechanisms of policing, enforcement, and social exclusion related to illegalisation. What is of interest here is that, as globalisation makes the dynamics of criminalisation increasingly international, this internationalisation also includes the creation of global labels of crime and deviance. As Catherine Dauvergne (2008: 18) observes:

[A]s "illegal" emerges as a globally meaningful identity label, the characteristics of all those nations against which this other is imagined also tend to merge. The line between having and not having can no longer be easily conceived as fitting around the border of *a* nation and must instead fit around the border of *all* prosperous nations, creating a global understanding of "insiders" and "outsiders".

In other words, while class interests have traditionally been seen, particularly by Marxist scholars, as a driver of state criminalisation policies, when it comes to migration the process still seems to be related to social inequality; however, the inequality is now globalised.

What this means on the individual level is that "the accident of being born in the global South" becomes a legal handicap for the citizens of these countries, particularly disadvantaged ones (Dauvergne, 2008: 17; Aliverti, 2012). This legal handicap stems from the assumption that there are different categories of states: those whose citizens' mobility is desirable (and is in fact something to be encouraged, as tourists, students, and professionals), and those states who are literally black-listed. As mentioned earlier, this understanding is based on a conception of law and illegality as grounded, geographically and geopolitically contextual, rather than universal, abstract, and immutable. According to it, illegality is not a relatively fixed property or status that a given individual holds, but rather "a condition that any given individual can flit in and out of depending on the relation between his and her movements and activities and the movements and activities of national, international and/or transnational agencies" (Squire, 2011: 7). Kubal (2013: 556) thus points out the example of tens of millions of Eastern Europeans who between 2004 and 2007 migrated to the "old" EU member states and de facto became "illegal workers", since they only had the right to reside but not to work. Unsatisfied with the binary opposition between legality and illegality, several scholars have resorted to alternative concepts such as liminal migration (Menjivar, 2006) and semi-legality in order to frame the various "in between" statuses (Kubal, 2013).

For scholars and academics, the ambiguous and contested nature of immigrant illegality may seem self-evident. However, for many migrants it is precisely the apparent firmness of such categories and their strong association with criminality that are among the most difficult aspects of detention or involvement in court proceedings. After a visit to a detention centre at Oslo airport, the Norwegian Parliamentary Ombudsman (Sivilombudsmannen, 2015) wrote that "[m]any of the detainees felt that they were treated like criminals, even though they had not been convicted of a crime". Khosravi (2010: 94) points out how illegality can become forcefully embodied and internalised by migrants through the sense of shame and guilt of being "an uninvited, unwelcome guest, an undesirable person". Therefore, it is not simply the harshness of border control measures which is at stake, but also the fact that the label of criminality becomes in Erikson's (1966: 7) phrase "the major identifying badge" of a person. Consigning a person to the category of "deviant" means that one is "sifting a few important details out of the stream of behavior he has emitted and is in effect declaring that these details reflect *the kind of person he 'really' is*" (ibid., emphasis added). Consequently, many migrant groups have directed their strategies of contestation at showing their positive contribution to society and refusing to allow the label of illegality to overshadow other aspects of their existence, such as their economic value to a society, their sense of belonging, school performance, and contributions to their local communities (Coutin, 2005).

The very term "illegal", as Dauvergne (2008: 16) points out, also "underscores a shift in perception regarding the moral worthiness of these migrants". This is not surprising, since moral censure is one of the defining features of criminal law (Garland, 1990; Von Hirsch, 1996). It is at this point, however, that the incongruous nature of the link between criminality and unauthorised migration becomes apparent. According to Lucia Zedner (2013), the criminalisation of immigration offences departs from ordinary principles of criminalisation – particularly the harm principle. Although a "necessary condition of criminalization is that some non-trivial harm is risked or caused by the offender", Zedner (ibid.: 51) points out that "in respect of many immigration offences it is unclear what the harm, or putative harm, is". The sentiment is echoed in many testimonies by migrants who have an acute sense of the injustice of the label and proclaim that they have "done nothing wrong". Or, as one detainee in Trandum, the Norwegian closed detention centre, remarked: "Nobody chooses where they are born."[10] Interestingly, similar sentiments have also been voiced by police officers responsible for pursuing immigration offences, who feel that they are not dealing with "proper criminality". One

Norwegian police officer interviewed in our project put it this way: "Well, it is important that our society does not become flooded [by irregular migrants], but it is not like a criminal you are burning to catch. You don't get a feeling that you are helping someone" (Mohn, forthcoming).

The officer addresses one of the central issues discussed in this book – that the coupling of migration and illegality is often met by moral ambivalence and discomfort. For those working within the system, the contested nature of illegal migration raises a number of questions about the purpose and legitimacy of the institutional settings they are in (Bosworth, 2013). For others, the very concept of illegal migration represents a point for sustained normative critique, expressed in a refusal to accept the categories of illegality and of "illegal migrants". As Schrover et al. (2008) point out: "Migrants can never be illegal themselves, only their activities can be regarded as such." In public and political discourse, a moral veneer is often added to the prosecution of immigration offences by stressing potential security and economic implications of border violations. The "illegality" of immigration is thus not simply a result of transgressing immigration law, but denotes a more pervasive and insidious connection between migration, crime, and other issues, including national security. Despite heavy criticism, the concept of "illegality" in recent years has therefore had a profound impact on the nature of political and legal thinking about migration. Punishing the "deviant immigrant" (Melossi, 2003) sends potent symbolic political signals. In the post-9/11 climate, migration has become ever more securitised (Huysmans, 2006; Bigo et al., 2013), and has legitimated a complex process of exclusionary practices, in which "various forms of security provide an organizing principle around which territorial and social inclusion and exclusion are drawn" (Guild, 2009: 190).

The discussion above reveals how their unauthorised status, defined by the authorities as illegality, forms the foundation of the processes of institutional and legal construction of crimmigrant others. This foundation is layered with additional considerations, such as othering and exclusionary practices based on insecurity, race, or – as we shall see in Chapter 3 – social class and poverty. As Nicholas De Genova (2013: 1180) observes, "The castigation of 'illegals' thereby supplies the rationale for essentializing citizenship inequalities as categorical differences that then may be racialized" (see also Reiter and Coutin, 2017; Bosworth et al., 2018). We shall see in Chapter 4 that, in the EU context, the definition of irregular migration as a security threat and a question of combating organised crime justifies the use of some of the harshest policing approaches and state coercive measures.

The deviant act of unauthorised border crossing and residence is essentially defined by the premise of global inequality, which encourages the free cross-border movement of some groups and creates insurmountable legal and economic obstacles to the movement of others. In Chapter 2, we will see that from this basic premise a plethora of offences is derived, such as illegal entry and re-entry, overstaying, and use of false documents (Aliverti, 2013; Mitsilegas, 2015). We will also see that the desire of state authorities to control unauthorised movement is creating other categories of transgressions and penal controls, such as the duty to report, spatial enclosures, and orders to leave designated areas and countries. Several observers have pointed out that the social status of illegality brings migrants an increased risk of economic exploitability and of inability to access various rights which they may be entitled to (Melossi, 2013a). The category of illegality is therefore not simply a juridical matter, but a life-determining identity label which deeply affects people's everyday existence (Fangen and Kjærre, 2013; Reiter and Coutin, 2017; Bendixen and Wyller, 2019).

Deportability

For an "illegal immigrant", in the US context often referred to as an "illegal alien", rule-breaking is close to being an existential condition (Menjívar and Kanstroom, 2014). In that respect the crimmigrant other resembles other deviant figures, such as Foucault's (1977: 251) delinquent, "who is to be distinguished from the offender by the fact that it is not so much his act as his life that is relevant in characterizing him". Similarly to the delinquent, also the crimmigrant other can be seen as a distinct penal subject that emerges as a product of particular legal and institutional arrangements and rationalities. Crucially, however, the deviance of the crimmigrant other is shaped by another social condition, which distinguishes him or her from other groups of deviants and outsiders that have been traditionally portrayed in criminological and sociological literature. As a non-citizen, the crimmigrant other is potentially deportable. This means that he or she will not just be sanctioned by a community by means of various forms of social censure, punishment, or consignment to specially designated (correctional) institutions. For his/her perceived deviance, the crimmigrant other can be, and often is, sanctioned by complete and permanent exclusion from the community. As Reiter and Coutin (2017) point out, deportees are cast into a category of total excludability akin to social death, where all their community networks and social ties are cut off by punitive administrative actions. In the post-war European context, such systematic use of penal power for the purpose of permanent social exclusion can be seen as a departure from long-standing traditions that have, despite notable exceptions, come to distinguish European from US penology (Daems et al., 2013). Deportees, Reiter and Coutin (2017) suggest, resemble prisoners subjected to prolonged social isolation in US maximum security prisons. They are subjected to processes which are not legally defined as punishment, and yet have the drastic effect of excluding them from the social contract and placing them "beyond the boundaries of society" (ibid.: 594). The perceived severity of such measures, as we will see later, greatly depends on the ties that deportees have to a community and the length of their stay (Strømnes, 2013).

Chapter 2 and Chapter 3 will examine in greater detail how state deportation regimes are marked by a duality of the sanctioning systems: the administrative and the penal. The crimmigrant other's deviance can be sanctioned either by banishment or penal sanctions or, quite often, by both. The slide from punishment to expulsion modes is the defining trait of crimmigration law (Stumpf, 2006; García Hernández, 2015). The following statement by a Norwegian police officer illustrates the connection:

> You should not forget, let's say that someone is caught for big theft for example, then there's a criminal case, but at the same time we produce a charge for a breach of immigration law, because one knows that a criminal charge will lead to deportation. So we also produce an immigration charge which will be "picked up" by us later on.
>
> *(OPD-015)*

The statement shows how the production of illegality is strongly connected to the production of deportability. The crimmigrant other is both punishable and deportable. The state will often choose both avenues, or may choose deportation with punitive intentions. Deportation has thus become one of the central penal technologies and, as we shall see in Chapter 2, marks the changing purpose of penal power (Bosworth et al., 2018). Most Northern states have in the past decades significantly lowered the threshold for deportability (Stumpf, 2006; Brouwer, 2019).

Several observers have pointed out, though, that (like illegality) deportability is not simply a status assigned to specific groups and individuals, but rather a process producing social conditions which make irregular migrants deportable (De Genova and Peutz, 2010). The creation of such conditions not only entails extensive policing and surveillance practices (Weber, 2013), but also has significant foreign policy aspects. For example, in Chapter 4 we shall see how EU countries tailor their foreign policy to co-opting states in the global South to participate in their deportation schemes and take back their unwanted citizens. The cooperation of the Southern state – indicated by the signing of return agreements (Janmyr, 2016) – is, therefore, one of the preconditions of deportability. Although a distinct legal condition, deportability is far from an achieved objective. In fact, most states manage to deport only a small proportion of migrants who had been designated as deportable (Van Houte and Leerkes, 2019).

De Genova (2002) suggests that the size of populations of unauthorised migrants makes their deportation an unrealistic option. Consequently, he contends, one of the main elements of state deportation practices is the creation among unauthorised migrants of heightened awareness of their deportability. Their daily life may become overshadowed by constant anticipation of deportation and efforts to avoid it (Galvin, 2015; Hasselberg, 2016). As a consequence, these groups are less capable of challenging their exploitative working conditions, and less likely to do so (De Genova, 2002; Melossi, 2013b). As we shall see in the next chapter, states are also investing considerable efforts in creating institutional settings and arrangements – including imprisonment – that are conductive to "voluntary" return (Johansen, 2013).

Deportation entails in many respects the production of fear. It does not only involve sending unwanted populations out of the state's territory, but sends political signals to those inside the territory who could potentially be deported, as well as to those outside state territory who are considering unauthorised journeys (Hasselberg, 2016). In his seminal contribution on the subject, De Genova (2002: 439) in fact defined deportability as a sociopolitical condition of fear that makes legally and illegally resident migrants vulnerable to harsh work conditions: "Migrant 'illegality' is lived through a palpable sense of deportability, which is to say, the possibility of deportation, the possibility of being removed from the space of the nation-state" (ibid.).

This rationality of inducing fear – usually associated with general crime prevention – permeates the field of so-called migration management. Pain and suffering inflicted on certain groups is employed to encourage conformity to state expectations by others. Yet, as with criminal sanctions such as imprisonment, the suffering caused by deportation means that whole families suffer. The separation may mean families being split up, fathers (and sometimes mothers) being separated from their children, the break-up of established community ties and links with relations, or the loss of a job or educational opportunities. As one deportee from Norway (Strømnes, 2013: 48) put it:

> The most important thing for me is to go back home and hug my children and embrace them. To be with my family, that is the most important thing for me. Because they telling me that they want to take me to Africa I have not been there for over 10 years. They tell me that they want to take me to Africa … I have nothing there, the only thing I have is my family.

Reiter and Coutin (2017: 570) describe the experience as "a form of social disintegration: ties to others are cut off and prior identities stripped away, often with devastating consequences for individuals' sense of self". Naturally, how traumatic the experience is depends on the depth and length of social ties with the deporting country as well as the strength of connections to the country of origin.

The next two chapters will address in greater detail the concrete micro-level practices of crimmigration control and deportation enforcement. However, we also need to take a closer look at the macro-level social dynamics behind these practices. As Erikson (1966) points out, one of the main reasons for the social production and sanctioning of deviance is the desire to maintain a community's boundaries. Similarly, the dominant understanding of deportation sees the practice as "facilitating the construction of the established boundaries of membership in contemporary states" (Gibney, 2013: 219). Penal power thus becomes one of the central social mechanisms shaping the nature of membership in contemporary societies. Deportability – like illegality – is a historically and socially contingent category: "just who is entitled to protection from deportation is a matter of debate and dispute because membership is not merely a legal category and is not simply confined to formal citizenship" (Gibney, 2013: 221). In Chapter 3, we will see how the Norwegian authorities have used certain policies to expand the "pool" of deportable populations. In recent years, most Northern states have enacted laws which have lengthened the list of acts punishable by deportation. Who is deportable is to some extent dependent on public sympathy and social perceptions of membership and belonging. Long-staying children (exemplified in the US by so-called DACAs)[11] and residents (such as the Windrush generation in the UK) can often be perceived as members and, although exposed to deportation due to their lack of formal citizenship status, are thus to some extent protected from it by public perceptions that they belong. Despite their "illegality" in a formal sense of the word, these groups have largely managed to mobilise public opinion and public and political support to protect them, even if unable to make a complete transition to "legality".

These examples also show that deportees, far from being powerless against the state, are often active agents in challenging their own deportability (Coutin, 2005). They point to the fact that border practices are best approached "as relational sites of political struggle, rather than simply as sites of biopolitical control" (Squire, 2011: 15). Nor is the crimmigrant other a monolithic category; it includes a variety of groups marked by different shades of deviance. The category's instability and contingency make it open to constant negotiation – both to expansion due to political pressures, which results in new groups being added to it, and to resistance, when alternative notions of belonging can come into the ascendant and eventually expand legal categories.

The spectacle

The discussion above shows the importance of public discourse and community perceptions in defining deviance and in the actual shaping of crimmigration control in a given society. Drawing on the work of Guy Debord (1994), Nicholas De Genova (2013: 1182) argues that today the border is a spectacle: "the spectacle of border enforcement yields up the thing-like fetish of migrant 'illegality' as a self-evident 'fact', generated by its own supposed act of violation". Also other observers have pointed out the spectacular and ritualistic performative aspects of contemporary border enforcement (Andreas, 2000; Andersson, 2014). However, as Ruben Andersson's (2014) analysis of the Spanish border makes clear, the border spectacle not only affirms the notion of migrant illegality, but also transforms it into something different and bigger – into a human avalanche. "The prey-like migrants of the borderlands gather here in two distinct human 'avalanches' – either a huddle aboard sinking boats or a frightening horde 'assaulting' the fences of Ceuta and Melilla" (ibid.: 138).

In 2015, the dramatic rise in the numbers of asylum seekers became systematically associated with terrorism and thus raised demand for militarised modes of intervention. This association is apparent in the statement of the NATO Secretary General Jens Stoltenberg, in May 2015: "Of course, one of the problems is that there might be foreign fighters. There might be terrorists also trying to hide ... to blend in among the migrants."[12] Such perceptions paved the way for the subsequent EUNAVFOR naval intervention against migrant smuggling, which will be addressed later in the book. The threatening nature of the avalanche – frequently referred to as a flood or a crisis – went hand in hand with the prominence of media images of border enforcement and the building of militarised fences. The imagery of invasion played, for example, a prominent role in the Hungarian government's response to the 2015 crisis (Canveren and Akgül Durakcay, 2017). Such associations not only define migration as a security issue, but also depict the irregular migrant as one of many. His or her individuality is, therefore, reduced as it seen as part of a larger group movement.

Nevertheless, the border spectacle is two-sided (Andersson, 2014). The spectacular nature of cross-border mobility encompasses not only the threatening, militarised and law-enforcement aspects, but also the humanitarian ones. "The visual economy of clandestine migration" (ibid.: 142) thus also involves the production, distribution, and consumption of images of migrant suffering and death, such as the powerful image of Alan Kurdi mentioned in the opening pages of this book. Such images and discourses establish a different kind of otherness for the migrant and appeal to different sensibilities. The duality of the threatening and the humane is often structured along lines of gender, age, race, and nationality. The images of suffering therefore often involve children, and create narratives about innocence and blamelessness, which stand in stark contrast to associations of fraudulence, "fortune hunting", and predatory behaviours ascribed to faceless and nameless dark-skinned male bodies. Yet, as Bridget Anderson (2013) points out, whether migrants are portrayed as dangerous offenders who should be deported or as victims in need of rescue, the two opposing notions are united in their conception of migrants as uncivilised others. Or, as Toni Morrison (2017: 39) observed about these two views of the other, "In either instance (of alarm or false reverence), we deny her personhood, the specific individuality we insist upon for ourselves." In the final chapter of this book we shall examine the implications that such notions of subjectivity have for our understanding of membership and justice.

The mediated images of migration have a remarkable ability to sway public sentiments. One male Red Cross volunteer described his change of heart after having seen the image of Kurdi's dead body in the following way: "It was that image that changed my mind. After that, I knew I had to do something." He was not alone in feeling in this way as the "crisis" created massive mobilisations for migrant welfare within the civil society (Barker, 2018; Bendixen and Wyller, 2019). However, this power of highly mediated events to sway public sentiment may be even more effective in turning European publics towards the tough-on-migration stance. Holzber et al. (2018: 545) suggest that the heated response to events on New Year's Eve in Cologne in 2015, in which the allegations of sexual abuse conducted by groups of men of Middle Eastern and North African origin, was the defining moment that contributed towards a U-turn in Germany's border policies. The crimmigrant other is thus not only a security threat, but also a potential sexual offender and a threat to gender relations (Ewing, 2008).

The coverage of irregular immigration in Western media is contentious and polarised (Thorbjørnsrud, 2015). By their choice of "different sets of frames, the news media tend to reduce the complexity of an issue by presenting it in an easy-to-understand, interpretive package" (ibid.: 778). Brouwer et al.'s (2017) extensive study of media discourse in the Netherlands shows that they consistently use the term "illegal" to describe irregular mobility, and that they frequently associate it with the word "criminal". Despite these negative representations, the authors nevertheless point out the complexity of connections between media portrayals and policy change and suggest that "the framing of migrants as criminals is a more diffuse process in which the media seem to follow rather than fuel politics and policy" (ibid.: 100). It is beyond the scope of this book to address in detail the intricate dynamics of migration politics (see, inter alia, Huysmans, 2006; Geddes and Scholten, 2016). However, for the purposes of our discussion, it is pertinent to explore potential similarities between the current dynamics of "tough on migration" border politics and populist penal policies, which at various points in the late 20th century shaped the use of state penal power, particularly in the Anglo-American context. European countries are turning towards what has elsewhere been termed a "hot climate" – against soft, liberal politics – becoming more openly politicised and no longer insulated from the pressures of populist politics. This is the case also in traditionally "cool" Scandinavian countries (Todd-Kvam, 2018). As Green (2008: 79) points out, hot penal climates are marked by a high degree of press, public, and political interest in penal issues, and tend to foster moralistic language and produce inhospitable environments for deliberative consideration (see also Loader and Sparks, 2011). Not unlike "tough on crime" policies, the border has become a site of symbolic politics and an opportunity to wow the electorate with promises of firmness, security, and protection.

The symbolic promises of protection are particularly visible in the proliferation of border walls (Brown, 2010), which have become prominent objects for affirming political authority. Not only in the United States, but also in numerous European countries. In fact, the attraction of symbolic border politics has been strongly felt even in countries which have traditionally defied the onslaught of populist penal politics, such as the Scandinavian countries. In January 2016, for example, the Norwegian authorities decided to start returning to Russia Syrian and Afghani asylum seekers, who had crossed its Arctic border at Storskog. The move – described by some observers as Norway's "arctic freeze" – drew harsh criticism from the UNCHR and civil society actors. Images of asylum seekers being driven back to Russia on shaky bicycles in temperatures below –20 degrees Celsius seemed out of keeping with Norway's humanitarian traditions. Nevertheless, they sent a powerful signal to the domestic electorate as well as to potential asylum seekers. A few months later, the country built a 200-metre-long symbolic border fence.

The border spectacle is therefore spectacular not only in its imagery of floods and suffering, but, increasingly, also through the exhibition of spectacular acts of exclusion. Often such acts, like the Norwegian Storskog incident, have limited effect as migration-reducing tools. Only a few asylum seekers were actually returned to Russia on bicycles. Similarly, the highly publicised Danish jewellery law has been very rarely applied. Nonetheless, such events, like border walls themselves, offer an opportunity for the display of state sovereign power. Yet, as Wendy Brown (2010: 25) succinctly observes, such displays are just as much a sign of decline of state sovereign power as they are a projection of its strength: "the new walls often function theatrically, projecting power and efficaciousness that they do not and cannot actually exercise and that they also performatively contradict". Similarly, De Genova (2013: 1189) suggests that the "dirty secret" of the border spectacle is the porosity of the border and the abject inclusion of irregular migrants as "illegal" labour (see also Melossi, 2013a).

Knowledge

Although the border spectacle transforms irregular cross-border movement into a matter of crisis and invasion, a threat to national security and even to national existence, the perception of migrant illegality as a "natural fact" is further strengthened by other, much less emotive and "cooler", forms of representation and knowledge. Earlier we saw how migrants' identities are inscribed in processes of state bureaucratic production of knowledge. Their bodies are subjected to a myriad of technological, bureaucratic, and scientific practices. For example, in several European countries it is standard procedure for immigration authorities to DNA test family members or to X-ray the hands and teeth of young asylum seekers in order to verify their age. Although fiercely contested with regard to their scientific value and ethics, these measures show the intimate connection between medical knowledge, immigration control, and notions of suspicion and potential fraud (Heinemann et al., 2016).

Miriam Ticktin (2007) points out that, in such settings, medical staff function as "biopolitical gatekeepers". Through the intertwining of the medical gaze and border policing, the state uses its extensive knowledge apparatus not only to create the crimmigrant body as an *identifiable body* and enhance the legibility of strangers entering its territory, but also seeks to protect itself from *the contaminating body* – a body that poses a potential biopolitical threat to the social body of the society he or she migrates to. Fear of the contaminating migrant body may thus support the establishment of seemingly humanitarian facilities, such as health clinics for irregular migrants (Villadsen, forthcoming). Migrants picked up in the Mediterranean Sea by a rescue boat are met by officials wearing protective face masks due to fear of contagion and disease. Frontex ships, such as *Siem Pilot*, are scrupulously disinfected after every mission, and their personnel are always required to move through a disinfecting area which divides the migrant areas of the ship from the crew area. One of the leaders of a police unit responsible for processing asylum seekers in Norway describes this perception of danger:

> We are not health personnel and are in principle not supposed to get that type of information. We are not supposed to ask about it either, of course. But one is clearly interested in asking: are you contagious? Is it advisable to use a face mask? Do you have tuberculosis, HIV? Preferably treat everyone – just like in prisons, they have the same problem there – treat everyone as if they were contagious. Use gloves. Do not let anyone cough directly at you. If someone is coughing a lot, use a face mask. Always be careful about blood.
>
> *(Police Immigration Unit, leadership, 1)*

The crimmigrant body is thus deeply marked by institutionalised notions of danger and suspicion which, as the quote above reveals, resemble those applied to criminal offenders. Such perceptions are frequently intertwined with established notions about race, gender, and ethnicity. The migrant is a bearer of potential danger and illegality at the border, as is made obvious by the frequent focus on racial and ethnic minorities in police stop and search practices (see, inter alia, Parmar, 2011: 209; Van der Woude and van der Leun, 2017; Bowling and Westenra, 2018; Brouwer et al., 2018). Such practices often rely on statistics to support the suspicion and the subsequent checks, as well as to give them a scientific veneer. Gundhus and Jansen (2019) show how, in September 2015, in the immediate context of the so-called migration crisis, Norwegian police launched "Operation Migrant". Focused on prediction of worst-case scenarios, the operation was the first national intelligence project designed to systematically operationalize pre-emptive and precautionary thinking. Migrants – and migration as a phenomenon – became constituted as potentially risky subjects, defined by intricate connections between the objectivity of statistical expert knowledge and suspicious "fantasies and imaginations" of state agents (ibid.).

Like many other illicit and politically sensitive activities, irregular migration is characterised by an intricate "politics of numbers" (Andreas and Greenhill, 2010). However, while in the case of many such activities numbers may be hard to come by, irregular migration is accompanied by the incessant production of statistics and a deep governmental thirst for knowledge. Governments wish to obtain detailed knowledge about the actual and potential size of the "threat" in its many modalities and variations. And, while US studies have "routinely shown that there is little (if any) link between immigration and crime" (Piquero et al., 2016; Sampson, 2008), some European studies suggest that migrants and their locally born children are more likely to perpetrate crimes than the rest of the population (Skardhamar et al., 2014).

Such calculations are not always unproblematic in the eyes of the public and the agencies which produce them. For example, after it took office, the current Norwegian government, and its right-wing Progress Party Minister of Justice, made repeated requests for statistics on immigrants' involvement in crime. When a report eventually came out (Andersen et al., 2017) the political response focused on the (relatively minor) over-representation of certain groups, instead of on the generally positive overall trends. The Ministry also chose to focus on the data without adjustments for the age and gender of the population, thus even further accentuating differences between "natives" and "immigrants". Within this type of "politics of numbers" immigrants are treated as a distinct and knowable entity which is then compared to the majority population, despite the fact that their "diversity is so great that it is questionable whether one should treat immigrants as one single group at all" (Skardhamar et al., 2014).

Statistical knowledge and society are mutually constructive (Sætnan et al., 2011). The very act of counting is a social act and represents a specific form of viewing. As Sætnan et al. (2011: 1) demonstrate, "in the act of counting we do not stand neutrally outside the 'object' we count, but rather (to some extent) enter into it, redefine it, change the stakes that affect it". Therefore, while the difference between the native and the immigrant population is in some cases a substantial and legitimate concern for the public and for the political authorities alike, it is also a central element in the shaping of social identities and, ultimately, in the work of othering. It reinforces a perception of criminality as a marker of the difference between immigrant and native populations – an inherent quality of their existence, which casts a long shadow over several generations. In the case of the Norwegian report (Andersen et al., 2017), the debates about over-representation were mainly about second and third generation immigrants, most of whom are – in legal terms – Norwegian citizens. As we shall see in Chapter 5, this differentiation between "natives" and crimmigrant others, members and non-members, has vital implications for the nature of citizenship and the traditional systems of rights and social inclusion in a society.

In order to grasp the processes of social production of the crimmigrant other, we need an understanding of the dynamic interactions between the statistical practices and governance styles of various actors involved. The processes of othering are not carried out simply by heated political and (social) media discourses about migration, crime, and terrorism, but are crucially supported and complemented by various types of knowledge practices and forms of expertise, and the conjunction of the two. Like Foucault's delinquent, the crimmigrant other comes into existence through historically specific constellations of power and knowledge (Foucault, 1977) which shape the "thing-like" quality of his or her otherness. Such processes are by no means novel (Melossi, 2015). As Piquero et al. (2016: 1416) point out, "[d]iscussions and – more realistically – misperceptions about the relationship between immigration and crime are as old as criminology itself".

While some state agencies may find the official practice of mapping out offenders' ethnicity questionable (Skilbrei, 2019), most states devote considerable monetary resources towards producing scientific knowledge about various connections between ethnicity or nationality and crime. For example, an examination of yearly Frontex reports reveals that the agency regularly produces statistics on the "Top ten nationalities" for a series of illegal activities, such as use of false documents, irregular border crossings on sea and land, and the like. The following table of top ten nationalities of "illegal border crossings" from the 2018 Frontex *Risk Analysis* report may be seen as typical of its kind:

TABLE 1.1 Frontex statistics of "illegal stay".[13]

	2014	2015	2016	2017	Share of total	% change on prev. year
Place of Detection						
Inland	366 467	632 453	409 889	352 507	81	ttī14
Air	33 793	41 179	50 347	46 387	11	ttī7.9
Land	15 511	18 527	23 486	29 980	6.9	28
Land Intra-EU	3 929	5 763	5 938	5 232	1.2	ttī12
Sea	901	681	578	1 680	0.4	191
Not specified	2 372	51		0	n.a.	n.a.
Between BCPs°	2 160	720	1680	:	n.a.	n.a.
Top Ten Nationalities						
Ukraine	15 786	22 652	28 996	32 599	7.5	12
Morocco	28 416	29 731	30 042	29 857	6.9	ttī0.6
Albania	21 248	28 926	24 127	24 800	5.7	2.8
Iraq	5 802	61 462	31 883	21 705	5	ttī32
Afghanistan	22 365	95 784	50 746	21 492	4.9	ttī58
Algeria	14 778	14 948	17 274	19 886	4.6	15
Pakistan	12 804	23 179	19 573	19 840	4.6	1.4
Tunisia	14 765	12 919	11 382	15 912	3.7	40
Nigeria	7 661	12 386	14 838	14 995	3.4	1.1
Eritrea	32 477	39 338	24 655	13 010	3.0	ttī47
All Other	249 031	358 049	238 402	221 690	51	ttī7.0
Total	425 133	699 374	491 918	435 789	100	ttī11

Source: Frontex (2018)

Frontex is by no means alone in producing "top nationalities" statistics. The genre has become common in police reports and in analytical products provided by various governmental agencies. It could be suggested that the "top nationalities" provides a matrix for understanding the state and its knowledge-based production of the crimmigrant other. It is a device for the production of typologies of immigrants, based on their involvement in illegal and unauthorised activities.

Our interviews with police officers and state officials revealed that not only individual member states, but also Frontex at the EU level, invested considerable resources into developing systems for collection, recording, and exchange of information about migration. Expensive and technologically increasingly advanced systems such as JORA (Joint Operations Reporting Application) and Eurosur (European Border Surveillance system) were talked about exclusively in positive terms because of their perceived ability to enhance states' abilities to see, record, analyse, and predict risky trends and events related to migration. As one officer described:

> Eurosur is the glue in the whole thing, for common borders, common responsibility. You make a data system that enables everyone to see the picture. No one can come and say "I did not know that". All analyses are in there, so you cannot go in and make your own analysis. It is directed by Frontex, how it should be done and it is done according to a model … So when I sit here now and look at images, I am informed about what is going on in Spain: a lot of drug traffic. A lot of people coming to Italy. And a lot of people coming to Greece. And I can see how this develops from day to day.
>
> *(FRN 8)*

These powerful abilities to see and collect knowledge about migratory movements and illicit activities stand in stark contrast to how European states and their agencies have handled the issue of migrant mortality. As pointed out earlier, Europe's Mediterranean border accounts for the vast majority of migrant deaths recorded globally (IOM, 2017: 6). Yet, there are no official public bodies hat have taken on responsibility for systematically collecting data on migrant mortality or for identifying the dead (Weber and Pickering, 2011; Aas and Gundhus, 2015). Since 2013, the International Organization of Migration (IOM) has been collecting such data through its Missing Migrants Project. However, in the absence of robust and reliable reporting mechanisms and limited resources, "data on migrant fatalities are, at best, estimates and at worst, serious undercounts" (IOM, 2017: 21; see also Last et al., 2017).

Conclusion

Collection of data about migrant mortality, and the inadequate efforts to identify the dead, accentuate the distinction between the citizen and the alien. Although some EU states, such as Greece and Italy, have invested significant efforts towards identification efforts, these are still largely unable "to identify a significant fraction of the dead" (IOM, 2017: 71). Such administrative knowledge gaps would be unthinkable with regard to the citizen population. As a subject of knowledge, the migrant is first and foremost "a risky subject" rather than "a subject at risk" (Rose, 2010), a security threat that can potentially be subjected to the use of state penal power.

This chapter has outlined five distinct aspects of the crimmigrant other as a penal subject: the crimmigrant body, illegality, deportability, the spectacle, and knowledge. These aspects touch upon legal, techno-scientific, and emotive aspects of the subject. Migrants are constructed as "illegal" and as a security threat to a collective "we", while the "ongoing irruption of media spectacles around migration speaks to the ways in which the immigration evokes strong political affect around commonsense imaginings of national belonging" (Vukov, 2003: 340). The following chapters of the book will argue that these commonsense imaginings of the national and the foreign are not simply structured around notions of security, which is the usual focus in scholarly literature, but also about morality, notions of blame, innocence, and deservedness. In Chapter 2, we will see how such perceptions structure the growing use of various modes of penal control.

It should be pointed out, though, that the aspects of penal subjectivity addressed in this chapter are by no means exhaustive. They could, in addition to moral and cultural otherness, also include racialization and exploitability. There exists a substantial body of work documenting the intersections of race and migration control (see, inter alia, Bosworth and Flavin, 2007; Weber and Bowling, 2012; Bosworth et al., 2017, 2018; Parmar, 2019) as well as criminalisation and economic exploitability of migrants (Calavita, 2005; Melossi, 2013a; Vecchio, 2015). While the following chapters will show how those subjected to penal power at the border are poor, racialised, and marked by colonial legacies, this book also needs to acknowledge its own limitations in terms of providing a comprehensive account of these issues.

Notes

1 https://ec.europa.eu/home-affairs/sites/homeaffairs/files/what-we-do/poli cies/european-agenda-migration/background-information/docs/2_hotsp ots_en.pdf
2 In a staff working document on the implementation of the Eurodac regulation.
3 www.amnesty.ie/hotspot-italy-abuses-refugees-migrants-eus-approach-ma naging-migration/
4 Translation by the author.
5 Source: www.eulisa.europa.eu/Publications/Reports/2017-088_2016%20Eur odac%20Annual%20Report.pdf
6 www.eulisa.europa.eu/Publications/Reports/2018%20VIS%20reports.pdf
7 https://id4d.worldbank.org/
8 www.nidsenter.no/en/about-us/about-norwegian-id-centre/
9 Although the distinction between the "mobility exporting" and "mobility importing/restricting" countries approximately reflects the global North–South division, this is not absolute and can also be seen within countries, for example in the former Yugoslavia or Italy, or the EU itself (in the case of Roma).
10 www.nrk.no/livsstil/slik-bor-de-som-skal-sendes-ut-av-landet-1.13770138
11 "DACA" stands for "Deferred Action for Childhood Arrivals".
12 Source: www.nato.int/cps/en/natohq/opinions_119822.htm
13 Source: Frontex (2018).

2

BORDERED PENALITY AND CRIMMIGRATION CONTROL

> The point of increasing penalties is, after all, that it should not be attractive to come back to Norway after deportation. And we hope to see this effect sooner or later – that people will think it is not a good idea to come back here, because they know that if they come here, that means a year in prison right away.
>
> *(Police officer, Oslo Police Department, oreigners' section)*

The role of punishment in modern society is changing. Traditionally, punishment has been regarded as a reaction to a wrongdoing. Its purpose has been either to redress the harm done, deter future crime, isolate offenders from society, or reform them in the process – or all of the above (Garland, 1990; Von Hirsch, 1996). Today, the traditional purposes of punishment have been overshadowed by another objective: border control. As the police officer's statement above reveals, states are increasingly using penal power to deter migration and to make themselves less attractive to unwanted migrants. Contemporary penal institutions have gained an additional purpose, which is to control mobility. Growing police efforts are devoted to performing border controls, both inside state territory and on its borders (Weber, 2013; Van der Woude and Brouwer, 2017; Parmar, 2019).

Criminal law is used not only to deter crime, but to deter mobility (Aliverti, 2013; Mitsilegas, 2015); European prisons are warehousing growing numbers of immigrants and preparing their inmates, not for reintegration, but for expulsion from society (Bosworth and Kaufman, 2011; Kaufman, 2015; Ugelvik and Damsa, 2017). Controlling unwanted mobility has become a driving force behind many traditional penal strategies, as well as an impetus towards penal innovation. This chapter examines these developments.

Chapter 1 outlined central aspects of the crimmigrant other as a penal subject, and we shall now see how these features interact with state penal measures. We shall examine three main modalities of penal power – criminalisation, policing, and imprisonment – and see how they are being used for the purpose of controlling unwanted mobility, and how these dynamics are fundamentally reshaping the nature of penal power in Europe. Finally, the chapter will examine deportation once more – as a particular penal measure – and examine how it shapes the nature of membership in contemporary societies. However, first we need to look at some of the underlying social dynamics behind the use of penal power over immigrants.

Bordered penality: the power to punish and the power to banish

Most traditional accounts of penal power are based on the assumption that punishment is about what Linda Bosniak (2006) terms the "already presumed members" – namely, citizens. Usually this assumption is unspoken and the citizenship status of those subjected to penal power remains unaddressed. A central element of punishment has always been exclusion, albeit temporary, from the presumed moral community. This book, however, is about what happens when penal power is exercised over people who find themselves not only on the moral, but also on the territorial and formal borders of membership (Aas and Bosworth, 2013; Kaufman, 2015; Barker, 2018). It argues that, when subjected to state penal measures, non-members, or those whose hold on membership is tenuous, encounter a different landscape from citizens. Citizenship, therefore, is of central importance for understanding how and why states use penal institutions.

As we saw in Chapter 1, the key difference between non-citizens and citizens – or between crimmigrant others and other types of deviants – lies in the centrality of deportation for the former. Crimmigrant others are deportable. They can be completely territorially excluded, for several years or a lifetime, not just from a country but from the entire European continent. The penality directed at non-citizens thus departs from ordinary sanctions by having an additional purpose, which at times becomes predominant. Penal intervention aims to guard not only society's moral boundaries but also its territorial ones. It functions as border control in an extended sense, defining and defending the boundaries of membership (Barker, 2018). The primary focus is, therefore, not on moral censure, but on *who has the right to be in the country*. As the statement by a Norwegian police officer quoted above makes clear, the state's objective is not only to expel undesirable groups and individuals, but to prevent them from coming back to the country. Although perceived as one of the least punitive societies in Europe, in 2014 Norway, for this reason, trippled the maximum penalty for breaches of the entry ban from six months' to two years' imprisonment.

The crimmigrant other is subjected to a distinct type of penal power: a *bordered penality* (Aas, 2014); this represents an intertwining of two forms of state sovereign power: the power to punish and the power to banish. Sovereignty is, as Wendy Brown (2010: 52) observes, "a peculiar border concept". It denotes both supremacy and autonomy; it is understood as the state's ability to be "a decisive power of rule and as freedom from occupation by another" (ibid.). These two meanings and functions have traditionally belonged to the separate spheres of internal and external security. The role of criminal law and policing has been to preserve internal security, to establish the sovereign's supremacy and the moral order of the society, in short to create a well-*ordered* and -disciplined society (Foucault, 1977; Simon, 2007). The sphere of external security, on the other hand, has traditionally been governed by military security and international relations, together with border security and immigration law; the task here has been to preserve the state's territorial integrity and autonomy. Traditionally, border control has sought to maintain clear boundaries between the inside and the outside of the state – the maintenance of a *bordered* society (Aas, 2013a).

Although inhabiting separate domains, border issues and crime control have some common features. They share the language of protection and security and, as Juliet Stumpf (2006) observes, both criminal and immigration law traditionally act as "gatekeepers of membership", defining the terms of social inclusion and exclusion. Questions about who belongs, and what kind of rights they have, are embedded in penal sanctions as well as in decisions to expel and deny entry. As the intensification of globalisation in recent decades has destabilised the established boundaries between internal and external security, policing, and soldiering, and the domains of immigration and criminal law, the distinction between the two aspects of sovereignty has become increasingly unclear (Andreas and Price, 2002; Stumpf, 2006). The growing mobility and the influx of non-citizens into the territorial domain of the nation state is producing fragmentation and to some extent dissolving the (national) penal domain by mixing elements of the "internal" and the "external", thus creating novel configurations of the penal (Aas, 2013a). As is shown by the growing numbers of foreign prisoners in European prisons and crime statistics (Aebi et al., 2019), and various policing strategies directed at non-citizens, (domestic) punishment is becoming increasingly internationalised, taking on the symbolic and practical functions of border control. The project of creating an "ordered society" through penal intervention has thus become increasingly intertwined with control of the border and the project of creating a "bordered society".

This intertwining and convergence of two formerly separate spheres has been described in socio-legal scholarship as crimmigration law. The term became widely known through Stumpf's (2006) seminal article "The Crimmigration Crisis: Immigrants, Crime, and Sovereign Power", in which she argued that we are witnessing the convergence of criminal law and immigration law (i.e. crimmigration law), which can be seen in the increasing criminalisation of immigration offences and in the growing similarities in their enforcement (see also McLeod, 2012). While these two spheres of law used to operate quite separately, with separate of courts, lawyers, procedures, and policing agencies, this is no longer the case (García Hernández, 2015). Crimmigration scholarship has opened an important avenue for understanding the growing use of penal power and coercive measures against populations of migrants and non-citizens (see also Guia et al., 2013; Van der Woude et al., 2014, 2017 for a European perspective). It has highlighted the central importance of membership for the operation of the law and for defining the rights and justice to which individuals have access. As we shall also see in Chapter 5, crimmigrant others do not get the same level of rights and the same quality of justice as citizens. The guarding of membership is also the animating force of crimmigration control and defines its political prominence and the intensity of punitive sentiments, which often have an impact on the severity of crimmigration control measures.

However, some scholars of borders and migration control have been reluctant to use the term "crimmigration". This may be partly due to the fact that the term is often applied uncritically and that the convergence of immigration control and crime control is seen as a process of merger. Empirical studies, on the other hand, reveal that, far from seamlessly merging, the two spheres – although strongly influencing each other – often continue to retain their distinctive features and demand nuanced examination (Moffette, 2018). In Chapter 1, we saw that notions of migration and crime do not always fit comfortably together; this is also felt by for those working within the system. As Chapter 4 will show, they can produce a considerable amount of moral discomfort and resistance. Others have also questioned the novelty of the developments outlined by the crimmigration thesis and pointed out the similarities between the treatment of migrants and other racialised groups in the US context (Garner, 2015). There is, therefore, much to suggest that, despite growing similarities and convergences, we need to be analytically attuned to the distinctions between the two aspects of sovereignty – the ordered and the bordered – as well as keeping in mind their historic and socio-political antecedents.

Bordered penality, nevertheless, creates a need for new frames of understanding, and a reconsideration of some of the central assumptions about punishment which are deeply rooted in the established conceptions of "normal penalty". In other words, it requires a change of perspective within studies of punishment and criminal justice (Bosworth et al., 2018). The intertwining of the ordered and the bordered fundamentally changes the nature of penal power, making it into a hybrid, which often raises the question as to whether we are any longer dealing with penal power and penal institutions. Is it imprisonment when migrants are placed in closed detention centres? These institutions often look like prisons, and make migrants feel as if they are in prison, but they lack the institutional discourses and legitimation which animate imprisonment regimes in most European countries (Bosworth, 2013).

The issue has been particularly prominent in the heated debates about whether deportation can be defined as punishment (Kanstroom, 2010). It is not so defined by most national and international legal systems. Nevertheless, as Chapter 3 will show, in practice, state authorities often use deportation with punitive intentions and as a means of addressing the problem of crime. More importantly, deportation may have an equally devastating impact on deportees and their families as criminal sanctions, yet immigration law does not usually give those subjected to it the right to free legal aid (Kaanstrom, 2010; Vazquez, 2012). How, then, should we talk about this severe form of state infliction of pain, whose purpose is to sanction transgressions, manage the crime problem, and resolve membership issues? In the face of this challenge, the inadequacy of the language we traditionally use to describe punishment and penality becomes apparent. The term "punishment", in modern times, has acquired specific connotations with prison. Influential works such as *Discipline and Punish* (Foucault, 1977) have equated punishment with imprisonment, making it the main focus of criminological attention and neglecting other forms of penality such as fines and community sanctions (Bosworth et al., 2018).

Bordered penality, on the other hand, requires that our understanding of punishment should move away from the shadow of the prison, and develop a language for the emerging forms of state infliction of pain which are designed to maintain a bordered society (Bosworth et al., 2018). In such a context, the notion of penal controls may be more productive than that of punishment. As Garland (2013b) observes, the notion of "punishment" suggests that the phenomenon in question is primarily "retributive" or "punitive", thereby misrepresenting penal measures that are oriented to other goals such as control, correction, or compensation. The main objective of penal controls directed at the crimmigrant other is to control the movement and identity of persons on whom state authorities do not want to lose their grip. One public prosecutor working on a project focusing on Romanian citizens in Oslo described this strategy thus:

We start quite often with arrests. We present them for an imprisonment hearing, and most of them stay in pre-trial detention until the
case comes up for trial. The case is not actually finished with until
they are convicted and then deported. Our cases are quite unusual,
because, in the first place, all interrogation and all the other work goes
on via an interpreter ... And, as I said, we imprison many of them.
They are not just imprisoned once. Often they are imprisoned again
and again, and remain in pre-trial detention until they come to trial.
This is because of the danger of absconding, you see? If you let them
go, they disappear out of the country.

(MAJ4)

The quote is a good illustration of how bordered penality works in
practice, and how imprisonment is applied, quite extensively, in order
to control unwanted movement.

Finally, when the power to punish and the power to banish become
intertwined, this challenges not only the dividing lines between the
spheres of crime control and immigration control, but also distinctions
between punitive and parsimonious societies. In Europe, particularly,
where the use of state penal power has been marked by a certain level of
ambivalence and restraint, and a commitment to human rights (van Zyl
Smit and Snacken, 2009), border control brings a sense of urgency and a
greater willingness to use the state's coercive means in order to contain a
threat. In fact, when the power to punish and the power to banish become
intertwined, it appears that the latter may be reinvigorating the former. As
we shall see in Chapter 3, this dynamic is particularly salient in Scandinavian countries. The dividing lines that students of penality should be aware
of are, therefore, not only those between neoliberal and welfare societies
(Cavadino and Dignan, 2006), but also between open and closed ones.

Criminalisation

The urge to control and banish the unwanted migrant has then become an
impetus for penal intervention. The term "criminalisation of migration" is
used to denote the growing presence of migrants and foreign citizens in
the criminal justice system and the general severity of border enforcement
regimes. This broad and uncritical reference to criminalisation tends to

obscure a more nuanced understanding of the concept and its "deeper and more precise theoretical legacy".[1] The concept refers to a series of definitional processes which, on different levels, result in migrants being classed as criminal offenders and certain acts as being criminal. The previous chapter outlined illegality as one of the defining features of the crimmigrant other. The "accident of birth" in a country in the global South carries a number of consequences. From this basic premise follow a plethora of offences –illegal entry and re-entry, overstaying, etc. – along with intricate processes of control and penal intervention (Aliverti, 2013; Mitsilegas, 2015).

In recent years, several Northern states have expanded the catalogue of immigration offences. In the UK, as Ana Aliverti (2012) points out, the expansion has been considerable. Since 1997, on average, Parliament has passed a piece of immigration and asylum legislation every two years. By means of these legislative changes, criminal law is increasingly used to punish transgressions of a web of legal technicalities, which regulate the conditions of stay for non-citizens. Illegality, therefore, is not a static condition: it can be better described as a process of illegalisation (De Genova and Peutz, 2011), involving often complex rules about applying for permits, extensions, meeting intricate documentation conditions, entry bans, and the like.

Other countries, like Norway, have made less use of state legislative power to increase the numbers of immigration offences, and have instead introduced more stringent law enforcement and harsher penalties for existing offences. In the US, illegal entry and re-entry have gone from being relatively minor categories of offences to crimes which now dominate US federal courts (García Hernández, 2015). As Menjívar and Kanstroom (2014: 10) report:

> In 2011 alone, some 188,000 "known criminal aliens" were removed from the United States; many of them were lawful permanent residents and were in the "criminal alien" category only because they had been prosecuted for immigration violations that were formerly routinely handled through civil deportation processes.

Immigration-related prosecutions outnumber all other federal criminal prosecutions, including drugs and weapons prosecutions (Stumpf,

2006). According to Eagly (2010: 1281), not "since Prohibition has a single category of crime been prosecuted in such record numbers by the federal government". European studies have still to document similar trends, although Melossi (2013b: 424) reports that "between 70 and 80 percent of the migrants who are arrested, reported, convicted or detained in Italy are 'undocumented'". The prosecution of immigration offences often serves other purposes than punishment of these particular transgressions. As Aliverti (2012) points out, the role of criminalisation is often symbolic and the offences themselves are not enforced. The creation of these criminal offences may be read as an attempt to appease the wrath of the electorate and the media about the "immigration problem": "By introducing these offences, the government send[s] a message that the situation is under control" (ibid.: 417).

Criminalisation of immigration offences often has several other effects, which cannot simply be reduced to numbers of actual enforcements and days or months of imprisonment for breaches of immigration law. The state uses the enforcement of immigration offences as a lever to achieve other objectives, such as deportation or combating terrorism. As Lazarus et al. (2013: 473) note, both the US government's war on terror and UK immigration law were used "to justify indefinite detention of foreigners suspected of terrorist activity, especially those who could not be deported to their home countries". As we shall see in the next chapter, the field of bordered penality opens the way for the considerable use of discretion by enforcement agents, who are able to "change tracks" between criminal and administrative proceedings. Also, other studies have documented that extensive and unregulated discretionary power of state agents are one of the hallmarks of crimmigration enforcement (see, inter alia, Legomsky, 2007; Gundhus, 2016; Van der Woude and van der Leun, 2017). Criminal prosecution is therefore only one among several options, and is often "reserved for those foreigners for whom the primary sanction – expulsion – cannot be carried out. In these cases, a criminal prosecution and conviction facilitate administrative proceedings leading to removal" (Aliverti, 2012: 417).

The selective and highly erratic prosecution of these offences militates against the predictability and certainty of criminal norms. Penality directed at non-citizens is governed by different parameters than when criminal law is directed at citizens. As Menjívar and Kanstroom (2014: 2) observe, when it comes to punishment, in most modern legal systems, it "is the conduct that counts, not legal status. In immigration law, however, the relationship between legal conduct and status is inherently quite complicated." State use of criminal law is intimately connected to questions of who has the right to stay in the country. Illegality thus comes close to becoming an existential condition (ibid.) and, as Zedner (2013) points out, many immigration offences lack a sufficient culpability requirement. Individuals are being punished due to no or limited fault of their own. Immigration offences also present a challenge to several other central principles of criminal law, such as the harm principle and proportionality (Aliverti, 2012; Zedner, 2013). The instrumental use of criminal law to pursue immigration policy objectives seriously distorts its use to censure really serious wrongs (Aliverti, 2012).

Criminal law is, as Lucia Zedner (2013: 41) observes, "predicated on the figure of the citizen". Its application to non-citizens is a departure from established principles and connects it to mobility control and membership issues. The question of mobility control thus often overshadows traditional considerations, such as the proportionality or legitimacy of criminal sanctions. We shall see in Chapter 3 that Norway, for example, has introduced harsher penalties and more stringent prosecution of so-called "mobile property offenders", where the cross-border mobility of an offender in itself becomes an aggravating circumstance (Flaatten, 2017).

This desire to control and penalise unwanted movement is also creating a number of other categories of transgressions and control measures. The Dublin Regulation, which still forms the controversial backbone of the EU's allocation of asylum seekers, penalises so-called "asylum shoppers" by preventing them from applying for asylum in the country of their choice. Similarly, the EU–Turkey deal, signed to bring an end to the "crisis" of 2015, in effect confined applicants for international protection to a limited number of Greek islands which, as Iliadou (2019) observes, are in many ways resembling prison islands. Most immigration systems require asylum seekers to report, or to leave designated areas and countries, or detain them in camps and closed detention centres. The objective of this web of controls – which due to their reliance on penal power can be termed penal controls – is to stop, direct, prevent, or induce movement in certain directions. The authorities may, for example, use extensive police force and criminal sanctions to disperse people from irregular encampments such as the so-called Jungle near Calais.[2]

The transgressions committed by migrants caught in this web of penal controls are primarily *spatial* rather than *moral* transgressions. They are moving and staying in certain spaces against state wishes, yet the moral reprehensibility of their actions is highly questionable. For example, by applying for protection in a Southern European country, an asylum seeker is exercising his or her legal right. Yet, by leaving this country because of difficult living conditions and poor prospects of achieving protection – a decision which may certainly be understandable from a humane point of view – an individual's movements become unauthorised. Due to this complicated relationship between the right to territorial presence and transgression, several authors have pointed out the inadequacy of the binary terms of legality/illegality, authorised/unauthorised, and documented/undocumented (Kubal, 2013; Menjìvar and Kanstroom, 2014).These notions direct attention not only to the fluidity and elasticity of immigrant illegality, but also to the myriad of bureaucratic practices by which states themselves "actually engage in perpetuating the legally ambiguous modes of incorporation" (Kubal, 2013: 555).

Policing

The fluidity and expandability of the category of illegality has important implications for the nature of other aspects of bordered penality, including law enforcement. The field of migration policing has recently seen a remarkable growth. For example, the budget of the European Border and Coast Guard Agency (Frontex) skyrocketed from €6 million in 2005, when the agency was established, to €320.1 million in 2018. Its staff numbers are set to more than double in the next few years.[3] Frontex's budget is more than twice the size of Europol's (€135.7 million in 2018), and clearly reflects the EU's political priorities. The US Immigration and Customs Enforcement (ICE) is now the largest investigative arm of the US Department of Homeland Security (Stumpf, 2006), while, in Norway, at one point the Police Immigration Service had grown to become half of the size of Oslo district police force.

These examples serve as an indication of the changes that the prominence of border control has made to the field of policing. They show the growing resources invested by Northern states in the control of the crimmigrant other. As Chapter 3 will show in greater detail, this focus and these resources have been central to the production of immigrant criminality. Most of the police officers interviewed in our project clearly recognised the change of focus and actually talked about the growing demands for the "production" of immigration-related cases. This is how one officer in Northern Norway described the new state of affairs:

[Before] it was more like that: cases came in and one took up those that came in, and it was almost random how one discovered things. The way we do it now is that we have a scheme involving what we call the responsible [*jourhavende*] investigator. The week that you are responsible, you have the responsibility for going through all the police registers, that is all the databases in which the police register information … It was different in the past; it was not something one focused on. It was like at the end of the year, "Yes, we have this many expulsion cases." Now, right from the start, that is from January, we go through what we have to produce, what is expected of each one of us, and our unit has to produce 75 expulsion cases. This does not mean that we will deport 75 people, but we have to produce 75 expulsion cases that we instigate.

(Police officer, Borders and Foreigners unit, Tromsø police district)

Importantly, these changes are not only a question of political pressure and influence, or of a growing inflow of funds, personnel and equipment; the changing nature of the tasks performed is also an element. Migration policing involves a number of tasks and modalities, such as pre-entry level controls, detecting entry into state territory, monitoring and ensuring migrant compliance with the conditions of their visitor's visas and/or other permits, along with policing documents, and, not least, deportation (Gundhus and Franko, 2016). There is now an extensive body of work thoroughly documenting the nature of migration and border policing in various countries in the global North (see, inter alia, Pickering and Weber, 2013; Weber, 2013; Brouwer et al.,

2018; Armenta, 2017; Parmar, 2019), and at the transnational level (Bigo et al., 2013; Aas and Gundhus, 2015). It is beyond the scope of this chapter to summarise this scholarship or describe in detail the many facets of policing of borders and mobility. Our focus must be on the processes through which perceptions of crimmigrant others structure police practices, making them the focal point of police suspicion.

Previous discussion has signalled one particular aspect of bordered penality and mobility control: the importance of identity. For the crimmigrant other, establishing who he or she is (as regards origin, citizenship, the right to stay, the nature of travel, etc.) often takes precedence over other considerations. Looking for documents and investigation of documents thus become a central task for policing agencies (Weber and Bowling, 2012; Gundhus, 2016; Van der Woude and Van der Leun, 2017). And, while we noted earlier that distinguishing between members and non-members is an essential requirement for successful administrative ordering of society, it also involves adopting a suspicious attitude, which produces suspicious identities. There is therefore a reciprocal relationship and tension between identification and identity. "The question 'who is this person?'" leaches constantly into the question 'what kind of person is this?'" (Caplan and Torpey, 2001: 3). As Morrison (2017: 22) observes, the "process of identifying the stranger has an expected response – exaggerated fear of the stranger".

In recent years this dynamic has led to the prevalence of police ethno-racial profiling; immigration policing has had a role in exacerbating the problem (Weber and Bowling, 2012; Parmar, 2011; Fassin, 2013; Van der Woude and Van der Leun, 2017). Police discretion can thus often turn into discrimination (Holmberg, 2000; Van der Woude and Van der Leun, 2017), which on a structural level can be deeply damaging for levels of trust among minority communities (Brouwer, 2019). The prominence of the immigrant as the object of police attention can be partly ascribed to the fact that incongruence, as Loftus (2010) points out, often forms the basis of police suspicion. Police officers' on-the-spot decisions about who may be involved in crime are frequently shaped by stereotypes "about particular social groups and situations, and invariably result[ed] in patterns of differentiation along distinctions of class, age, gender, sexuality and ethnicity" (ibid.: 15). As a stranger "who does not fit in", the immigrant becomes a seemingly natural focus of stop-and-search practices.

However, immigration law adds an additional element to this age-old tendency to focus on people "who do not fit in". For police officers, in their capacity as street-level bureaucrats, the possibility of using administrative law opens up alternative avenues of intervention (Van der Woude and Van der Leun, 2017). A racialised other who is stopped on suspicion of involvement in crime can also be a person with suspect permission to stay in the country, and vice versa. The crimmigrant other is, therefore, potentially the object of dual suspicion and the suspicion of irregular mobility can always conveniently morph into, and merge with, other forms of criminality and unwanted behaviours that police are trying to control (ibid.). Vigneswaran (2013: 123), for example, shows how South African police "resort to laws concerning human mobility as a 'default' response to a range of crimes that they are unable to effectively control", such as illegal street trade in counterfeit music and films. Similarly, Jahnsen and Skilbrei's (2018) study of prostitution policy shows how police combine criminal law and immigration law in different ways, thus producing exclusionary outcomes for foreign women.

In Europe, so-called mobile property offenders (often from Eastern Europe), have become a high policing priority in several countries, including Denmark and Norway. The two countries have developed special police projects to target the problem (Sausdal, 2018): units have been equipped with skills and resources to tackle cross-border aspects of policing, including linguistic skills and expertise in international cooperation mechanisms. Police focus on mobile foreigners is underpinned by a heightened perception of danger, which distinguishes them from native offenders. As one officer in our study put it:

> One of the challenges connected to foreign groups is that they are so incredibly mobile. A Norwegian property offender in a way focuses on his immediate surroundings, on where he lives, whereas these groups travel across the borders of districts and are more mobile.
>
> *(POD 10 in Gundhus and Franko, 2016: 502)*

Such perceptions of the danger posed by foreign offenders have not only justified the use of more extensive and coercive policing and surveillance methods but can also, as David Sausdal's (2018) study of Danish police shows, produce a pessimistic sense of imminent social decay and nostalgia for the good old days among officers.

The extensive body of work on police ethnic profiling points to the long historic traditions which join police focus on race and ethnicity (Weber and Bowling, 2012); it is also the case that such processes are not necessarily seamless or self-evident. As the earlier quote from the Norwegian police officer shows, the police force had to be sensitised to the importance of immigration control. It was required to "produce" more deportation cases through a top-down process, which changed the unit's priorities and perceptions of "proper" police work and "proper criminality". In such a situation, where the importance of immigration control may not be self-evident to the officers, ideas about dangerous foreign offenders lend a sense of urgency to the task, making it seem important for the protection of the nation, and mirror popular and media discourses about the need to fend off an imminent threat (Brouwer et al., 2017). The various practical and operative ways in which crime control and mobility control are merged thus result from a particular imagination, which makes the crimmigrant other a "natural" focus of police intervention (Gundhus and Jansen, 2019). As Vigneswaran (2013: 126) observes, "developing a narrative of criminal mobility is a subtle and complex discursive exercise, requiring the exercise of an official's imagination."

However, when analysing these processes of metamorphosis and redefinition that affect border control and traditional law enforcement, it is not enough, as Van der Woude and Van der Leun (2017) point out, to focus solely on the individual officer's perceptions and possible prejudice. One also needs to take into account intricate organisational dynamics, which are present at local, national, and supranational levels. Institutionally, the morphing of the crimmigrant other from one kind of criminal to another enables cross-fertilisation between various fields of policing. In the present political climate, migration control brings a sense of urgency and vitality (and much-needed funds) to traditional law enforcement agencies. Border control agencies, on the other hand, have gained power by redefining themselves as crime fighters, and have tapped into the authorisations, modes of operation, and legitimacy open to traditional law enforcement agencies (Brouwer et al., 2017). As the EU*observer* reported recently:

Frontex has effectively become a law enforcement agency. Focus on migration has morphed into drug smuggling, document fraud, terrorism, and cigarette smuggling. It has even seized arms. "I would not object if you define us as a law enforcement agency at EU level," Fabrice Leggeri, the agency's chief, told EUobserver on Tuesday (20 February).[4]

The remarkable transformation of Frontex will be addressed in greater detail in Chapter 4. What we can note at this point is the blurring of institutional and professional boundaries between previously distinct fields of policing. Border policing is, as Pickering and Weber (2013) point out, by nature transversal. It crosses established boundaries, not only geographical ones, but also the institutional ones between various policing actors and public/private divides, thus opening up "spaces of governance which are ripe for colonization" (ibid.: 94). Migration and global mobility challenge the presumption that policing is about the creation of order among fellow citizens of a national community (Weber, 2013). It raises questions about who the public is and about what happens to the police and policing when its activities are targeted specifically at non-citizens. More precisely, what are the consequences for the police when they are increasingly given the task of distinguishing citizens and non-citizens, legitimate and non-legitimate members of a community?

Imprisonment: houses of banishment

A similar question can be asked about the next aspect of bordered penalty – namely, what happens to penal institutions when those who are detained in them are no longer citizens? Consider the following description of the Trandum immigration detention centre near Oslo airport, provided by the Norwegian Parliamentary Ombudsman (Sivilombudsmannen, 2015, my translation):

One of the main findings during the visit was excessive attention to control and security at the expense of the individual detainee's integrity … Several described the humiliation of undergoing a body search on arrival and after all visits. The body search entailed the removal of all clothing and that the detainee had to squat over a mirror on the floor so that the staff could check whether they had concealed items in their rectum or genital area. The detainees perceived it as especially upsetting that a full body search was conducted after all visits, even when staff members had been present in the room during the visit. Many were also frustrated that they were not given access to their mobile phone and that they were locked in their rooms during evenings, at night, and for shorter periods during the day.

The detention centre uses largely the same security procedures as the correctional services, including procedures for locking detainees in and out of their rooms, the use of security cells and solitary confinement, and room searches. In some respects, as in the case of full body searches after visits, the procedures appear to be more intrusive than in many prisons.

Trandum is surrounded by high fences and barbed wire; it looks very much like a prison and, for practical purposes, it functions like a prison. Detainees are called "inmates" and are subjected to strict security measures and locked into their cells at night. They have strictly allotted times for recreation and are not allowed to use mobile phones. However, unlike other Norwegian prisons, Trandum until recently also housed children and families. What distinguishes the institution from a prison is its purpose: in a prison, the aim among others, is to reintegrate prisoners into society, whereas in Trandum "they are on the way out" (Ugelvik and Ugelvik, 2013). We could say that, while prisons have traditionally been called reformatories or "houses of correction", institutions like Trandum are different. They can be described as *houses of banishment*. This is made very evident by the institution's strategic placement right by the airport runway, with the loud sound of planes landing and taking off providing a constant reminder of the destiny of its inmates.

Trandum is by no means unusual. Immigration detention centres, although not historically a novelty, have seen a dramatic expansion in the past two decades in the countries of both the global North and global South (Cheliotis, 2013; Bosworth, 2014; Turnbull, 2017). The term "immigration detention centre" covers a variety of institutions and there are considerable jurisdictional differences in the length of detention and composition of the detained populations. In some jurisdictions, such as the UK and Norway, the detention of minors is allowed under some circumstances, whereas in others, for example Italy, it is strictly forbidden (Campesi, 2015). It is beyond the scope of this book to address the comparative aspects in detail. What is of interest here is the nature of the institutional arrangements which are being put in place to control the crimmigrant other.

A large body of scholarship has outlined the similarities and differences between immigration detention and imprisonment regimes (see, inter alia, Ugelvik, 2013, Ugelvik and Ugelvik, 2013; Bosworth, 2014; Turnbull, 2017). Although institutions for immigrants deprive their inmates of their liberty, they are driven by a different set of rationalities and do not have the objectives traditionally ascribed to imprisonment – namely, correction and reintegration into society. Instead of aiming to reintegrate and to produce the normalised subjectivity of a citizen, Bosworth (2012: 130) observes: "British immigration removal centres fall short of the familiar justifications of custody, namely rehabilitation, deterrence or punishment ... The centres can only produce what has already been made: non-citizens." Rather than aiming to reintegrate inmates into the nation, the purpose of the emerging institutional regimes, and the therapeutic work conducted in them, is designed to ease and encourage inmates' return to their presumed land of origin. Departure – whether coerced or voluntary, termed "deportation", "expulsion", or "return" – is the desired objective towards which the state is directing its efforts, and which, from the detainees' perspective, is the main cause of stress and resistance (Bosworth, 2012).

Detention may serve a number of purposes, such as preventing absconding prior to deportation, determining detainees' identity, seeking their cooperation, or wearing down their resistance to "voluntary" return (Campesi, 2015; Brouwer, 2019). However, while detention centres and other crimmigration institutions often have a strong resemblance to prisons and criminal justice institutions, critics have pointed out that they lack a legitimating discourse and the awareness of due process and rights, which is normally found in criminal justice (Bosworth, 2013). These institutions are also less transparent and several countries do not regularly publish official data about them. In addition to the heavy emphasis on security which had, for example, made the Trandum detention centre into an institution resembling a high security prison, immigration detention has several other features which increase levels of frustration among detainees. At one point, Trandum had to be temporarily closed down because of damage done to the property. There were also recorded cases of serious self-harm and attempted suicide. Such occurrences are not uncommon (Weber and Pickering, 2011).

In detention centres, the state deprives migrants of their liberty to control unwanted mobility or to induce them to move in a certain direction. And, while such practices may fall short of traditional understandings of punishment, and are better described as the penal control of mobility, they nevertheless reveal the productive nature of penal power. Penal power should be studied not only for its repressive effects (of which there is plenty of evidence in immigration detention), but also, as Foucault (1977) reminds us, for its productive intentions. As pointed out by Bosworth above, immigration detention produces non-citizens. The state's intention is to shape the detained non-citizens into individuals who are prepared to leave, and to give up their claims to residence and aspirations to membership of the country (Brouwer, 2019). The state's intentions are, therefore, directed outwards, beyond state territory (Aas, 2013a). The rationality has been described by Didier Bigo (2006) as banoptic: instead of the traditional panoptic disciplining and training of souls (Foucault, 1977), the priority is banishment and territorial exclusion (Aas, 2011).

Bordered penality thus represents a shift from a panoptic to a banoptic penality. While panoptic rationalities have long provided a blueprint for understanding imprisonment and its physical and moral architecture, banopticism moves the attention from moral reform and control of the soul to control of cross-border movement. The crimmigrant other, it would appear, is first and foremost deportable, rather than reformable. To be precise, state penal institutions are concentrating their efforts on inmates' deportability, rather than their reformability. However, it would be misguided to underestimate the moral aspects of bordered penality. The crimmigrant other is frequently perceived as a moral threat to the nation and his or her social exclusion is a product of the interplay between administrative and punitive sanctions and institutional arrangements. Several scholars have documented the circulation of populations between immigration and criminal justice institutions.

Campesi (2015: 431) reports that around 25 per cent of those in Italian pre-removal detention centres have been in prison. Similarly, Bhui (2016: 268) reports that about a third of immigration detention centre places in the UK are occupied by ex-prisoners, while 400 immigration detainees are held in prisons.

The foreign offender is, therefore, a transgressive figure who circulates between immigration detention centres and traditional prisons (Turnbull and Hasselberg, |2017). European prisons are no longer domestic institutions, but increasingly house large groups of so-called foreign offenders (Bosworth and Kaufman, 2011; Kaufman, 2015; Ugelvik, 2017; Aebi et al., 2019), many of whom await deportation after their sentence. In the past two decades, there has been a dramatic rise in the numbers of foreign citizens in prison populations: the percentage is on average 20 per cent in most Western European countries and a staggering 73.8 per cent in Switzerland.

The reasons for the variations in the figures are manifold and reflect, among other things, differences in the percentage of foreign citizens in the general population and their involvement in illegal activities, the use of prisons for housing immigration detainees, as well as differences in immigration law and in law enforcement practices, which may target certain types of offences and offenders. Nevertheless, what Table 2.1 clearly shows are the remarkable differences between Eastern and Western Europe, which will be further addressed in Chapter 3. Western European countries are imprisoning large numbers of foreign citizens, many of whom are of Eastern European origin. According to data obtained by the EU*observer* in 2016,[6] there were 11,511 Romanian citizens imprisoned abroad (almost half of the Romanian national prison population), while the number of Albanian citizens in European prisons (5,722) in fact exceeds its national prison population.

In important ways these trends are reshaping the nature of imprisonment in Europe. Ugelvik (2017), for example, describes the everyday difficulties prison authorities face in housing foreign offenders. It is important to note that the banoptic rationalities described above are not only guiding immigration detention institutions but are also reshaping traditional imprisonment regimes which now have hybrid purposes and populations. They are creating novel institutional arrangements, such as special prison wings or special prisons dedicated to housing foreign

TABLE 2.1 Foreign nationals in prison population[5]

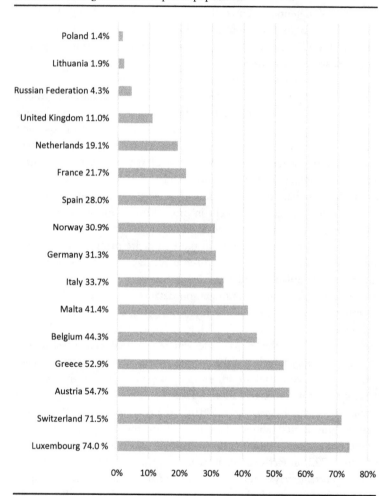

Source: World Prison Brief. URL: http://www.prisonstudies.org/info/worldbrief/wpb_
stats.php?area=all&category=wb_foreign

offenders which have been established in the UK, Norway, and the Netherlands (Ugelvik, 2013; Kaufman, 2015; Brouwer, 2019).

Norway opened its prison exclusively for foreigners in Kongsvinger in 2012. While it seems to retain the commitment to welfare that is characteristic of Scandinavian imprisonment regimes, the institution itself is the creation of a particular mentality which differentiates between "natives" and "foreigners". Kongsvinger is, as Ugelvik and Damsa (2017) observe, a crimmigration prison which inflicts upon its penal subjects a distinct set of pains of imprisonment. Among them is a sense of differential treatment that may be acutely felt by those imprisoned in the institutions and producing a sense of injustice.

Deportation

The placement of the crimmigrant other in a different imprisonment regime is a result of distinct bureaucratic and political rationalities that differentiate between categories of "native" and "foreign" offenders. Several of the criminal justice actors we interviewed also expressed a perception that ordinary penal measures do not deter foreign offenders and that therefore stricter measures are needed. Similarly, Sausdal (2018) reports a view widely held by Danish police officers that their country's prisons not only did not deter foreign offenders, but in fact attracted criminals, who saw them as "kindergartens" or "five-star hotels". The crimmigrant other's difference from the native population somehow demands the infliction of higher level of pains and harsher conditions in order to achieve deterrence. As one Norwegian police officer (in Franko and Mohn, 2015: 171) put it:

> To foreigners it doesn't matter as much if they are put in prison. It does not feel like punishment. Many are in this country only to commit crime. So, what is the countermove for the police? We have to use deportation … This is a change from when I attended police college. Then, crime prevention was prison – individual and general prevention. For Eastern Europeans, prison is like a hotel where they get a daily allowance. Yes, OK, they are kept away from society for a while. But with deportation they will be kept away in the long term!

The quote not only demonstrates the view that the crimmigrant's otherness means that he or she does not experience pain in the same way as the native citizen, but also shows how deportation emerges as an alternative form of crime prevention. One former Norwegian minister of justice expressed this very clearly in a parliamentary debate:

> I have seen a change of direction towards greater use of deportation in order to prevent people from returning again and again and committing serious crimes. Statistics also show this ... in terms of numbers of deportations since 2007, which have grown considerably. This also means that the police are more conscious that they have this as a tool in their toolbox. My impression is that the police use it as often as they can, and I think we can expect a continuation of that trend.
>
> *(Storting, 9 December 2013)*[7]

Earlier, we identified deportability as one of the defining features of the crimmigrant other as a penal subject – one that is reshaping the nature of the penal measures he or she is subjected to, from panoptic to banoptic bordered penality. The following paragraphs will look at deportation and ask several questions. What kind of penal measure is it? Is it a penal measure at all? Can it be called punishment? Despite what the previous quotes might suggest, deportation is not often described as a crime preventive measure in such clear terms. In fact, its fate has been to inhabit the indeterminate, hybrid terrain between administrative and criminal law (Kanstroom, 2010).

Deportation is not defined as punishment in most national and international legal systems. In 2000, in its landmark judgment *Maaouia v France,* the European Court of Human Rights clearly established that immigration decisions were not subject to Article 6 of the European Convention on Human Rights that lays down fair trial guarantees. Consequently, decisions on deportation (unlike criminal punishments) can be taken by administrative authorities without the persons affected having a right to have their claims heard by an independent judge. According to Marie-Bénédicte Dembour, *Maaouia* v. *France* has had profoundly negative implications for migrants' rights, and can be seen as one of the failures of the Strasbourg system to provide justice for migrants (more on that in Chapter 5).[8] Although in some countries deportation decisions are taken by specially appointed judges, such decisions do not generally entail the same levels of rights, and this is particularly true of the right to free legal aid. In *Padilla* v. *Kentucky* (2010), the US Supreme Court partially acknowledged the problem and decided that criminal defence attorneys must advise their clients about the immigration consequences of a guilty plea (Kanstroom, 2010). The wording of the decision clearly acknowledges the centrality of deportation for criminal penalties: "[A]s a matter of federal law, deportation is an integral part – indeed, sometimes the most important part – of the penalty that may be imposed on noncitizen defendants who plead guilty to specified crimes."

Deportation is thus marked by difference from traditional punishment (applied to citizens), as well as by some similarities with conventional understandings of what constitutes a penal measure. Deportation can be described as one of "invisible punishments", which occur outside of traditional sentencing, through the diminishment of the rights and privileges of citizenship (Travis, 2002). However, there is much to suggest that, in fact, it meets some of the five criteria of punishment defined by H.L.A. Hart (2008) in his influential *Prolegomenon to the Principles of Punishment*:

1. It must involve pain or other consequences normally considered unpleasant.
2. It must be an offence against legal rules.
3. It must be of an actual or supposed offender for his offence.
4. It must be intentionally administered by human beings other than the offender.
5. It must be imposed and administered by an authority constituted by a legal system against which the offence is committed.

According to Beth Caldwell (2012), deportation's link to punishment consists of several elements: its legislative intent, its severity of impact, its nexus to crime, and its historical use. As we saw above, statements by various Norwegian criminal justice actors made clear that they have come to consider deportation as a "new tool" in their toolbox of crime prevention measures. Governmental papers describe it as a form of protection against "persons who can represent a danger to society"

(Franko and Mohn, 2015). It was also suggested that "the use of deportation can have a general preventive effect. The threat of deportation can in itself prevent disorder and crime" (ibid.). Deportation's kinship with punishment lies not only in its rationalities of justification, but also in its extensive use of similar measures. Involuntary deportations frequently involve temporary or longer periods of deprivation of liberty, house searches, the use of handcuffs, and other coercive methods of policing. However, it should be borne in mind that a large proportion of deportations (often called returns) are voluntary rather than executed by force, even though voluntary and forced aspects of deportation are often interconnected and difficult to distinguish.

Why, then, has deportation received so little attention from scholars of punishment? Much of the answer may lie in the close association, in both the criminological and popular imagination, between punishment and imprisonment (Bosworth et al., 2018). In order to acknowledge the penal and punitive nature of deportation, we therefore need to redefine our concepts of penality and break its long-standing association with prison. What Malcolm Feeley reminds us about the past is worth noting here. He points out (2002, in Bosworth et al., 2018: 36) that:

> Transportation was a significant feature of English penal policy for over two centuries, and constituted its most significant form of serious sanctioning for half this period. It operated as the dominant form of severe sanctioning for a period longer than the modern prison has existed.

This turns our attention to forms of penality beyond imprisonment, as well as to the colonial aspects of penal power, which will be further addressed in Chapter 4. If we expand our understanding of penality to include deportation, this means that we should also adjust our understanding of punitiveness to match. In Chapter 3, we shall see that countries with low levels of imprisonment and high levels of crimmigration sanctions, such as Scandinavian societies, raise the question as to whether these societies can really be called non-punitive (see also Franko et al., 2019).

Deportation, then, should be considered as regards both its difference from traditional punishment, especially imprisonment, and its similarity to it. When it comes to similarity, deportation and imprisonment have in common the fact that they inflict pain not only on those subjected to them, but also on their families and loved ones. In the same way that othering and the production of crimmigrant others represent a form of social splitting, this also involves the breaking up of families and community ties. For deportees, the perceived painfulness and injustice of the sanction is often related to the strength of the ties that bind them to the country they are leaving behind (Brouwer, 2019). Deportation entails exclusion from the community, as well as a disruption of family life which, due to geographical separation, is often more drastic than that brought about by a prison sentence (see, inter alia, Coutin, 2007; Brotherton and Barrios, 2009; De Genova and Peutz, 2010). Interviews with deportees reveal that it is those with children that are particularly affected by deportation: they experience it as painful and unfair (to the extent that they would prefer to serve a prison sentence). The practice has serious implications for the right of children to family life (Dembour, 2015; see also Chapter 5). One father, interviewed by Strømnes (2013: 43), said:

> If you are a father, you have responsibility for your kids, my kids does not have anything to do with this, you cannot punish my kids, because is taking me to [his country of origin] is punishing my kids, they have not seen me for 27 months, I have only talked by phone, I call two time every week. (man, Africa)

Others, with weaker ties to the country, acknowledged the legitimacy of their deportation and did not see it as punishment:

> No, it is not punishment. They have the right to throw me out because this is not my home country. It is not punishment, it is right. It is like, for example, if a person comes into my house without invitation, I would throw them out right away. (man, North Africa)

(Strømnes, 2013: 50)

The argument has been made so far that deportation is a penal intervention. It is often carried out with the explicit political purpose of preventing crime and is not just an intentional infliction of pain (Christie, 1981), but in many cases it is also experienced as painful. Like imprisonment, deportation involves severe deprivations, which are often experienced as deeply exclusionary. The perceived severity of such deprivation greatly depends on the strength and depth of the ties deportees have with the deporting country.

Penal alienage

In the above we have seen the practical differences between penal regimes for citizens and non-citizens, as regards, for instance, the prison conditions and forms of policing that they are subjected to. We also noted the differences in the productive nature of penal power. Foucault's influential account describes penal power as disciplining of the modern soul – the soul which was "not born in sin and subject to punishment, but is born out of methods of punishment, supervision and constraint" (1977: 29). Bordered penality, by contrast, produces something other than the disciplined soul. It produces *penal alienage*. Deportation, as Mathew Gibney (2013: 219) points out, "serves as a practical reminder of the worth of citizenship". By means of the power to banish, the sovereign prerogative to decide on who is considered a member of society is exercised in the penal field. Deportation gives penal power a distinct meaning. It involves termination of membership. For non-citizens, membership is probationary, as Stumpf (2006) observes, and can be revoked through punishment.

Bordered penality is intimately connected to issues of membership (Barker, 2013, 2018). It is directed at non-members, as well as at those whose hold on membership is tenuous or who appear to be what Zedner (2013: 46) terms "stunted citizens". In contemporary societies, there are further distinctions than those between citizens and non-citizens. Individuals can possess various statuses, which bring them closer to, or further from, full membership of a national community. They can be long-term or short-term residents, carriers of dual citizenship, asylum seekers or fully recognized refugees, citizens of other EU or EEA states, and so on (Guild, 2009). For these different groups, penal power can have a variety of consequences (Aas, 2013a), among others:

a   Loss of residence or denizenship status due to breaches of criminal law and immigration law (Aas, 2014).
b   Loss of possibilities for inclusion for those with legitimate claims – for example, those with refugee status – through cancellation of their claims to protection due to overriding concerns with security and crime prevention (Westfeldt, 2008).
c   The questioning of the membership status of formal citizens, who are prevented from enjoying full benefits of equal membership through frequent penal control, such as racial profiling (Brouwer et al., 2018).
d   Loss of citizenship status for refugees due to accusations of fraud (Brekke et al., 2019), or for dual citizens due to involvement in terror-related activities (Zedner, 2016).

Bordered penality forces us to recognise how penal power can have different consequences and effects on individuals depending on their membership status. Some groups - for example, unwanted Romanian citizens of Roma origin – may be punished *in order* to facilitate their deportation. Punishment is a necessary precondition for the termination of their denizenship of various EU states. For others – for example, Nigerian citizens involved in the drug trade – deportation may be used *instead of* punishment (Aas, 2014). Residence status and length of residence, nationality, family ties, etc., can to some extent provide protection from alienage for some groups whose membership is, nevertheless, precarious. Interestingly, in Chapter 3 we shall see that it is precisely groups which possess certain forms of formally acknowledged membership and protection (recognised refugee status, so-called denizenship, and dual citizenship) that penal power has particular importance for, in that it can revoke their membership. Since, in principle, EU and EEA citizens have the right to live and work in other EU and EEA countries, their membership can only be revoked through criminal sanctions and on security grounds. Thus, in her analysis of decisions of the Swedish Immigration Board on individuals with recognised refugee or equivalent status, Lisa Westfeldt (2008) discovered that a criminal conviction could constitute grounds for deportation even in cases where the Board noted its opinion that there was a continued risk of persecution in the country of origin.

Bordered penality thus reveals the contested nature of citizenship and how negotiations about membership play out amid the exercise of penal power. This form of penality demands a thorough analytical understanding of citizenship and an acknowledgment of the centrality of citizenship in questions of crime and punishment (Barker, 2013). In Chapter 4, we shall see how, on a global level, there is a carefully worked out gradation of states according to the security risk presented by their migration, or what might be termed their "deviance". These intricate global hierarchies of citizenship crucially inform how contemporary penal power is exercised over non-citizens.

The discussion above also reveals that the crimmigrant other is by no means a unitary category and can belong to a number of groups that have different legal and social statuses and "shades of deviance" ascribed to them. As Linda Bosniak (2006: 10) points out, the category of "alienage" can be misleadingly unifying: "In objective terms, the people who comprise the group of aliens are socially divided in many significant ways." And it is precisely suspicion, and the focus on criminality, which may give the state leverage to move people from one category to another. The following quote from a police officer in Oslo serves as an illustration of how penal power is intentionally used by the state to cancel claims to membership, or possibilities of legal re-entry, for people who are perceived as unwanted:

> It was probable that he [Afghan citizen] gave false personal information, I guess. And yes, you can say that, if you give false information to the police you have committed a criminal offence. This is grounds for deportation the moment he gets a negative response on his asylum application. It means that he can be sent out with a ban on coming back again; as opposed to being sent out and coming back the next day as a tourist. This is something that we sometimes keep in mind, because it happens that, in a manner of speaking, one knows what is going on. That you, my friend, smell like trouble.
>
> *(Oslo Police District, operative, foreigners' section)*

Racialised otherness: allotting membership in a divided world

While the quote above may serve as a useful illustration of the intertwining of immigration law and criminal law, it does not make explicit one vital element of the equation – namely, that who "smells like trouble" is strongly shaped by racial, gendered, and other categories. The individual in question was a male citizen of Afghanistan and probably poor. Several observers have pointed out the racial antecedents of crimmigration control and suggested that, by focusing solely on issues of citizenship and migration, the crimmigration thesis overlooks important elements of race and racial discrimination, which are shaping contemporary crimmigration control measures (Garner, 2015). Hindpal Bhui (2016: 267) points out the influence of colonialism on current immigration control policies and remarks that they "can best be informed by a broader historical conception of 'racism'". Nicholas De Genova (2018) goes as far as to suggest that the European "migrant crisis" can best be understood as the equivalent of racial oppression in the United States and that it deserves to be framed as an issue of "black lives matter". By addressing them simply as migrants, De Genova argues, we are encouraging a process of de-racialisation.

There is by now an extensive body of scholarship on racial profiling and its intersection with border policing (Weber and Bowling, 2012; Brouwer et al., 2017, 2018; Bosworth et al., 2018; Parmar, 2019) However, in the European context, the widespread social marginalisation and use of penal power over Eastern European citizens, particularly the Roma population shows, that "whiteness" and race are contingent categories (Brouwer et al., 2017; Yıldız and De Genova, 2018). As Bhui (2016: 276) observes, Eastern European citizens can also be "subject to a racialised framing as 'other'. Their whiteness is not seen as a motivation for inclusion, rather their cultural difference is seen as a criterion for exclusion."

Race may often appear to be the elephant in the room in matters of border control, but this may partly be due to its complicated interconnections with other types of othering and exclusion. For this reason, Bosniak (2006: 134) argues that the subordination of non-citizens needs to be analysed on its own terms and "needs to be regarded as something more than a mere proxy for other forms of oppression". While penal alienage resembles other forms of subordination and racialised social exclusion, it also has distinct features connected to issues of citizenship. As Bosniak (ibid.: 11; emphasis in original) points out:

Alienage presents real difficulties for antisubordination theorists. While it shares some characteristics with other forms of social subordination, it can also appear to be a different species of exclusion altogether: not social disadvantage but, instead, an instance of constitutive boundary maintenance, a necessary condition for preservation of the community *within which* the struggle against social subordination takes place.

Bordered penality, therefore, requires a conceptual apparatus which captures how and why distribution of membership becomes so salient for understanding contemporary patterns of social exclusion and the use of state power and coercion (Barker, 2018). It cannot be understood as yet another axis of social subordination, but demands an understanding of how and why "disadvantage based on alienage is both like and unlike other forms of disadvantage" (Bosniak, 2006: 11). The position of the crimmigrant other forces us to come to grips with many layers of othering which may be impossible to pin down exactly, not least because they play out differently in different local and national contexts. Such layers are built around the particular position of the crimmigrant other which can be, at the same time, that of a "subordinated insider" as well as a "national stranger" (ibid.).

The conundrum of the crimmigrant other lies to a large extent at the intersections of citizenship, class, race, gender, religion, and cultural belonging, which are difficult (if not impossible) to take apart. It demands an acknowledgment of the powerful historic legacies of colonialism and their continued influence both on contemporary notions of race, self, and identity, and on the trajectories of global inequality, which shape contemporary deportation regimes and hierarchies of citizenship. It also brings to the fore the continued salience of the connections between criminalisation, class, and poverty (De Giorgi, 2013; Melossi, 2013a). This is recognised in what one police officer we interviewed in Oslo said about his work:

> What you talk about as crimmigration – which we see quite a lot of – this, in our view, is mainly just poor people ... The problem of poverty is something that takes up a lot of our resources. The

more serious organised crime I think is something we could have solved in a different way – for example, by cooperating with Nigeria. Our goal, however, is to make Norway less attractive to come to.

(OPD2, police officer, Oslo organized crime unit)

Marxist traditions within migration studies have kept a sharp eye on these material aspects of social control and the way bordering practices make people not only deportable, but also exploitable (Calavita, 2005; Melossi, 2013b). Melossi (2013b: 428) suggests that the legal regime of migration can best "be understood – almost literally – as a quite traditional maneuver of authoritarian intervention on the labour market". While not producing the disciplined working subject *within* the penal institutional practices, the penal control exercised over migrants produces a more submissive, docile, and cheap workforce outside the penal domain, in society at large. Immigrants' social exclusion, criminalisation, and racialisation is, as shown by Kitty Calavita's (2005) careful study, closely connected with their role as cheap labour: "Law plays a central role in this alchemy of economics, race, identity and exclusion"' (ibid.: 165). It will be the task of Chapter 3 to show how this "alchemy" works in one particular national context.

Conclusion: the power to uproot

This chapter has outlined the construction of the crimmigrant other through various modalities of penal power, shaped by the rationality of border penality. Throughout history, states have attempted to control the movement of the mobile poor by coercive means. The control of the crimmigrant other in the context of contemporary North–South relations echoes the historic practices of colonial penality (Feeley, 2002, in Bosworth et al., 2018). This issue will be further addressed in Chapter 4. Affluent states, particularly (but not exclusively) in the global North, are preventing citizens from poorer states establishing residence in their territories and making claims on their resources. Through the creation of penal alienage, state-sanctioned penal power aims to prevent unauthorised movement and remove people to other states' territories. The construction of the crimmigrant other thus has a number of productive effects. These include the daily reinstatement of an unequal global order and its hierarchies of citizenship (Basaran and Guild, 2017) and, more importantly, as Morrison (2017: 24) succinctly observes, "the illusion of power through the process of inventing the Other". The control of the border and the use of penal power over the crimmigrant other are vital tools used to reassert state authority (Bosworth and Guild, 2008).

Bordered penality is built on an idea of national belonging. The crimmigrant other is a "failed citizen" who does not belong to the national "community of value" (Anderson, 2013). Such an order rests on a certain belief in the neatness of categories of belonging and striving for purity and order. Mobility represents a disorder which interferes with the nation state's sedentary predicament (Gundhus and Franko, 2016). However, as much as the productive effects of border control tend to be seen in scholarly literature in terms of control of movement and a reinstatement of the nation state's need for order, we should recognise the extent of secondary movement and "disorder" that are produced by such efforts. In 2017 alone, EU countries transferred 23,715 asylum applicants among themselves (Eurostat),[9] while in 2016 they deported 176,223 individuals to countries outside the EU, 45 per cent of those were forced returns (Frontex, 2017). This considerable amount of state-induced mobility highlights the fact that states are not only trying to fend off unwanted movement, but are also active in the process of strategic creation of movement to strengthen their sovereignty (Gundhus and Franko, 2016). Such activities are not only "tying" people to the territories they properly belong to, or returning them to their "proper sovereigns", but also uprooting them. When the state becomes a producer of movement, rather than creating order, it generates complex processes of uprooting which reverberate throughout societies, families, and local communities (Brotherton and Barrios, 2009; Kanstroom, 2012). As Chapter 1 pointed out, deportation is best seen as a process. As Coutin (2015: 674) puts it:

> Deportation is not a discrete event; rather, it begins long before an individual is apprehended, through the myriad practices that make someone vulnerable to deportation in the first place. As well, deportation continues long after an individual is returned, through the difficult process of readjustment, the ripple effects on family members and the continued prohibition on entry.

The crimmigrant other is, then, subjected to multiple processes of uprooting and social separation with negative social, economic, and existential implications (De Genova and Peutz, 2010; Vigh, 2016). This makes many deportees eager to escape the places they are deported to by relying on their skill in illicit mobility, one of the few resources at their disposal. State-induced movement may thus propel people into further movement and participation in the illicit economy of movement, thus creating conditions of permanent circulation (Vigh, 2016). Weber et al. (2019), for example, show the extent of intra-European deportation practices and movements related to, among others, the Dublin Regulation. The desire to prevent "refugees in orbit", in fact, creates people in orbit – people for whom circulation has become a way of life – and who, through this circulation (some of it state-sponsored), gain an expertise in mobility and illicit border crossings, which they may then also offer to others (Vigh, 2016).

One of the core traits of crimmigrant others, therefore, is not only that they are deportable, but also that this deportability often entails uprooting. This means that families can be split up between different countries, individuals can be uprooted from places where they have spent much of their lives and established a community ties and a sense of belonging. The penal power to banish is also the power to uproot and, as we shall see in the following chapter, making claims on the resources of the welfare state.

Notes

1 www.crimeandjustice.org.uk/publications/cjm/article/theory-and-politics-criminalisation
2 www.theguardian.com/world/2018/dec/01/french-police-step-up-calais-refugee-evictions
3 https://euobserver.com/justice/141062
4 https://euobserver.com/justice/141062
5 Source: World Prison Brief. www.prisonstudies.org/info/worldbrief/wpb_stats.php?area=all&category=wb_foreign
6 https://euobserver.com/investigations/135659
7 www.stortinget.no/no/Saker-og-publikasjoner/Publikasjoner/Referater/Stortinget/2013-2014/131209/7/
8 https://blogs.brighton.ac.uk/humanrights/tag/maaouia-v-france/
9 http://appsso.eurostat.ec.europa.eu/nui/show.do?dataset=migr_dubto&lang=en

3

"HARD-ON-THE-OUTSIDE, SOFT-ON-THE-INSIDE"

An inclusive society with an exclusionary edge

> We will continue to fight for a strict and sustainable asylum policy, which secures the Norwegian welfare model!
> *(S. Listhaug, Immigration Minister, 22 November 2016)[1]*

Norway is one of the wealthiest nations in the world. It consistently receives high scores for its quality of life, gender equality, levels of education, health care, and the like. In many respects, it is a good place to live. The country also boasts one of the most humane penal systems – an achievement which government institutions and the general public seem to be proud of. It has therefore been seen as exemplifying the much-discussed Scandinavian exceptionalism (Pratt, 2008; Pratt and Eriksson, 2012), a penal style characterised by an inclusionary and welfare-oriented approach to social problems (Smith and Ugelvik, 2017; Bendixen and Wyller, 2019).

However, despite historically low levels of recorded crime, Norway now has record levels of imprisonment. Although still considerably less punitive than most Western countries, in recent years the Norwegian criminal justice system has undergone profound transformations and has been at the forefront of innovations in bordered penality and crimmigration control (Aas, 2014; Ugelvik, 2013; Ugelvik and Damsa, 2017).

The country has set in motion a series of exclusionary measures directed against those deemed to be non-members. The current right-wing government has made deportation a strong political priority (Franko and Mohn, 2015; Gundhus, 2016). For several years running, the police had been given high targets for deporting unwanted foreign citizens and there is reason to believe that Norway has become one of the "deportation leaders" among EU states (Van Houte and Leerkes, 2019). This chapter offers a detailed and empirical description of the processes on the ground that create penal alienage in a society, and in a penal system, otherwise characterised by its lenience and its inclusive welfare orientation (Bendixen and Wyller, 2019). While reflecting the general trends outlined in the previous two chapters, this chapter also shows the specific contextual and cultural dynamics underpinning the notion of the crimmigrant other. It reveals that there are, in practice, numerous national variations of bordered penality and crimmigration control that require detailed empirical analysis. Moreover, it raises a question about possible drivers behind the expansion of crimmigration enforcement, which has in the US context been seen as strongly related to the rise of more exclusionary and punitive penal policy (Stumpf, 2006). The Scandinavian context challenges such explanations and points instead to the intricate relationships between membership, the welfare state, and social exclusion (Aas, 2014; Barker, 2018).

Building a deportation machine: "a snowball which keeps on rolling"

Today, approximately 17 per cent of the Norwegian population are immigrants or the children of immigrants.[2] In 2017, almost 34 per cent of prisoners were foreign citizens. This is a considerable rise from 11.5 per cent, the figure only 12 years before that. The figure is even higher for remand prisoners, which regularly exceeds 50 per cent. Norway is one of the few European countries to have a prison just for foreigners: Kongsvinger prison houses only foreign citizens (Ugelvik, 2013), and now has both male and female sections. In recent years, Trandum, the closed detention centre near Oslo airport (mentioned in the previous chapter), has undergone considerable expansion. In 2003, this former military barracks was converted from an open asylum centre into a prison-like institution, run by the newly established Police Immigration Unit (PIU).[3] The Unit itself has also been greatly expanded, with its number of employees rising from 135 in 2004 to approximately 950 in 2016, becoming almost half the size of the country's largest police district.

The remarkable growth of Trandum and the PIU is symptomatic of the development towards what might be termed crimmigration control in Norway. As we shall see in the rest of the chapter, this development encompasses not only criminalisation strategies, but most notably the development of particular imprisonment regimes and policing approaches directed at non-citizens. The bordered forms of penality, described in Chapter 2, take various shapes and develop in different ways. In 2013, for example, Parliament unanimously increased penalties for breaches of re-entry bans from six months to a maximum of two years' imprisonment, with one year being the standard sentence. Since then, the number of foreign citizens imprisoned for breaking immigration law has risen dramatically. According to Statistics Norway, unconditional prison sentences for breaches of re-entry ban have grown from less than 1,000 prison days a year before 2009 to 74,000 prison days in 2016.[4]

The development of such forms of penality, however, is exemplified more than anything else by the extensive focus on, and the use of, deportation. This is evident both in the steep increase in deportation orders issued by the Norwegian Directorate of Immigration (UDI), and in the numbers of forced returns actually carried out by the police and the PIU, particularly between 2013 and 2017. The numbers of deportation orders are shown in Figure 3.1, which provides data on expulsion or deportation decisions handed down for breaches of criminal law and immigration law. Figure 3.1 reveals a steep growth in deportations related to criminal sanctions, particularly those imposed on EU and EEA citizens (dark grey columns). These developments are not proportional to recorded crime patterns (Mohn, 2013). As I shall proceed to show, they are the result of sustained top–down political pressure and of internal changes in the police and its culture. In the past ten years, Norway has effectively built what Sigmund Book Mohn (forthcoming) terms a "deportation machine".

The intense focus on deportation is even more visible in Table 3.1, which provides an overview of deportation decisions actually carried

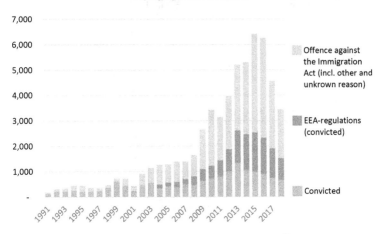

Expulsion decisions (with re-entry ban) in Norway, by legal ground. 1991-2018

FIGURE 3.1 Deportation decisions in Norway 1991–2018[5]

Source: Sigmund B. Mohn and UDI (Norwegian Directorate of Immigration) annual reports (1991 – 2018). Medium grey and dark grey columns represent deportations decisions given for breaches of criminal law (dark grey columns represent deportation decisions arising from breaches of criminal law by the EU and EEA, which are legally established by a special legislative framework)

out, including forced returns, which at times even exceeded the numbers of expulsion decisions. Between 2007 and 2016, the number of forced returns almost quadrupled, rising from 2,187 to 8,078. Although deportation numbers are notoriously difficult to compare across jurisdictions (since states may use quite different terms for such practices), there is reason to believe that Norway is actually one of the European leaders in deportation (Van Houte and Leerkes, 2019).

This remarkable quantitative change was accompanied, as well as made possible, by a profound qualitative change within the police in terms of its views on deportation and border control in general. The change of mentality can be described as twofold: it has to do with raising the status of immigration work among the officers and increasing the level of expertise and knowledge about the field

TABLE 3.1 Returns by Main Categories (2007–2016)[6]

Year	Asylum – rejected	Dublin-procedure	Expulsion/rejection	Total – forced	Assisted re-turn (IOM)	Total
2007	552	561	1 074	2 187	443	2 630
2008	437	805	1 084	2 326	568	2 894
2009	651	1 463	1 226	3 343	1 019	4 359
2010	1 226	1 979	1 410	4 615	1 446	6 061
2011	1 482	1 503	1 759	4 744	1 813	6 557
2012	1 397	1 114	2 390	4 901	1 753	6 654
2013	1 275	1 408	3 283	5 966	1 889	7 855
2014	1 804	1 680	3 775	7 259	1 622	8 881
2015	1 559	1 144	5 122	7 825	1 167	8 992
2016	1 385	1 346	5 347	8 078	1 456	9 534

Source: Norwegian Ministeries: https://www.regieringen.no/contentassets/005e1d69ad51419584 51b8770552dab9/immigration-and-integration-20162017.pdf

(Gundhus, 2016). The Norwegian justice authorities have actively promoted an understanding that deportation reduces crime. The political "will to expel" has aimed to change priorities and traditional mentalities, which did not see immigration control as a central aspect of police work and considered it quite unrelated to crime control and crime prevention. Issues of immigration control, therefore, had to be moved from the administrative domain to that of criminal law and crime control. One officer in a police immigration unit in Oslo spoke about the changed status of his work:

> Yes, I can say that there has been a change. Because when I started here, and perhaps the first two years, we did not work with this in mind at all. Crime was like not an issue. Yes, we took cases from the stations and processed them, but we ourselves were not actively in crime prevention work … In those days we were part of the asylum system.
>
> *(OPD, foreigners' section)*

This change of mentality meant that border control units and tasks were upgraded to "crime fighting", and ordinary units had to be made aware of the value of immigration work. To this end, the Police Directorate, encouraged by the Ministry of Justice, began systematically organising so-called deportation seminars, in which local police authorities were made aware of the "deportation potential" in their criminal registers. Police officers were taught how to use immigration law, how to check documents, and how to spot fake ones, and given training in other aspects of immigration control. One of the interviewees, who works in the Police Directorate, charged with organising the deportation seminars, described the objectives as follows:

> Even though we do not manage to catch their [police officers'] attention completely, I think that if we have managed to bring in some new thoughts that come to mind when they are patrolling and making checks, then a lot has been done. And something must have happened, because numbers have gone up 35 per cent … Yes, deportation [numbers]. We hope that we are contributing

towards that. If you talk about it – there is something about that – you make people see the importance.

(Police Directorate 11)

This change of mentality was central to shifting the bureaucratic production of deportation cases (and deportable individuals) into a higher gear. It was, however, achieved through the implementation of another bureaucratic change, which was essential for the smooth running of the machinery. This came about when the justice authorities and police leadership made deportation one of the central performance indicators for each police district (Gundhus, 2016). This meant that, from then on, the everyday practices of policing were measured not only according to how many traffic stops were performed, how many drug cases were worked on, how many arrests were made, or what the police response time to incidents was, but also according to how many deportation cases they produced. Deportation became incorporated into the existing systems of new public management and was thus subjected to governance by numbers (Gundhus, 2016).

This move was introduced by the Labour government in power at the time, and enjoyed broad political support. It then received a further push by the current right-wing government that came into power in 2013. A large number of our interviewees pointed out how important it was for changing police priorities and making the force more focused on immigration issues and deportation, in the way described in the following account of a senior officer of the Police Immigration Unit:

Traditionally, I think, police have worked on criminal cases, investigations, public order – immigration cases never used to have high status within the police … And when the police investigated a case and had someone sentenced, they tended to think: "Now, I have done a good job, I am finished." And they did a good job, for sure, but the administrative bit was missing. So what happened after the report that showed that over half of the local districts hadn't had a single deportation case was that we recommended to the Police Directorate that the districts should be measured on this. And the Directorate followed up on it, and now the districts are measured every year on deportation cases, and they are behind a lot more deportation decisions.

(Police Immigration Unit, leadership, 1)

The decision to make deportation a police performance target accelerated the trend towards making immigration control an integral part of the criminal justice system. Our informant above described it as a "snowball which keeps on rolling". However, it is important to bear in mind that this involved a systematic change which included all parts of the system. Police officers on the ground were thus required to increase their "production" of deportation decisions, and expel as many people as possible in order to meet their performance targets. At the same time, the Immigration Directorate – responsible for the actual legal production of such decisions – lowered the threshold of offences for which individuals could be deported. The Directorate even opened a "hotline" in order to support the police with immediate administrative assistance.

Due to this systematic political investment, the threshold of turning into a crimmigrant other was considerably lowered for an immigrant living in Norway, and the net of controls in which one could be caught became wider. This is described as follows by one police officer working in an immigration unit in Oslo police district:

And this threshold has actually become lower over the years. We cooperate with the UDI [Immigration Directorate] to find out where exactly is the limit so that we can get deported most of those who commit crime. And they wish actually to have a pretty low threshold. And for those who are not EU citizens it is a pretty low threshold; perhaps it is not necessary to have more than a few thefts in a shop and you get deported.

(P1)

In 2002, as Figure 3.1 shows, only 457 individuals received a deportation order as a consequence of a criminal offence, but by 2012 the numbers had increased fourfold to 1,866, and rose even further in the subsequent years. They declined, though, in 2018 mostly due to the record low numbers of asylum seekers. A similar trend has also been observed in the US, where, after legislative changes, deportation became "the consequence of almost any criminal conviction of a non-citizen" (Stumpf, 2006: 5). Also, other European countries have in recent years prioritised deporting criminal offenders (Gibney, 2013; Brouwer, 2019), As we shall see below, this connection between even minor crimes and expulsion from the country became particularly significant for non-citizens of Roma origin.

Focusing on the "usual suspects"

Many of the police officers and public prosecutors we talked to described the changing attitude to the use of immigration law in their daily work as matter of "changing tracks" or "having two hats" and alternating between them. The two "hats" – the criminal law one and the administrative one – can be selected at the officers' discretion (see also Jahnsen and Skilbrei, 2018). The trend is illustrative of the large discretionary powers that are built into crimmigration modes of control (Sklansky, 2012; Van der Woude and Van der Leun, 2017). The advantage of being able to choose freely between the criminal and administrative options was that they could adjust their strategies according to their objectives and the availability of resources. A non-citizen can thus first be kept on remand under immigration law (for example, on charges of illegal stay and unclear identity), and then kept in the same institution on criminal charges. The end result can be either a criminal penalty, a deportation decision, or both.

Figure 3.2 shows the results of a police operation directed at the open drug scene in central Oslo. The figures are an illustration of what bordered penality looks like in practice, in terms of the categories of persons subjected to police intervention and the nature of coercive state measures directed at them. The operation ran over several years and targeted non-citizens – 531 in total were arrested in 2011. Although the arrests occurred in conjunction with drug-related activities, by far the most common response was a deportation order – criminal charges were brought against only nine individuals.

Criminal law is applied not only to punish, but also to deport, while deportation is used both for immigration purposes and because an individual is seen as a law and order problem (without it being necessary to prove this with criminal law procedural means). As one police

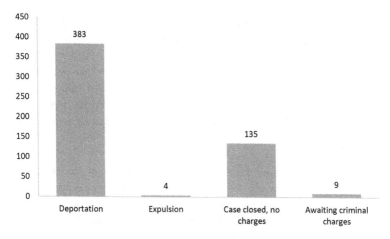

FIGURE 3.2 Results of the campaign against the open drug scene in Oslo (2011)
Source: Aas (2014)

prosecutor (OPD 1) said in an interview: "We were breaking our neck on criminal cases." As a consequence, his division chose to use the administrative track more actively. The authorities also see deportation as a more cost-efficient way of dealing with minor offences. As one interviewee from the Police Directorate observed:

> Well, we measure their performance on deportation and we see that there has been a remarkable growth. And I think that this is economically a rather efficient way of dealing with these cases, to get a deportation order and a return. At least this is our argument, that it is cost-efficient in terms of the system as a whole. If you have a criminal case, it is much more complicated, plus you end up with a conviction and a sentence, which costs a lot of money.
>
> So you have to prioritise the cases you have and take the important ones, while you take the other ones the other way. Otherwise you have to let them go, and this is what happened before, right. Instead of using the administrative track, they were let go and did it again.
>
> *(Police Directorate 10)*

The statement is illustrative of the position of the crimmigrant other as being subjected to a double suspicion, as mentioned in Chapter 2 (see also Jahnsen and Skilbrei, 2018). However, the strategy of changing between tracks according to what was most convenient was not used only for minor offences. An officer from a section working on West African organised crime networks explained his preference for using deportation instead of traditional penalties thus:

> I see no reason why we should spend a lot of money putting them in prison here, when we can fly them out. I can see that this is what is being done now, and I do not understand why. They do ten or twelve years inside and continue just as before. We can send them to [Kurdistan] instead.[7]
>
> *(OPD 2)*

The preference for deportation was supported both for economic reasons (deportation being seen as a cheaper and less time-consuming way of addressing crime problems) and because of deterrence objectives (deportation hurts more). It supports the arguments, presented in Chapter 2, that in practice deportation is often used as a penal measure, with similar objectives to criminal penalties.

However, one of the consequences of the changing-tracks approach is that the main focus is on the person, with the objectives of the law becoming of secondary importance. The legal framework can be chosen according to convenience and thus loses its power to guide police action. Instead, it becomes a posteriori justification. David Alan Sklansky (2012) describes this approach as "ad hoc instrumentalism". It is, he says

> a manner of thinking about law and legal institutions that downplays concerns about consistency and places little stock in formal legal categories, but instead sees legal rules and legal procedures simply as a set of interchangeable tools. In any given situation, faced with any given problem, officials are encouraged to use whichever tools are most effective against the person or persons causing the problem.

The approach is well exemplified by the following statement from an officer from Oslo police district, who explained his unit's thinking in this way:

> What we are looking for is "Is this a person who does criminal activities in Oslo?" If we think that he is behaving in a way which suggests that he is committing crime, then we go in and do an immigration check to find out about his identity and background. And then you can quickly have a look at his phone activities. Like "Have you got white? have you got coke?", right? Then we understand that he is "of interest", that he is doing shady business. And then it is natural that we take a step towards the criminal law track. What happens next is that we either discover that he has drugs on him, or if he doesn't, we can start asking questions about immigration law. And then you can quickly see, for example, if he has been in Norway long, and if he is hiding information about his means of sustenance in Norway, and all that is relevant for immigration law. And then we arrest him on immigration law, first and foremost because we see that he is involved in crime, but we cannot prove it in criminal law.
>
> *(OPD 015)*

In such an approach, prosecution becomes personal. It means, as Justice Jackson (in Sklansky, 2012) puts it, "picking the man and then searching the law books, or putting investigators to work, to pin some offense on him".

These statements make clear how the crimmigrant other emerges as a result of a specific focus of police suspicion and attention. However, such on-the-ground practices were also supported by more general perceptions of foreign citizens as particularly criminogenic. The aforementioned government proposition to increase penalties for breaches of entry bans was explicitly directed at a particular imagined class of criminal foreigners. The proposition clearly stated that increased penalties would:

> contribute to the reduction of other types of criminality in Norway, since a large proportion of those who are punished for

breaches of the entry ban are also reported for or convicted of other types of crime. In addition, those who will breach the entry ban will, for a longer period than before, not be able to commit new offences while they are in prison. This effect is likely to be substantial.

(Prop. 181-L., 2012–2013: 20–21, my translation)

The passage reveals how the notion of the crimmigrant other arises from a perception of foreign offenders as being a particular class of criminal offenders, who represent a substantial burden for the nation state. One of our informants described this reasoning thus:

There has been a report which is actually quite interesting reading and which you should look a bit more closely into. The same way some people try to find out how much crime costs society, they have calculated that it costs a good deal to have illegals – persons illegally in the country, who commit crime. Many of these commit a lot of crime. And this is something that makes one want to get them out of the country.

(P1)

While the notion of the criminal foreigner is a not uncommon feature of political, media, and social media discourse, the discussion above reveals its practical configurations in the bureaucratic production of knowledge and in discourses which have powerful and direct implications for everyday practices of policing and control. The informant above reveals the perceived connection between staying in the country without proper documents and criminality. From this point of view, irregular migrants have numerous overlaps with criminal offenders and are talked about as "illegals" – that is, "persons illegally in the country, who commit crime".

Penal power between East and West

In Norway, as in many other Western European countries, the notion of the criminal foreigner has frequently been applied to Eastern European citizens (Brouwer et al., 2017; Sausdal, 2018). The "usual suspects" are often citizens of Romania, Lithuania, Poland, or other Eastern European countries. In the last ten years the Norwegian police have developed several projects directed specifically at Eastern European offenders. In a project against pickpockets in Oslo, over 90 per cent of those arrested were foreign citizens, mainly of Romanian origin (Norsk Politi, 2013).

Not surprisingly, therefore, Eastern European citizens are among the largest categories of foreign nationals in Norwegian prisons. In 2018, the Norwegian Correctional Services reported the following ranking of "nationalities" in Norwegian prisons (Kriminalomsorgen, 2018):

Norway 2208 (405 on remand)
Poland: 133 (66 on remand)
Romania: 103 (53 on remand)
Lithauania: 82 (34 on remand)
Albania: 77 (35 on remand)

In this respect, Norway is by no means unusual, but rather reflects a general trend, as we saw in the previous chapter (Aebi et al., 2019). Frontex statistics (2017: 56) consistently show that Eastern European citizens (both those from the EU and from third countries) are among those most frequently expelled from the EU. In 2016, 27,201 Albanian citizens were successfully returned to their country of origin, as were 20,970 citizens of Ukraine (ibid.). These trends are partly a result of the EU expansion in 2007 which, in principle, enabled free movement for citizens of the newly accepted member states.

However, the focus of the Norwegian authorities on Eastern European citizens residing in the country was not just a natural consequence of their rising numbers. The Eastern European citizen also emerged as a distinct type of criminal offender, namely a so-called mobile property offender. As mentioned earlier, the Supreme Court has made sentences for this group of offenders considerably harsher (Flaatten, 2017). They have also become the target of special police actions and a priority for individual districts. This is described by one officer working for a motorised patrol unit:

Among other performance targets, we have ones for how many mobile property offenders we take. But we are a bit overwhelmed with the numbers at the moment, because we also have a special patrol unit which just works on that. Because of that we leave it to them a bit and hope that they can manage to meet the targets for the district. But we need to gear ourselves up and catch a few more. It is better now than it was before, though if one starts digging into a case you can soon lose numbers. Our group needs to have at least 20 measures per day and if you spend two or three hours on a case, then this is not possible.

(FRN 5)

For a number of years, mobile property offenders from Eastern Europe have been the target of special police projects and action forces, which rely on the use of novel surveillance methods (see also Sausdal, 2018 for a Danish example), and which have also led to closer police and justice cooperation with counterparts in the offenders' countries of origin. This is how one of our interviewees in the Justice Department describes the situation:

Just that, how are you going to handle this? How are you going to cooperate with Poland, Lithuania, or Romania about what we call mobile property offenders? All this is coming over other borders where there is no control. OK, we have police cooperation agreements with Romania, with Bulgaria. We have prisoner transfer agreements with Lithuania and Poland. And why do we have them? It's because it is necessary to solve our national crime problems. And if you talk to those [working] on the project "Borderless" in [the districts of] Vestfold, Telemark, Asker, and Bærum, you will probably find people who think it is completely natural to call colleagues in Klaipeda in Lithuania and work with them.

(Justis 2, lawyer)

Such initiatives that seek to control unwanted mobility have made everyday practices of policing in Norway thoroughly globalised (Gundhus and Franko, 2016). The aim of the Norwegian authorities has been to design a system which can monitor and catch large numbers of such offenders, and then swiftly process them and deport them. One officer from Northern Norway described this change:

> So, if there are any special incidents, or if we have urgent depor-
> tation cases (which we hardly ever had before), but on which there
> is now special focus – and this is most likely to be Eastern Eur-
> opeans, who do property crime – there it is a low threshold for
> deportation. This came about after an instruction from the Immi-
> gration Directorate. It is called a directive and it says that, in the
> case of minor offences, related to petty theft, or theft, and the
> person otherwise has nothing to do with Norway, that is no job,
> no place of residence, no income, no health insurance, that type of
> thing. Well, then the threshold for deportation is low. And in such
> cases a person can be arrested and deported in two days. Average.
> This is a change of focus from before.
>
> *(Police officer, Tromsø PD)*

Eastern European offenders in many ways appear to be paradigmatic criminal aliens, but they have a distinct position within the criminal justice system. Since many of them are EU citizens they possess, in principle, a type of formally acknowledged membership and protec-tion (so-called denizenship). And this is why punishment gains parti-cular importance, since it leads to revocation of their membership and the creation of penal alienage. EU and EEA citizens have, in principle, the right to live and work in other EU and EEA countries, but their membership is precarious; it can be revoked through criminal sanc-tions and on security grounds. In practice, as the quote above reveals, offences leading to the creation of penal alienage and deportation do not have to be considerable and can even be punishable by fines. Therefore, while third country citizens – for example, Nigerians – can be expelled solely through the use of immigration law, EU citizens, by contrast, need to be punished first, before they can be expelled from the country. Our investigation revealed that, in the case of EU citizens, criminal law and immigration law are mostly applied *cumula-tively* – deportation is added to the (increasingly severe) prison terms – rather than *substitutively*, as in the case of the campaign against the open drug scene mentioned above. The approach was described by the leader of the pickpocket project in the following way:

> We have an express investigative procedure in order to get the offenders convicted while they are in pre-trial detention. Once convicted, they are transferred to imprisonment, while we start a parallel deportation case. When the prison sentence has been served, they are often out of the country right away, and they can also get an entry ban of two to five years.
>
> *(Norsk Politi, 2013)*

Such an approach features a strong reliance on imprisonment, before trial and as punishment. It also entails, of course, heavy reliance on deportation and entry bans in order to prevent future mobility. Figure 3.3 shows that it is precisely for EU and EEA citizens that we have seen a particular growth in expulsion orders linked to criminal sanctions, while immigration law represents a more frequently applied form of social exclusion for non-EU nationals.

It is important to remember, though, that these patterns of the use of penal power are very much shaped by issues of gender, social class, ethnicity and race. Membership or denizenship can become more precarious because of other forms of social exclusion. This is particularly apparent when one looks at the situation of the Roma population in Norway. Figure 3.2 shows that Romanian citizens are one of the largest groups who are expelled and, as we saw earlier, the third largest group of foreign inmates.

Romanian Roma became a visible feature in Norwegian public space after EU expansion and received considerable public attention, particularly because of begging. Their presence has been a hotly debated issue; it is often referred to in media discourse as a "wave" and the country is described as being "swamped" (Johansen, 2016). In 2017, an influential documentary, entitled *Lykkelandet* ("The Land of Happiness", my translation) was shown on the main Norwegian public television channel, and depicted Roma begging as part of organised crime, whereby naive Norwegians were lured into financing luxury lifestyles in Romania. Although the Vagrancy Act had only recently been abolished, the Roma presence in Norwegian cities caused the country to

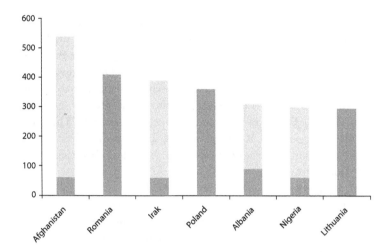

FIGURE 3.3 Deportation decisions by nationality and grounds, top seven nationalities, 2016. Dark grey columns depict violations of the Penal Code,
light grey columns depict violations of the Immigration Act[8]

Source: UDI (Norwegian Directorate of Immigration), https://www.udi.no/statistikk-
oganalyse/arsrapporter/tall-og-fakta-2016/faktaskriv-2016/hvem-ble-utvist-fra-norge-i-
2016/(accessed: August 20, 2019)

begin to reconsider reintroducing penal measures directed at beggars
and vagrants. Although no general prohibition on begging has in fact
been implemented, the Roma have been subjected to a number of
control strategies, particularly because of their campsites and irregular
way of life.

Historically, Norway has a long and problematic relationship with
travellers and the Romany population (Engebrigtsen, 2012). For this
reason, the country's relations to the Romanian Roma have been, as
Johansen (2016: 169) observes, "characterized by a combination of
sympathy and bad conscience, on the one hand, and repulsion and
antipathy, on the other". The poverty of many Romanian Roma is
thrown into relief by Norway's affluence, and has given rise both to
penal interventions and, importantly, to several humanitarian initiatives. This peculiar intertwining of penal and humanitarian forms of

governance will be further discussed in the Chapter 4. It should be pointed out, though, that their situation in Norway displays a number of similarities with the situation of Roma in other European countries (Barker, 2017). According to Yıldız and De Genova (2018: 425) a critical examination of Roma marginalisation, racialisation, and criminalisation in Europe brings into focus broader questions about Europe, European-ness, and European citizenship. They suggest that the contested Roma politics of mobility should be understood "as a constitutive feature of the sociopolitical formation of the EU" (ibid.).

Just as penality, in general, reveals the limits of social solidarity (Garland, 2013a), the construction of the Eastern European crimmigrant other reveals a split within Europe and the limits of its project of free movement and, ultimately, shared identity. The Eastern European crimmigrant other is symptomatic of what Etienne Balibar (2010) describes as Europe's cosmopolitan difficulty – its need to "deal with its *double otherness*, or its internal otherness and external otherness, which are no longer confronted in absolutely separate spaces". The perceived criminogenic nature of the East serves as a vehicle for the creation of boundaries within Europe and has created a rift in European identity. Although possessing formal membership, their cultural differences (expressed in a perceived criminal lifestyle) becomes a justification for social exclusion and subject Eastern European citizens to racialised framing as "other" (Bhui, 2016).

This is by no means a new development. In *Uses of the Other*, Iver Neumann (1999) points out the historic importance of "the East" for the collective identity formation of Europe. And, although the geographic markers of the East have gone through profound political changes, the developments described in this book suggest that the dynamic remains the same. Cut loose from its geographical point of reference, "the East", Neumann (1999) suggests, has become a generalised social marker in European identity formation. Thus discourses about crime and the use of penal power have a productive role in identity formation.

It should be borne in mind, though, that while these processes may be seen as undermining the value of European citizenship, their implications seem to be far more complex. As we shall see in Chapter 4, controlling the crimmigrant other has also served as an impetus for EU integration and considerably accelerated the speed of inter-European criminal justice cooperation. The trend was visible in the intensified EU cooperation that several of our informants mentioned as a tool for solving the crime problems associated with Eastern European citizens. A police station in an affluent part of Oslo even had police officers from Romania stationed there to assist them in their work of controlling unwanted mobility (Gundhus and Franko, 2016).

Beyond exceptionalism

Developments described in this chapter do not only consist of practical penal measures; they rest upon specific cultural perceptions about Norwegians and "foreigners", their social circumstances and values. During a parliamentary hearing the country's Minister of Justice said: "Since there is a trend that increasing numbers of foreign criminals come to Norway to help themselves with our riches, it is important that deportation measures work well and in a preventive way."[9] Several of our interviewees pointed out Norway's affluence and "attractiveness" as the background for the introduction of various penal measures. As one jurist employed in the Justice Department observed: "With all the money flowing around in this country it is clear, as I said, that Norway is an attractive country to do crime in" (Justis 2). The country was often referred to as a "honey pot" and Norwegians seen as the naive owners of many valuables. The leader of the Oslo police pickpocket group explained:

> A combination of naive Norwegians, a lot of valuables, and a low risk [of being apprehended], made Oslo one of the worst cities in Europe for pickpocketing. But we have managed to turn this trend around … Before many of them managed to get away with writs. They are shocked now when they see that we react more quickly and with severer penalties. At the same time, we will take a parallel route on the administrative track to get a deportation order.[10]

The above statement reveals cultural perceptions about Norway and Norwegians as naive owners of valuables, falling prey to foreign offenders. It also shows that the lenience of the Norwegian penal system is perceived as a risk that needs to be countered, both by the use of immigration law, and with stricter penalties. As we saw in the previous chapter, cultural perceptions that Eastern European offenders regard Scandinavian prisons as "hotel[s] where they get a daily allowance" are quite commonplace (Sausdal, 2018). The state, therefore, needs to inflict higher levels of pain in order to achieve a desired level of deterrence. In several judgments during the last decade, the Norwegian Supreme Court considerably raised sentencing levels for pickpocketing and for so-called mobile property offenders, which are crimes considered to be largely committed by foreign citizens (Flaatten, 2017).

There are many indications that these cultural changes are contributing towards heating up of the penal climate (Todd-Kvam, 2018). The Norwegian prison population has steadily increased over the past two decades. Throughout the post-war period, Norwegian prison figures had generally not exceeded 60 inmates per 100,000 inhabitants, but they rose from 57 in 2000 to 73 inmates per 100,000 inhabitants in 2016.[11] In actual numbers, this means that Norway had 33 per cent more prisoners in 2016, despite the fact that levels of recorded crime have seen a significant decline in the same period. In 2017, Statistics Norway reported a 27 per cent decline in levels of recorded crime since 2002; in fact, this was the lowest level in 25 years. The decline was particularly significant in property crime, but was also visible in most other categories, apart from sexual assault against children.[12] To sum up, then, the post-2000 period in Norway has been marked by high levels of immigration and population growth, record low levels of recorded crime, and record high levels of imprisonment. The development of bordered penality seems to be contributing towards increased punitiveness and the creation of a harsher penal climate.

It has been customary to describe the Scandinavian penal climate as exceptional (Pratt, 2008). Few societies can match Scandinavian countries in their commitment to welfare (Pratt and Eriksson, 2012), particularly if this is set against the late modern punitive and security tendencies to be seen in Anglo-American countries. Despite some trends to the contrary, elements of the idea of reintegration have retained their historic centrality in criminal justice and prison service ideologies (Smith and Ugelvik, 2017). Norway has been no exception to the Scandinavian norm. Its prisons have become popular with foreign visitors engaged in penal tourism, particularly the island prison at Bastøy. On one of his visits, the influential US documentary maker Michael Moore summarised the prison system's attitude towards prisoners as "how can we make them good neighbours".[13] He described Norway as a society which "operate[s] with a sense of we" (ibid.) and puts high value on social inclusion. This stance is epitomised by the Norwegian Labour Party's popular slogan "Alle skal med" (imperfectly translated as "Everybody in").

Despite the fact that, since 2013, the right-wing Progress Party has been in government and held the position of Justice Minister, penal welfarism has remained unchallenged by and large, at least as far as citizens are concerned. As John Todd-Kvam's (2018) recent analysis reveals, however, non-citizens have become the focus of a range of populist penal policies, including those described in this chapter. Rather than being immune to punitive sentiments (and exceptional in that regard), Norway has thus seen the development of penal populism that is bordered. The Progress Party "does populism" by focusing on non-citizens (ibid.). This development is exemplified by a recent statement by the Justice Minister, Tor Mikkel Wara, who made this comment on a proposal to extend the legal authority of the police to detain non-citizens in the course of border control:

> Border and immigration control are instruments in the war on crime. And it is important there should be clear rules that provide a basis for necessary control. I also detect strong support for the proposals for new legal authorities during the hearing.[14]

The Minister's statement is interesting on several levels. It stresses there is a general consensus about the necessity of stricter immigration control measures. However, its use of the phrase "the war on crime" is quite remarkable in the Scandinavian context, and clearly marks a departure from welfare-oriented penality. To employ a metaphor of warfare in the context of domestic governance (whether it is a war on crime, drugs, or terror) indicates, as Jonathan Simon (2007) observes, a move towards particular means and rationalities of governance. Such a style of governance uses fear of crime to gain legitimacy for policies which may challenge democratic forms of governance and welfare-oriented approaches to social problems.[15]

These changes have perhaps been most palpable in Norway's changing relationship to the international human rights regime. As mentioned earlier, in January 2016, the justice authorities, in a highly controversial move, started pushing back asylum seekers, some on bicycles, who had crossed its Arctic border with Russia at Storskog, amid freezing temperatures. Later, the country started to build a symbolic steel border fence at Storskog, presumably to halt future flows of refugees. Like Denmark's controversial "jewellery law", Storskog was an articulation of symbolic politics through which the authorities have been sending the message to the domestic audience that they are "tough on migration", and trying to change the country's "soft" and inclusionary image on the international stage. Since the war, Scandinavian societies have been branding themselves as humanitarian superpowers and champions of human rights, but immigration control objectives are now leading to a kind of "negative nation branding" (Gammeltoft-Hansen, 2017). Norway's controversial former immigration and justice minister, Sylvi Listhaug, even suggested that the European Human Rights Convention should be challenged in order to prioritise security of Norwegian citizens.

These developments can be seen as an indication that, mainly through its focus on controlling non-citizens, the Norwegian political climate has become a "hot" climate or, at least, is heating up. While criminal justice has been previously quite insulated from direct political pressure, this is no longer the case. As Green (2008: 79) points out, hot penal climates are marked by a high degree of press, public, and political interest in penal issues, and tend to foster moralistic language and produce inhospitable environments for deliberative consideration. Cool penal climates, on the other hand, are "characterized by comparatively minimal interest in penal issues, lower levels of punitive sentiment, and more opportunities to foster policy deliberation" (ibid.). Since the Progress Party's arrival in power, there has been hyperactivity in the justice domain, which is a departure from the previously slow pace and sober tone of Norwegian criminal justice politics. Several of our interviewees were in no doubt about the political nature of the changes their work has been subjected to. One leader of a police immigration unit in Oslo described them as follows:

> It may be in the nature of a right-wing government to have a major focus on this [deportation]. Perhaps a bit more of a focus than others, other parties. And the Progress Party was, after all, one of the drivers behind the increase of resources for the Oslo police district.
>
> *(OPD)*

These changes may not be immediately apparent to an outside observer. Norway still has among the lowest levels of imprisonment in Europe. The populist aspects of its public discourse, despite lively social media debates, do not come close to the shrill tone of political discourse seen in the US and some other European countries. Norwegian bordered penality still operates within the general "coolness" of its penal climate. The developments described in this chapter are in a sense invisible, under the radar of legal and normative debates about punishment, yet very much part of the everyday practice of the police and the courts. This is partly related to the fact that bordered forms of penality are, in general, not considered part of the legitimating discourse which mostly informs ordinary criminal justice practices (Bosworth, 2013). There can, however, be no doubt that the change in practice results from an intentional political strategy, as is evident in the systematic nature of deportation seminars and in the fact that deportation has been made into a key police performance indicator.

Norwegian punitiveness is difficult to grasp because it relies on a different form of penal power – a different "what" of punishment – from the one usually discussed in criminological and penological texts and textbooks (Aas, 2014). Punishment is generally inextricably linked to the idea of imprisonment, and prison figures are taken as the main indicator of state punitiveness. Prisons have the virtue of being "visible embodiments of society's decision to punish", while, as we saw in the previous chapter, deportation represents an invisible punishment (Travis, 2002: 15), which can have equally devastating effects on the lives of deportees. While not formally defined as punishment, the Norwegian authorities often use deportation in addition to, or interchangeably with, ordinary penalties, and sometimes see it as economically preferable and a more efficient way of addressing law and order issues.[16] Even if offenders are punished, the job has not been completed until they have been sent out of the country. Conventional measures of punitiveness are, therefore, generally poorly suited to recognising punitive and exclusionary aspects of Scandinavian societies, precisely because the punitive nature of the bordered is not immediately apparent through the traditional criminal justice frame (see also Franko et al., 2019). Prison figures clearly need to be seen in conjunction with deportations and immigration detention (Bosworth et al., 2018).

The situation we have described raises questions about some central assumptions about the nature of penal tolerance, and the connections between welfare and punitiveness (Barker, 2018). Bordered penality reveals the intrinsic boundedness of the welfare state, where its normative framework of social equality and inclusion reveals itself to be universal exclusively within the boundaries of citizenship. In this respect, Norway, like other Nordic societies, can be seen as a prime example of what Bosniak (2006: 16) terms "hard-on-the-outside, soft-on-the-inside conceptions of citizenship", where an understanding of membership as strictly bounded provides the necessary framework for the pursuit of equal/democratic citizenship within. This tendency finds its expression in a double-faced penal culture which is mild towards insiders and punitive towards outsiders (Barker, 2013).

The Norwegian penal state is, as Ugelvik (2013) observes, "a state with a double vision". The duality is evident in the institutional design of its imprisonment regime, where new confinement facilities have been created, designed exclusively for non-citizens, and, to a large extent, guided by different rationalities. The character of institutions like the Trandum detention centre and the Kongsvinger prison is determined by the fact that their inhabitants are not considered members of Norwegian society, and are not expected to return to the society which has imprisoned them. They are, therefore, beyond inclusion. The existence of a class of people who are considered beyond inclusion is particularly significant in a country where the idea of rehabilitation and reintegration has been the pillar of its prison service ideology. In theory, at least, it is assumed that a Norwegian prisoner will return to society, and the welfare state is willing to use its substantial muscle power to achieve that objective (Ugelvik, 2013) and to make him or her, as Michael Moore put it, "a good neighbour" (see above).

The control of the crimmigrant other, therefore, creates the paradox of social exclusion in an inclusive society. By undermining its inclusive nature, it sets the society at odds with its own self-narrative, whether this concerns its commitment to human rights and a reintegrative prison system or to a police force that is committed to serving the general public. These developments have not gone unchallenged. Several representatives of the police have expressed concern that focusing on immigration control and checking documents may threaten the traditionally high levels of trust in the police in Norway. This problem has been particularly acutely felt in Oslo, where a large proportion of the population is made up of immigrants and the descendants of immigrants, and where the police have invested considerable efforts in initiatives to win the trust of immigrant communities. Indeed, in 2016, Oslo's chief of police publicly declared that "Racial profiling is destructive for trust and can contribute to police losing trust, and therefore valuable information, from the society it is supposed to serve" (Oslo Politi, 17.3.2016).[17]

This understanding of immigration control as racial profiling mirrors the arguments of critical voices within immigrant populations and civil rights activists, who regard such controls as deeply discriminatory. Several voices within the police thus expressed a view of immigration controls as counterproductive as regards the anti-radicalisation and counterterrorism work that is being done in these communities. As one operative officer from Oslo we talked to put it:

> I do not think that they have managed to grasp the complexity of a diverse society, which Oslo has become, and what this in fact demands; which considerations one should bear in mind. And that an increased presence of the police in immigrant communities, which in a way just mind their own business and try to make the wheels go round, will be stigmatising and create an us-and-them attitude. This is dangerous, considering that one wishes to avoid radicalisation.
>
> *(Operational, OPD)*

Police discontent was most clearly expressed in several public statements made by the union of senior police officers. In April 2017, the leader of the union said:

> Frequent checks on individuals can be experienced as a burden. Having more resources for detection and deportation means there is extra pressure on police districts to deliver on the performance targets. Those who are to be deported do not, as a rule, wait in asylum centres. They have to be found. In some cases, the focus has been on residents, just to increase the numbers. Focusing on performance targets can lead to reduced trust in the police among people who feel they have been unfairly treated. It can be directly destructive of the reputation of the police.
>
> *(Leader of Norges Politilederlag, Geir Krogh, 20 April 2017)*[18]

On the ground, police officers often perceived the intense political demands and performance targets imposed on them as an interference in their professional judgment (Gundhus, 2016), as well as being generally damaging to the reputation of the police. The sentiments expressed in Krogh's statement may therefore have been prompted in equal measure by dislike of New Public Management techniques as well as a fear of losing public trust. Nevertheless, there is much to suggest that such concerns are well founded. In their comprehensive study of police legitimacy among immigrants, Bradford and Jackson (2018: 584) found that low levels of trust and difficult relationships between immigrant groups and state institutions such as the police "tend to be generated not by the 'cultural baggage' of the immigrants but by the actions and omissions of the institutions with which they interact and the larger state framework within which both exist". Police officers' concerns, therefore, indicate a well-grounded fear that their actions may be contributing towards the creation of social divisions within a society which has traditionally prided itself on high levels of unity and social cohesion. Another member of the police leaders' union said: "We have, until now, managed to avoid a development that we see in some countries with much discussed parallel societies. But we should have ongoing debate and awareness about this, if we are to succeed in the future "(Jan Erik Haugeland, NPL Øst, 21.4.2017).

The control of the crimmigrant other thus has profound social consequences and creates a number of paradoxes. Although "hard-on-the-outside, soft-on-the-inside" approaches may, at the outset, enjoy a considerable degree of public and political support, the boundaries between the "inside" and "outside" are far from clear in increasingly diverse societies.

Conclusion

On 17 May 2017, the Norwegian prime minister and foreign secretary interrupted their National Day celebrations to hold a press conference to welcome the release of Joshua French, a man with dual Norwegian and British citizenship who had been sentenced, in a shambolic criminal trial, to life in prison for murder in the Democratic Republic of the Congo:

> "I am very pleased to confirm that the Congolese authorities decided yesterday to transfer Joshua French to Norway," the Norwegian prime minister, Erna Solberg, told a news conference. "French came to Norway today and is now receiving the necessary medical follow-up. I am relieved that he is now in Norway."[19]

The story was covered by all the major national media outlets and became front-page news. The timing of French's return on the National Day was pregnant with symbolism: a long-lost son finally returns and is embraced by the nation. Reports generally expressed concern for his health and sympathy with the heroic suffering of his mother. The state authorities also declared that he would be immediately released and would not be serving the remaining part of his sentence in a Norwegian prison. Subsequently, French's story has been made into a movie and portrayed in numerous documentaries.

This book is obviously not about cases like that of Joshua French. Quite the opposite. It is about people who, like French, are convicted of crime, or associated with crime, but whom Norway – along with other Western counties – is doing its utmost to get rid of. The story of French's return is interesting, because it speaks to the central message of this book: the importance of citizenship and belonging in matters of crime and punishment. It shows that, in certain circumstances, the release of a "foreign offender" can become a cause for national celebration – a trigger for sympathy and solidarity – while at other times it leads to fear and social exclusion. While French and his companion may have been constructed as crimmigrant others in the Democratic Republic of the Congo, in Norway they were seen first and foremost as members, albeit marked by a certain level of notoriety and suspicion.

This chapter has shown how the use of penal power and the state's coercive apparatus is shaped by perceptions about membership and belonging. These perceptions also shape and define contemporary responses to mass migration. Penal power is used as a marker of belonging and as a means of policing the boundaries of membership in contemporary Europe. The building of border fences, draconian deportation measures, and disregard for the principles of the international human rights law have become central elements of populist political movements and politics aiming to curb migratory flows. These political sentiments have gained most visible expression in the US, with Donald Trump's campaign to build a wall against Mexico and with the US government's aggressive drive for deportation. However, this chapter has shown that these trends are, in less dramatic forms, also taking place in some European countries, including Scandinavian ones. Three decades after the highly symbolic fall of the Berlin Wall – seen as one of the defining moments of the new European identity – European states as diverse as Hungary, Greece, and Norway are enacting a different kind of symbolism and again erecting walls and border barriers (Brown, 2010).

The use of penal power has been, in the Anglo-American context, frequently linked to neoliberalism (Cavadino and Dignan, 2006), the demise of the welfare state (Wacquant, 2009), the diminishing state power under conditions of globalisation, and the state trying to cover up the demise of sovereignty by acting out on issue of crime (Garland, 2001). The argument has been extended to explain the recent prominence of immigration law within criminal justice. In the European context, punitive attitudes towards non-members have been linked to the resurgence of nationalism, giving rise to what Vanessa Barker (2018) terms "penal nationalism". Expulsion and denial of access thus serve to revitalise the nation state, which, as Bauman (1992) observed, needs nationalism for the primitive accumulation of authority. Border control and the nation state have been, throughout history, mutually reinforcing categories (Donnan and Wilson, 1999). When national identity appears threatened under conditions of globalisation, and when what has been termed "zombie state" needs to reassert its authority, the daily re-enacted divisions between natives and (criminal) aliens gain a particular political prominence (Schinkel, 2009).

While such explanations undoubtedly hold much purchase, they also bring to attention the importance of national and local difference and the need to avoid generic descriptions. What is of particular interest in the Norwegian context, described in this chapter, is that the state in question is by no means a hollowed out, neoliberal "zombie state", but rather one of the most ambitious and wealthiest welfare states in the world. In this case, the joint forces of criminal and immigration law do not simply aim to cover up the state's emptiness and declining sovereignty. Rather, bordered penality has an additional dimension, which also becomes apparent if we take a look at its historic origins. As Walters (2010: 91) points out, contemporary practices of deportation have clear affinities with the historic poor law, and involve "a certain reconstruction of its logic on a regional, and today a global scale" (see also Weber and Bowling, 2008). By re-enacting fixed and rigid conceptions of membership, deportation is "an instrument to defend and promote the welfare of a nationally defined population" (Walters, 2010: 86). As Vanessa Barker (2018: 1) points out with regard to Sweden:

The Swedish welfare state is based on a cracked foundation in which the core principles of equality, solidarity, and inclusiveness do not necessarily or always extend to others and outsiders. The principle of equality is foundational to the society and there is a long history of humanitarianism based on this belief. Yet, these core principles bump up against a countervailing logic of welfare state solvency and nationalized membership. The welfare state is a national project first and foremost, and will use its hard and soft power to uphold it.

Bordered penality is therefore not simply about revitalising national identity and keeping out the foreign and culturally different – although this clearly is a salient aspect – but about keeping out those who wish to make claim on the resources; about the protection of welfare rights for citizens. It is about the "right to be here" and hence about access to welfare and Northern wealth. Barker terms the phenomenon "welfare nationalism": "a place where the welfare state must be preserved and made sustainable for those on the inside by limiting access from the outside" (2013: 17; 2018). Similarly, Ceuppens and Geschiere's (2005: 397) descriptions of struggles over autochthony in the Netherlands – yet another traditionally tolerant society with an exclusive edge – reveal "attempts to reserve the benefits of the welfare state to those who really belong". Through the daily dynamics of defence and rearticulation, borders are constituted as both material forces and structures of imagination. By comparing their country to a "honey pot", Norwegian police officers see themselves as its guardians. The practices of bordered penality are thus "deeply rooted in collective identifications and the assumption of a common sense of belonging" (Balibar, 2010: 316), which structure the punitive attitudes towards non-members. In such a context, the crimmigrant other is defined by his or her lack of membership – as someone deemed not to belong – and also as a threat to the general welfare of the society, as someone representing a threat to the honey pot.

Notes

1   Source: www.dagbladet.no/nyheter/sylvi-listhaug-slar-tilbake-mot-kristoffer-joner—vi-lar-oss-ikke-stoppe-av-dette-hylekoret/65365851
2   Source: Statistics Norway, at www.ssb.no/innvandring-og-innvandrere/faktaside/innvandring#blokk-1
3   The unit is a specialised unit within the police force with the primary responsibility for identification of asylum seekers and deportation of foreign citizens without permission to stay in the country. The tasks of border policing are, in Norway, otherwise embedded in the general police force.
4   Source: www.ssb.no/sosiale-forhold-og-kriminalitet/artikler-og-publikasjoner/5-500-ar-ubetinget-fengsel
5   Source: Sigmund B. Mohn and UDI (Norwegian Directorate of Immigration) annual reports (1991–2018). Light red and dark red columns represent deportations decisions given for breaches of criminal law (dark red columns represent deportation decisions arising from breaches of criminal law

by the EU and EEA, which are legally established by a special legislative framework)

6 Source: UDI and the Police Immigration Service.
7 "Kurdistan" not meant literally.
8 Source: UDI annual report, 2012. URL: www.udi.no/arsrapport2012/ Statistikk/Tabell-13-Utvisningsvedtak-etter-statsborgerskap-og-grunnlag-2013/ Accessed: 21.8.2013.
9 Source: www.stortinget.no/no/Saker-og-publikasjoner/Publikasjoner/ Referater/Stortinget/2013-2014/131209/7/
10 www.politiforum.no/artikler/her-tar-de-lommetyv-nummer-163-og-164/ 385850
11 www.prisonstudies.org/country/norway
12 www.ssb.no/sosiale-forhold-og-kriminalitet/artikler-og-publikasjoner/his torisk-fa-lovbrudd-anmeldt-i-2017
13 www.nrk.no/vestfold/michael-moore-har-laget-dokumentarfilm-om-ba stoy-fengsel-1.12901926
14 www.regjeringen.no/no/aktuelt/vil-halde-tilbake-utlendingar/id2611652/
15 For the deployment of military preventive thinking in the filed of migration in Norway, see also Gundhus and Jansen's (2019) analysis of the "Operation Migrant".
16 For further discussion of the punitive aspects of deportation, and their legal implications, see, inter alia, Pauw (2000) and Vazquez (2012).
17 www.tv2.no/a/8298886/
18 www.politilederen.no/nyheter/1682-ukritisk-bruk-av-maltall-kan-skade-p olitiet
19 www.theguardian.com/world/2017/may/17/joshua-french-freed-norwa y-uk-congo

4

POLICING EUROPE'S HUMANITARIAN BORDERLANDS

But he also warned law enforcement officers their behaviour must be "exemplary" and reminded them that migrants were "people who have travelled continents; these men and women are human beings".

"It's a delicate mission and for it you must be exemplary and in absolute respect of professional ethics and absolute respect of the law. This means not waking people up in the middle of the night, not using teargas during mealtimes," he said. Any excessive behaviour, he warned, would be "punished".

(Report on Emmanuel Macron's visit to Calais, January 2018)[1]

Chapter 3 outlined the dynamics surrounding penal control at the national level; this chapter moves the analysis to the European level and examines the role of the crimmigrant other in the progressive securitisation and militarisation of the EU's border policies. The European mobility regime is examined to situate the crimmigrant other within the EU's classifications of hierarchies of citizenship. Such hierarchies reflect the deeply stratified nature of global mobility and are the backdrop against which notions of security, deviance, and illegality are forged within contemporary migration regimes. The chapter outlines the rise of Frontex, the European Border and Coast Guard Agency, and shows that, although the narrative of the crimmigrant other plays an important role in the resurgence of national forms of membership and belonging, the coupling of migration and crime has also created some different dynamics. The chapter looks at the integrative features of the EU's focus on border security, particularly as regards combating human smuggling. Migrant smugglers – depicted mostly as men from the global South – have become the epitome of contemporary organised crime and a motor of the vast expansion of the authority of EU policing agencies.

The chapter concludes by pointing to the duality of contemporary systems of European migration control and governance and to the centrality of humanitarian rationalities within them. As shown by the words of the French president, Emmanuel Macron, Europe has developed a regime of migration governance that combines humanitarian, penal, and military rationalities. It requires the use of increasingly militarised modes of control while stressing that the use of teargas is prohibited during mealtimes and that migrants should be seen as "men and women who are human beings". This duality is fundamental to the shaping of narratives about migration and can be seen in strongly divided, black-and-white thinking about migrants. The migrant smuggler represents one side of the division, while on the other is the notion of migrants as victims, as in narratives about trafficked women and children. Such notions demonstrate the intricate moral economy of exercising penal power at the border (Fassin, 2005, 2015). This chapter develops the theme by examining ethical and moral dilemmas inherent in such a system of border control. European border regimes can be described as humanitarian borderlands (Aas and Gundhus, 2015). They are marked by the duality of massive suffering and human need, on one hand, and extensive use of force which lacks traditional forms of legitimacy, on the other. This duality is explored through the accounts of people tasked with border policing, and it is argued that the narrative of the crimmigrant other helps chart this difficult moral terrain.[2]

Building a belt of protection: penal power in the post-colony

On 28 June 2018, after an emergency summit, the EU leadership announced agreement on a strategy to manage its migration challenges:

> In order to definitively break the business model of the smug-
> glers, thus preventing tragic loss of life, it is necessary to eliminate
> the incentive to embark on perilous journeys. This requires a new
> approach based on shared or complementary actions among the
> Member States to the disembarkation of those who are saved in
> Search and Rescue operations. In that context, the European
> Council calls on the Council and the Commission to swiftly
> explore the concept of regional disembarkation platforms, in close
> cooperation with relevant third countries as well as UNHCR and
> IOM. Such platforms should operate distinguishing individual
> situations, in full respect of international law and without creating
> a pull factor.

In addition to stressing its commitment to effective border controls the
statement outlines three elements which are the defining features of
the EU's external migration management strategy: a) the offloading of
the burden of migratory flows onto its neighbours, even though they
may have very poor human rights records; b) the use of language such
as "combatting organised crime", and "the business model of the
smugglers"; and c) the discursive importance of saving lives at sea. This
somewhat incongruous combination of elements is the main structure
within which the EU frames its responses to the irregular migration at
its Southern borders and will be addressed in the following sections.

In recent years, a vast body of scholarship has documented the centrality of the security discourse in the EU's responses to international
migration (Huysmans, 2006; Guild, 2009: Andersson, 2014). As Huysmans (2006: xi) points out, such a discourse is a "political technique of
framing policy questions in logics of survival with a capacity to mobilize
politics of fear in which social relations are structured on the basis of
distrust". Securitisation is thus not only a set of bureaucratic, legal, and
technological practices but also a discursive phenomenon which frames
migration, and immigrant populations, as security problems, rather
than, for example, humanitarian, developmental, or economic issues.
Such a perspective is exemplified in the aforementioned statement by
the Secretary General of NATO about the danger of terrorists trying to
hide among migrants. Similarly, Frontex clearly defines fighting terrorism as a central aspect of its mission, saying that "Frontex also

contributes to the fight against terrorism by assisting Member States in tightening controls at the external borders and supporting the detection of potential foreign terrorist fighters."[3] Europe is by no means unique in establishing such connections in popular and political discourse between the international terrorist and "the 'bogus refugee', an unscrupulous, queue-jumping economic migrant also tainted with the suspicion of criminality" (Pratt and Valverde, 2018: 138). The threats are not only criminality and terrorism – such people are also perceived as a crushing burden on state welfare systems, social services, and national cultures (Holzberg et al., 2018; Barker, 2018).

International migration has also been framed as a threat to the survival of the EU on a more fundamental level. The German chancellor, Angela Merkel, recently dramatically stated that the EU's future hinges on "solving the migration issue".[4] The perception that the fate of EU integration depends on how the continent handles migration has put the issue at the top of its political agenda.[5] For more than a decade, EU member states have been playing complicated "sovereignty games" (Adler-Nissen and Gammeltoft-Hansen, 2008) around migration and border control, in which the strategy of passing the buck to one's neighbour has seriously challenged the ideal of burden-sharing. Several countries have reinstated border controls and introduced measures which may threaten one of the main accomplishments of EU integration: free internal mobility (Casella Colombeau, 2017). These developments have raised serious doubts about the viability of Schengen, which has been one of the key stones of European integration in the field of Justice and Home Affairs.

Migration control is, then, changing contemporary Europe in very profound ways. This book does not aim to provide a comprehensive overview of these developments (for a more detailed analysis see, inter alia, Mitsilegas, 2015; Pijenburg et al., 2018; Carrera et al., 2019). What is of interest here is that Europe's response to migration has been a defining aspect of its identity, institutions, and mechanisms of government; the logic of the "dangerous migrant" has been central to this (Mitsilegas, 2015). The "migration security nexus" (Walters, 2008) has contributed in recent years to a considerable militarisation of the EU's borders, the rise of Frontex, and the development of a technological/military complex (Andersson, 2014). It is also fundamentally restructuring the EU's relationship with its neighbours

(Milivojevic, 2019; Stambøl, forthcoming). As a response to the so-called migration crisis, Europe has surrounded itself with an invisible wall, the human costs of which can be seen in the inhumane conditions suffered by migrants stranded in Libya, Turkey, and Greece, and also in the tragic numbers of migrant deaths mentioned earlier (IOM, 2017; Gammeltoft-Hansen, 2018).

The strategies of externalisation have no doubt been effective. In 2017, two years after the peak of the crisis, there were 204,300 irregular border crossings in the EU, a 60 per cent reduction from the previous year (Frontex, 2017). Norway, for example, received only 3,546 migrants, the lowest number since 1995. The national deportation machine (described in Chapter 3) thus has far less work to do, because violence and coercion have been outsourced to a protective belt consisting of Europe's border zones and to distant processing centres. The structures of bordered penality at the national level, therefore, need to be situated within the broader geopolitical system of global power relations, which at present is doing the lion's share of walling up and guarding the boundaries of membership. The EU has shifted from internal to external responses (Pastore, 2017), which have become the more important of the two. EU states are doing their utmost to transfer their migratory burdens to their neighbours and make themselves less attractive to migrants (Gammeltoft-Hansen, 2018). The EU has successfully used a stick-and-carrot approach to export its migration control agenda and co-opt its Southern and Eastern neighbours into doing its policing jobs, thus creating "law enforcement buffer zones" (Andreas and Nadelmann, 2006: 15; Milivojevic, 2019; Carrera and Cortinovis, 2019). This strategy was particularly visible during the 2015/2016 crisis, when the agreement with Turkey became the agent of the EU's intended solution, particularly as a consequence of its failure to achieve internal solidarity and burden-sharing among member states (Gammeltoft-Hansen, 2018).

Put bluntly, due to the political toxicity of migration and the unwillingness of member states to share the burden of migrants more equally, the EU's main strategy in recent years has been to shift the burden onto its neighbours, extraterritorialising de facto the European border (Aas, 2013a; Gammeltoft-Hansen, 2011; Carrera and Cortinovis, 2019). Such strategies are by no means peculiar to the EU; in their aim and nature they resemble the Australian Pacific Solution and the

American Caribbean Solution (Ryan and Mitsilegas, 2010; Weber and Pickering, 2011). As Mitsilegas (2010: 39) observes, there has been a "convergence between models of extraterritorial immigration control globally". These regions have become, to use Sanja Milivojevic's (2019) term, a "purgatory" for migrants and can be seen as a large-scale example of the use of penal control for the purpose of immobilisation.

This extensive use of penal power for the purpose of migration control challenges Europe's commitment to some of its fundamental values, such as the right to seek asylum and the right to life, this being most visible on its Southern borders. For example, in a judgment in *N.D. and N.T.* v. *Spain*, the European Court of Human Rights (ECHR 291 (2017)) ruled that the long-standing practice of pushing back migrants from the external borders of the EU is unlawful. The Court found that Spain's 2014 expulsion of migrants on the border with Morocco amounted to the collective expulsion of foreign nationals and was a violation of Article 4, Protocol 4 (prohibition of collective expulsions) and Article 13 (right to an effective remedy) of the European Convention on Human Rights.[6] The judgment indicates that, for several years, the EU has been actively pushing the boundaries of legality (Dembour, 2015; Gammeltoft-Hansen and Vedsted-Hansen, 2017).

The extensive use of policing and penal power on its external borders is underpinned by an influential perception that the migratory pressures there are a question of illegality. If we look at the statistics produced by Eurostat in Figure 4.1, we can see that the so-called crisis of 2015 is depicted as one of illegality.[7] Although most of the increase in that year could be ascribed to the influx of migrants from Syria (many of them with a right to apply for asylum), the label applied is that of illegality. Although several EU bodies have been critical to the use of the term, its law enforcement agencies seem to be reluctant to use alternative concepts. Frontex, for example, uses mixed terminology and its reports frequently speak of "illegal" border crossings (Frontex, 2017, 2018) despite the mixed nature of irregular migratory movements.

It is beyond the scope of this book to present a detailed overview of EU's external border policies (see Vaughan-Williams, 2015). Instead, I shall focus on one of my main arguments that the objectives of migration control, supported by a metanarrative about the crimmigrant other, create new forms of criminalisation and punitiveness. These

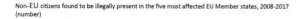

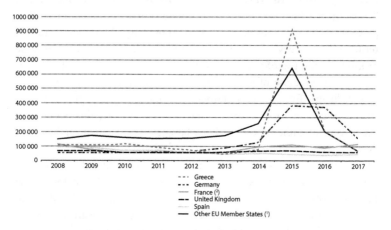

FIGURE 4.1 Eurostat statistics on non-EU citizens 'illegally present' in EU Member States

Source: https://ec.europa.eu/eurostat/statistics-explained/index.php?title=File:Non-EU_citizens_found_to_be_illegally_present_in_the_five_most_affected_EU_Membe_States,_2008-2017_(number)_1.png&oldid=391971

developments towards the use of penal power at the border are taking place in a particular geopolitical context. European states can be described as Northern penal states (Aas, 2013a) and are – in terms of criminalisation and penal control – crucially defined by their geopolitical position. Northern penal states are creating an elaborate legal regime that criminalises certain forms of movement, effectively rendering large parts of the world's population "illegal" (Dauvergne, 2008).

The European Union's efforts to combat irregular border crossings have led to the tightening of border controls in neighbouring regions (Milivojevic, 2019). These trends are particularly apparent in the Sahel region, where states such as Libya, Algeria, Morocco, and Tunisia have been encouraged to tighten legislation and increase legal sanctions against irregular migrants, and the facilitators of their journeys, in exchange for financial aid and cooperation (Andersson, 2016). Although these countries have a long history of migration, which forms part of their local economies and modes of being, they have been put under pressure to define these activities as clandestine and illegal (Stambøl, 2019). Julien Brachet's (2018) ethnographic study reveals that, since 2016, in Niger – a country heavily involved in trans-Saharan trade and traditionally hospitable to migrants – people have, for the first time, been punished for the newly created crime of human smuggling.

Geopolitics, therefore, matters in migration control, as well as in crime control (Andreas and Nadelmann, 2006). Earlier chapters have outlined the contingency of the label of illegality within national and local contexts, and this chapter reveals similar dynamics at the global level. Although the nation state is usually the main agent of crim-inalisation, it is important to acknowledge that states vary, and their interests in terms of criminalisation depend on their geopolitical posi-tion. Some states are more sovereign than others (Dauvergne, 2008: 172). Several historic and contemporary accounts of the inter-nationalisation of crime control have pointed out that what is illegal, and how it is policed, often depends on the political interests of certain states, most notably the United States and Western Europe (Andreas and Nadelmann, 2006; Jakobi, 2013). "The models, methods, and priorities of international crime control are substantially determined and exported by the most powerful states in the international system" (Andreas and Nadelmann, 2006: 10). A similar situation exists in the illegalisation and policing of migration. Spatialisation is, as Coutin (2005: 6) observes, "the key to both criminalization and to challenging how criminality is defined". It offers an opportunity to explore and embrace the situatedness of law – what Philippopoulos-Mihalopoulos (2010: 190) terms "law's spatial turn", as well as the articulation of politics through law. Extraterritorial border controls and the out-sourcing of asylum are, according to Gammeltoft-Hansen (2011), examples of doing "politics through law", where governments strate-gically seek to shift or deconstruct legal responsibilities otherwise owed by reference to law itself.

As the globalised dynamics of criminalisation become increasingly international, this internationalisation also includes the creation of globally meaningful labels of crime and deviance. These regimes consist not only of legal regulation, but also of various mechanisms of policing, enforcement and social exclusion related to the illegalisation –mechanisms which are becoming increasingly transnational in their nature. As Northern penal states, EU states (collectively and individually) possess the ability to externalise their domestic control functions and export their crime and migration control agendas to others (Aas, 2013a). The EU has thus established a substantial "EU Emergency Trust Fund for Africa" (EUTF) and earmarked €4.3 billion for the purpose of migration control.[8] It is financing a number of cooperations to support third countries in their "migration management". French police officers in Niger, for example, are working to equip "Saharan border posts with jeeps and night radar, computers, machines to detect fake identity papers and to take biometric fingerprints, and Internet access to retrieve Interpol files" (Brachet, 2018: 23). Similarly, Frontex seeks to "constantly develop reliable and effective networks of partnerships at the operational level with the relevant authorities of non-EU states".[9], [10] Although deeply problematic from a humanitarian perspective, particularly when it comes to the situation in Libya (Carrera and Cortinovis, 2019), this strategy is also clearly articulated in the aforementioned conclusion of the European Council summit, which states:

> As regards the Central Mediterranean Route, efforts to stop smugglers operating out of Libya or elsewhere should be further intensified. The EU will continue to stand by Italy and other frontline Member States in this respect. It will step up its support for the Sahel region, the Libyan Coastguard, coastal and Southern communities, humane reception conditions, voluntary humanitarian returns, cooperation with other countries of origin and transit, as well as voluntary resettlement. All vessels operating in the Mediterranean must respect the applicable laws and not obstruct operations of the Libyan Coastguard.[11]

Moreover, the EU has been exporting not only border control training standards and surveillance equipment, but also "unwanted aliens". In recent years, Frontex has chartered growing numbers of flights to countries such as Serbia, Nigeria, Kosovo, the Congo, and Iraq (Frontex, 2017, 2018). These flights are funded by Schengen states and help return to the global South various types of unwanted mobility, such as irregular migrants, foreign citizens who have committed criminal offences, and failed asylum seekers. In fact, so-called "Return Support" is now the second biggest item in the Frontex budget; it increased by 30 percent, from €39 million in 2016 to €53 million in 2017.[12] The deportability of the crimmigrant other is, therefore, part of an elaborate international regime for policing aliens (Weber and Bowling, 2008; De Genova and Peutz, 2010: Walters, 2010) and should be situated within the context of deeply unequal international relations. The return flights act primarily in the interests of the Northern states organising them. Many Southern societies greatly depend on remittances from their citizens abroad, and several observers have pointed out the detrimental effects caused by the return of "criminal aliens" both to the returnees and to their countries of origin (Brotherton and Barrios, 2006; Weber and Bowling, 2008). The flights are nevertheless supported by a political and legal arrangement in which many Southern states are more or less active participants.

Historically, these developments are nothing new and are clearly analogous to the penal, administrative, and military deportation practised by European colonial powers in the past (Benton, 2010; Walters, 2010; Anderson, 2016; De Vito, 2018). As Clare Anderson's (2016) extensive study reveals, from the 17th to the 20th centuries, approximately 380,000 transported convicts journeyed to locations across the British Empire. Most European colonial powers participated in some form of penal expulsion. These "punitive entanglements" (De Vito, 2018) should not be understood simply as penal strategies that enabled countries that deported convicts to save money on prisons and to get rid of unwanted populations – first and foremost they were a means of furthering their colonial enterprises and a form of colonial governmentality (Anderson, 2016). Contemporary practices of bordered penality, therefore, have clear neo-colonial dimensions. Today, as in the past, strategies of mobility policing are not only about fending off unwanted movement, but also, essentially, about the strategic production of sovereign power in a deeply stratified global order (Gundhus and Franko, 2016). In fact, contemporary deportation practices seem to surpass those at the height of the colonial era. While the Australian colonies were sent an estimated 167,000 convict men, women, and children between 1788 and 1868 (Anderson, 2016: 383), Eurostat reports that, in 2017 alone, 188,905 non-EU citizens were "returned outside of the EU". However, this was a reduction of 17.4 per cent on the year before, when 228,625 non-EU citizens were returned to states not belonging to the EU.[13] According to Frontex (2017, 2018), approximately half of the returns were so-called forced returns.

Global hierarchies of citizenship: from deviant states to deviant citizens

The figure of the crimmigrant other, then, should be understood within the context of racial and (neo-)colonial social relations (Basaran and Guild, 2017). The processes of its social production and related state modes of control share many similarities with past colonial "solutions" and are deeply involved with notions of race (Bhui, 2016; Bosworth et al., 2018). The figure of the crimmigrant other is produced in the context of pervasive global inequalities which determine individuals' ability to move across national borders. As Basaran and Guild (2017: 274) observe, "The 'colonial other' – othered by race, religion and tradition – remains also in the post-colonial order more closely scrutinized at international borders than his/her Western counterpart." While certain populations are systematically prevented from moving (their movements being defined as illegal), for others, there has been a systematic removal of barriers to movement. These inequalities are particularly visible in the case of the EU, where the removal of internal border controls has been one of the hallmarks of EU membership, while at the same time it is intrinsically connected to raising barriers against so-called third-country nationals.

Although the nexus between migration and insecurity has been a pervasive feature of the European border regime, it is important to bear in mind that its effects on different groups of travellers have varied markedly (Aas, 2011). Not all migrants are equal. European states have created fine gradations of migrants, resulting in intricate hierarchies of citizenship, which are central to the structuring of the use of penal power. Though one of the defining features of the crimmigrant other is that he or she lacks citizenship, this social condition has different effects on various categories in the hierarchy. Via the logics of securitisation, Northern states are developing increasingly sophisticated and technologically advanced practices of social sorting of mobility (see, inter alia,

Zureik and Salter, 2005; Broeders and Hampshire, 2013; Pickering and Weber, 2013; Milivojevic, 2019). Human mobility flows are, as Broeders and Hampshire (2013: 1207) point out, "accompanied by flows of personal data and biometrics which are used to identify and categorise passengers before arrival, and to differentiate treatments at ports of entry". Such databases systematically collect data on travellers who are considered suspicious by immigration authorities, who sort border crossers into so-called green, grey, and black hierarchies (ibid.).

On a global level, this approach has created a fine gradation of individuals and states according to the security risk represented by their migration, or what might be termed their "deviance". In the case of the EU, according to Guild (2009: 188–189), this grading has produced the following "typology of European inclusion and exclusion":

1. Citizens of states in Europe
2. EU citizens who are not nationals of the state where they are living (expulsion and exclusion possible only on the grounds of public policy, public security, and public health)
3. Citizens of the Union who are temporarily excluded (under time-limited restrictions on some nationals involved in the 2004–2007 EU enlargement)
4. Swiss, Norwegian, and Icelandic nationals
5. Turkish workers in the EU
6. Third-country nationals with long-term residence (they enjoy the same protection against expulsion as migrant citizens of the EU)
7. Third-country nationals whose country of nationality is on the EU's visa whitelist (e.g. US nationals)
8. Third-country nationals whose country of nationality is on the EU's visa blacklist but with which the EU has a visa facilitation agreement (e.g. Russia)
9. Third-country nationals whose country of nationality is on the EU visa blacklist and with which there is no visa facilitation agreement (e.g. China); there is a presumption that these persons pose a security risk and they must obtain a visa
10. Third-country nationals whose country of nationality is on the EU visa blacklist and whose country has been specified in the EU

> visa rules as a country of specific security concern by at least one
> member state

Such hierarchies of national exclusion are based on a pre-established racialised colonial ranking. It is this global hierarchy that determines national levels of protection and rights, including the various degrees of protection that individuals have against expulsion. While there may be national differences, most Northern states follow the norms associated with affluence, cultural, and political affinity, security, and cooperation with crime and immigration control objectives. Failure to cooperate is directly felt by the citizens of the "deviant state" (Milivojevic, 2019). Citizens of blacklisted countries (see number 8 above) are collectively seen as a potential security risk of some kind – illegal migration, criminality, political violence – depending on the state they are from. Such a risk can be neutralised by visa facilitation, if these countries offer the EU security reassurance in the form of a readmission agreement, whereby they will accept their citizens if they are expelled (Guild, 2009: 190). Milivojevic (2019: 74), for example, shows how, in order to "rescue" their visa liberalisation regimes, the Western Balkan states were asked to restrict mobility of certain groups of their own citizens, mostly of Roma and Kosovo Albanian origin. The main "strategies to restrict the movement of the local 'Other'" thus emerged: legal reforms that criminalised the abuse of visa-free regimes and racial profiling at border crossings (ibid.). By violating their own citizens' right to leave the country and to seek asylum, these countries effectively use penal power to comply with external demands.

In the Western Balkans example we see a more general pattern of the Northern legal production and creation of standards of conduct and governance, which is accompanied by Southern compliance and the adoption of standards in exchange for trading and mobility benefits, development funds, promises of potential EU membership, etc. We see here the constitution of two qualitatively different types of statehood: the *deviant state* (which may be cooperative or non-cooperative) and the *Northern penal state*, which is defined by its aim and ability to export its "crimmigration control" agenda. This tendency to evaluate a state's capacity to govern crime according to its ability to respond to issues on the international crime control agenda is neither new nor unusual

(Jakobi, 2013). One need only think of the US-sponsored war on drugs, the FATF (Financial Action Task Force), and the US State Department's ranking of countries according to their money laundering and anti-trafficking efforts (Andreas and Nadelmann, 2006; Jakobi, 2013). What is of particular importance, though, in the case of migration control, is that the deviance of the state has direct consequences for its individual citizens. In Chapter 1, we saw how Frontex, in its yearly *Risk Analysis* report, creates "Top ten nationalities" rankings of countries whose citizens are most likely to stay illegally, be refused entry, apply for asylum, use false documents, etc.[14] Other examples can be found in the domestic patterns of control in which a state's deviance "rubs off" onto its nationals, triggering the suspicions of the Northern state – it thus produces deviant identities for its citizens. Untrustworthy states produce untrustworthy identities. This happens most obviously through the increased focus on ID documents and identification (*Policing & Society*, 2011).

The figure of the crimmigrant other thus emerges at the intersection of unequal global power relations and broadly defined technologies of control. While these developments have received considerable scholarly attention, the importance of the logic of the dangerous migrant for the growth of these systems has been far less acknowledged. Examination of the EU's main large-scale information system – the Schengen Information System (SIS) – reveals that by far the largest category of registered wanted persons are "unwanted aliens". The system was set up for the purpose of law enforcement cooperation and external border control and enables state authorities, such as police and border guards, to enter and consult alerts on certain categories of wanted or missing persons and objects. At the end of 2017, the system contained 896,791 alerts relating to people, most of which – over 56 per cent of the total – were alerts pursuant to Article 24 of the SIS II Regulation (i.e. to refuse entry into or stay within the Schengen area) (EULISA, 2018: 10).

The unwanted migrant has thus become an animating force behind the development of rapidly growing systems of control, which has considerable economic and political resources at its disposal. As Ruben Andersson (2016) observes:

> At Europe's frontiers, an industry of border controls has emerged, involving European defence contractors, member state security forces and their African counterparts, as well as a range of non-security actors. Whenever another "border crisis" occurs, this industry grows again, feeding on its own apparent "failures".
>
> *(Andersson, 2016: 1055)*

Although it is commonly assumed that unwanted migration constitutes a threat to the EU project, we can see that it is also an important force animating and accelerating the process of European integration, as regards both the development of a common foreign policy, investments in technology, and the strengthening of EU policing agencies and cooperation between national police forces. Nothing demonstrates this trend more clearly than the rise of the European Border and Coastguard Agency, better known as Frontex.

The rise of Frontex

Frontex was established in October 2004 and became operational the following year.[15] Its overall mission is to promote and coordinate the management of the EU's external borders. It does so through its main activities: the coordination of operational cooperation between member states on the management of external borders, risk analysis, the monitoring of relevant research in control and surveillance of the external border, the training of border guards, and, most visibly, through major joint return operations, and technical and human operational assistance in air, sea, and land border initiatives (Gundhus and Franko, 2016). Frontex (whose headquarters is in Warsaw) has had strong political support from the European Commission for a steady growth in its tasks and responsibilities, and in its staff and resources. In its first year of operation, the agency's budget was only €19 million, which rapidly increased to €93.3 million in 2014 and to a staggering €322 million in 2018. In the course of 2017, its staff grew by a third to 488 and is expected to more than double, with the aim being to reach 1,000 by 2020 (Frontex, 2017: 2).

In addition to its staff, the agency has at its disposal approximately 2,500 officers in the European Border Guard Teams, and an extensive arsenal of technical equipment (Frontex, 2017). It carries out regular high-profile joint operations at airports and land borders and in the Mediterranean, particularly in Greece, Italy, Malta, Spain, and Cyprus.[16] The Frontex inventory of equipment, which the agency has at its disposal, in 2014 consisted of a total of 804 items, including 285 pieces of maritime equipment, such as coastal patrol vessels and boats, 96 items of equipment for aerial surveillance and patrols (helicopters and fixed-wing aircraft), 132 land border surveillance vehicles and patrol cars, and 291 items for border control, such as hand-held surveillance equipment and document-checking equipment (Frontex, 2014).[17] The organisation has also substantially upgraded its surveillance capabilities, most visibly through the development of the Eurosur system.

In 2016, the revised European Border and Coastguard Regulation came into force and made Frontex into the European Border and Coast Guard Agency,[18] greatly enhancing its authority. In addition to considerably increased staff numbers, the new agency gained the ability to purchase its own equipment. It was also given a mandate to send liaison officers to neighbouring third countries and launch joint operations with them, including in their territory. Most remarkably, the agency was given the power to intervene in a member state even if that state objected. In the past, Frontex had to get permission before operating in a country, but now it can intervene and deploy EBCG teams to ensure that action is taken on the ground, even when a member state is unable or unwilling to take the necessary measures. Frontex has also gained access to European databases, and is now far more closely involved in deportation through the deployment of so-called return intervention teams.

As we can see, Frontex is an important player in extraterritorial border control, a situation which was further strengthened by the 2016 revisions. The agency has developed an extensive network of partnerships at the operational level with the authorities in non-EU states, particularly in the Sahel and the Balkans, and exports border control training standards and surveillance equipment, while simultaneously expanding the geographical scope of its own activities (Andersson, 2014; Milivojevic, 2019). It has, for example, opened a risk analysis cell in Niger. The global North–South dynamics discussed above, which are also visible in the agency's major return operations, are thus essential for understanding its activities and modes of operation.

While this book cannot provide a comprehensive analysis of Frontex's legislative framework, tasks, and operations (see, inter alia, Fink, 2018), we will now briefly examine the transformations of sovereignty connected to the rise of the agency, and the role of the migration and crime nexus in these transformations. Frontex has seen not only a steady growth in its resources and personnel, but also a fundamental change in the nature of European borders and responsibility for their protection. One of its publications describes the current situation thus:

> For the first time, the European Border and Coastguard regulation clearly states that "the management of the external borders is a shared responsibility of the Union and the Member States". As a result, the Agency acts as the operational arm of the EU, and a partner for the Member States.
>
> *(Frontex, 2018: 6)*

The agency has thus become an actor with a considerable degree of autonomy and, on the basis of its risk analysis, can now intervene in a member state even if it objects. Establishing borders as a "shared responsibility" represents a remarkable shift from the situation during the early days of Frontex, though the idea of creating a common European Border Police or European Border Guard had, in fact, already been floated in 2001 (Neal, 2009). Following 9/11, European borders became framed within the securitisation discourse (Huysmans, 2006). However, as Neal (2009) argues, at that point the urgency of security did not override member states' concerns about sovereignty, so the controversial idea of having a European corps of border guards was quietly dropped. More than a decade later, in the immediate aftermath of the much-debated "migration crisis" and the terror attacks in Paris, the proposal for the creation of a European Border and Coast Guard was passed without much controversy. Migration pressures have, thus, brought about a major change in the ways European states conceive of their sovereignty. Paradoxically, it was precisely at a time when the protection of borders was seen to be a vital element in the resurgence of nationalism (Barker, 2018) that the formation of this supranational border force took place.

It could be argued that, while the drive for security post-9/11 was not enough to override member states' jealous guarding of their sovereignty (Neal, 2009), the intensified framing of migration as a matter of security (Guild, 2009) eventually succeeded in setting such objections aside. In the past decade, EU discourse has increasingly associated the issue of irregular migration with organised crime and the threat of terrorism. The anxiety of EU states about migration has thus also been increased by a sense of urgency conveyed by narratives about the prevention of terrorism and organised crime (Carling and Hernández-Carretero, 2011). The trend is visible in Frontex documents where "Crime, illegal immigration, human trafficking and international terrorism are all uttered in the same breath" (Neal, 2009: 350). Thus, its *Risk Analysis* report says (Frontex, 2018: 31):

> While stressing that many migrants detected for illegal border-crossing are persons who are eligible for international protection, there are many challenges at the EU's external borders in detecting those linked to terrorism, crimes, or those suspected of war crimes.[19]

An important element in the remarkable rise of Frontex is, therefore, its transformation from a border control actor – or, better, an enabler and coordinator for EU member states – into a fully fledged crime control and security agency. According to its own self-description, the agency has made a "move towards becoming an essential actor in law enforcement on the European level" (Frontex, 2017: 2). As its Executive Director, Fabrice Leggeri, explained (25 October 2018), "While Frontex is often perceived as only dealing with migration, we are now increasingly involved in the crucial fight against organized crime, including the scourge of terrorism."[20]

The redefinition of Frontex as a law enforcement and security actor has been accompanied by new powers being given to the agency. Under the new mandate, acquired in the revisions of 2016, members of the European Border and Coast Guard teams deployed at border crossing points have full access to various EU databases, including the Schengen Information System (SIS) (Frontex, 2017: 5). The fight against "illegal immigration" and organised crime is, therefore, accelerating the speed and complexity of European integration. As early as

2003, Walker (2003: 121) observed that the field of so-called Justice and Home Affairs had moved from being a "poor cousin of European integration" to the position of a senior member of the family, who was in some regards "vying for the mantle of head of the family". The rise and transformation of Frontex exemplifies this trend. Rather than only threatening the EU project, as is commonly assumed, unauthorised migration is in fact taking it to new levels of complexity and integration which were previously unthinkable.

The scope of Frontex's law enforcement mission has grown particularly in tandem with the increased focus on human smuggling discussed in the next section. In this context, *Smuggler Nation*, Peter Andreas's (2013) illuminating study of US law enforcement efforts directed at smuggling offers some interesting historic parallels with contemporary EU developments. It draws attention to the role of anti-smuggling initiatives in vastly expanding the policing authority and reach of the federal government (2013: xi):

> Smuggling, it turns out, has been as much about building up the American state as about subverting it. Through its long interaction with the underworld of smuggling, the United States has emerged not only with a sprawling law enforcement bureaucracy – and jails overflowing with convicted drug law offenders – but also as a policing superpower, promoting its favored prohibitions and policing practices to its neighbors and the rest of the world.

Andreas's study points to the productive nature of fighting illicit cross-border activities in terms of the expansion of the powers of state authorities, particularly policing agencies, and of their extraterritorial expansion (see also Andersson, 2014). The question arises as to whether we are now seeing similar developments in the context of the EU.

Fighting illegality: the evil smuggler

A substantial body of criminological scholarship shows how the expansion and legitimacy of the international policing system has greatly depended upon the creation of images of "worthy opponents" (Hobbs and Dunnighan, 1998). Seeing nation states and the world economy as being gravely threatened by organised crime has served as a pretext to "develop more intrusive, authoritarian, and muscular forms of law enforcement" (Abraham and van Schendel, 2005: 4; Aas, 2013b). In the context of EU border control, combating human smuggling, which typifies organised crime, has emerged as the main legitimating argument for the use of increasingly aggressive modes of enforcement. As Carrera et al. (2019) point out, countering migrant smuggling has been framed as one of the top political priorities of the EU in responding to the so-called refugee crisis which emerged in 2015. These efforts have had a profound impact on EU laws and agencies – not only Frontex, but also Europol, Eurojust, and EASO, as well as national policing efforts in member states (ibid.).

In June 2018, at the urging of the EU leadership,[21] the UN Security Council imposed sanctions for the first time on six leaders of human trafficking networks operating in Libya.[22] In addition to Frontex and Europol, the EU's most visible anti-smuggling effort has been the establishment of EUNAVFOR MED Operation Sophia in the Central Mediterranean (Carrera et al., 2019). Initiated in 2015, at the peak of the "crisis", the operation "recasts migration management as a priority of the EU military engagements" (Garelli and Tazzioli, 2018: 686). It "opened with the dispatch of five warships, two submarines, three planes, three helicopters and two drones" (ibid.) and now includes contributions from most of the member states. Operating in international waters

> The purpose of this operation is to disrupt the business model of smugglers by identifying, capturing and disposing of vessels used or suspected of being used by them, as well as to train the Libyan coastguards and navy and contribute to the implementation of the UN arms embargo on the high seas off the coast of Libya.[23]

Although one of its main objectives is to save lives at sea and to reduce migrant mortality, Sophia's model of border control is built on the insidious connection of migration with organised crime. It regards irregular migration as a fertile ground for the development of organised crime, which needs to be combated by all necessary means. Unauthorised border crossings, it is argued, support "the business model of smugglers". Garelli and Tazzioli (2018: 692) suggest that

EUNAVFOR, modelled on the counter-piracy Operation Atlanta off the Horn of Africa, introduces economic parallels between smuggling and maritime piracy. The figure of the smuggler thus becomes a catalyst for increasing militarisation, exchange of information between border and law enforcement agencies, the introduction of control measures usually reserved for the most serious forms of organised crime, and cooperation with international partners, all of which would, under normal circumstances, be deemed unacceptable. As Calogero Ferrara, an Italian prosecutor, said in a recent television interview: "I think we have to deal with smugglers in the same way we deal with mafia organised groups in the sense that they are merciless organisations, they operate for profit and are very structured ... one of the worst criminal activities in the world."[24]

Although empirical research on the subject is scarce, it has raised doubts about the "very structured" and organised nature of smuggling networks. In the case of Niger, Brachet's (2018: 29) ethnographic study reveals that "they are neither centralized nor possess any hierarchy", but are instead "rather fragmented and uncoordinated chains of actors". Rather than representing a novel development in terms of scale and organisation, the figure of the human smuggler emerges as the result of a "highly politicized interpretation of long-standing local and regional practices" (ibid.: 30). In her overview of existing research on human smuggling, Gabriella Sanchez (2018: 1) points out that, according to official data, "most people convicted for smuggling are in fact independent operators, often working on behalf of friends and family members, or who are migrants themselves trying to reach a destination." Therefore, rather than being under the control of organised crime, smuggling networks often reflect long-standing social relations and migration traditions (Sanchez, 2017, 2018; Maher, 2018).

Like other scholars in the field, Sanchez (2018: 3) points out that "reliance on smuggling emerges from the lack of accessible, legal and safe mechanisms for mobility". Illicit migratory industries, such as human smuggling and other forms of illicit facilitation, can therefore be seen as a form of "survival entrepreneurship" and innovation for those without access to legitimate opportunities (see also Andersson, 2014; Tinti and Reitano, 2018). Human smuggling is part of a broader spectrum of illicit activities, which Gilman et al. term "deviant globalisation", whose essence "is "regulatory arbitrage" – that is, taking advantage of the differences in rules and enforcement practices across jurisdictions in order to make a profit" (2011: 16). As Comaroff and Comaroff (2006) astutely observe, when the West is trying to impose its legal order on the chaotic nature of the post-colony, a form of resistance and a resource of the disadvantaged is "counterfeiting modernity" (producing fakes, false credentials, and illusions) (Aas, 2013a). For citizens of the global South, unauthorised migration, like other forms of deviant globalisation, "is both a powerful engine of wealth creation and a symbol of their exclusion and abjection" (Gilman et al., 2011: 4). Fortified borders and strict mobility regimes are thus an immense source of vulnerability and make their lives precarious. It should be borne in mind, though, that what puts people at risk is the condition of illegality related to their status as irregular migrants, rather than smugglers alone (Sanchez, 2018: 3).

Smuggling – as a form of deviant globalisation that the elaborate transnational order of actors and regulations is trying to suppress – is thus in many ways a product of its own making, driven by global inequality, and the economic opportunities created by border closures and the demand for illicit services (Andersson, 2014; Tinti and Reitano, 2018). The very logic of prohibition empowers the adaptive strategies of deviant entrepreneurs for whom "every prohibition is a business opportunity", thus creating illicit economies, which can offer a ticket out of poverty for individuals, families, and entire communities (Gilman et al., 2011; Aas, 2013b; Tinti and Reitano, 2018). For this reason, the participants themselves may not see these activities through the lens of crime and victimisation, and may not accept the categories of criminal and victim (Maher, 2018).[25] As Sanchez (2018: 2) points out:

> In many communities facilitating migrants' journeys is seen as part of a complex series of care, support and knowledge that help communities and their members move and survive. Together these practices may be known to be illicit, but legally do not constitute a crime.

As we have seen, Niger (like many countries around the world), until recently, had no laws criminalising smuggling.

Empirical research also shows that, far from the black-and-white images produced by media and policy discourse, the distinctions between smugglers and their "victims" (i.e. unauthorised migrants) are quite complex (Tinti and Reitano, 2018). Smugglers are often themselves migrants or asylum seekers, who provide services to friends, acquaintances, and family members by drawing on their past migration experiences (Stone-Cadena and Alvarez-Velasco, 2018; Maher, 2018). They are likely to be, or to have been, irregular migrants (Sanchez, 2017). As Stephanie Maher's (2018: 36) ethnographic study of Senegalese migration networks shows:

> Migrants in Senegal are often familiar with their handlers and are more likely to call them a friend (*ami*) than a criminal. Also, most migrants do not see themselves as "smuggled," which implies victimhood. Rather, they see themselves as making calculated choices to migrate based on a host of social factors.

Media discourse, by contrast, is marked by a "dichotomist script of smugglers as predators and migrants and asylum seekers as victims" (Sanchez, 2017: 10). Smugglers are often portrayed as men of non-Western origin, unscrupulous, profit-driven, and prone to violence.

There is much to suggest that, in the official migration discourse, the smuggler has been cast in the position of what Christie and Bruun (1985) influentially termed a "suitable enemy" (or a "good enemy", to translate the Norwegian term literally). Written in the 1980s in the context of the war on drugs, the authors argued that a suitable enemy is defined as dangerous, possibly diabolic and inhuman – an enemy that symbolises what is negative and evil, and the opposite of established values in society (ibid.). This position of moral depravity, Christie and Bruun point out, enables those waging war against the enemy to feel safe in their task, and silences any critical voices. This condition is exacerbated by the fact that, discursively, human smuggling is often not distinguished from human trafficking. The two phenomena are treated essentially the same despite the considerable legal differences between them (Segrave et al., 2018).

This harnessing of moral outrage related to smuggling has helped move human smuggling and trafficking towards the top of the EU's security agenda. The unprecedented UN sanctions against Libyan smuggling groups were passed as a result of international outrage following the publication of graphic images and footage of human slavery in Libya. An important point here is that irregular migration is not only being defined as a security threat but also framed in the language of morality: a matter of good or evil. A central tenet of this book is that the logic of (in)security is not adequate to understand the intensified policing and surveillance of Europe's borders. These developments are not simply a matter of protection against a perceived security threat, but also against a moral one. The policing of physical boundaries is, therefore, intrinsically connected to questions of morality and the policing of moral boundaries.

These moral aspects relate not only to the justifiability of waging a war against the enemy but, in the case of EU border policies, to where the responsibility lies for the most ethically problematic aspects of the present situation on the border, particularly the tragic loss of life at sea. In the official discourse, smugglers, as suitable enemies, have been made responsible for almost everything that is bad on the border, including loss of life at sea, terrorism, and human trafficking. The European Commission website thus declares:

> The loss of migrants' lives at the hands of smugglers in the Mediterranean Sea is an acute reminder of the need to tackle migrant smuggling, using all of the legal, operational, and administrative levers available. The fact that migrant smuggling networks are closely linked to other forms of serious and organised crime including terrorism, human trafficking, and money laundering increases this urgency even further.[26]

The evil smuggler has thus become a scapegoat at a moment of crisis, justifying a variety of interventions due to the urgency of his threat (again, the gender connotations are very clear). Putting the blame on the smuggler also eases the discomfort of state authorities responsible for border enforcement. As we shall see in the following sections, those performing the task of border control operate in a morally ambiguous terrain. When the blame for migrant deaths – the most problematic aspect of border control – is outsourced to the smuggler, this serves to create a moral high ground for the authorities. As the one becomes darker, the other becomes whiter by comparison. This line of reasoning is exemplified by the following description of a search and rescue mission, provided by an officer in an official Frontex brochure:

> I was on mission last week. It was Force 8 to Force 9. Thunderstorm with hail. We got the call that there was a search and rescue case. We started looking just as the weather got very bad. Out of twelve people who were reported missing, eight of them had been washed dead onto the shore. Among these there was a seven-year-old girl. This girl had been promised heaven in the European Union, but she had been cheated of her life. She paid to be dead. The facilitators, the people traffickers, left her to die. It's very painful, very distressing.
>
> *(Frontex, 2010: 35)*

The tragic deaths at sea are, as Brachet (2018: 28) observes, not interpreted as the unfortunate result of border control, but are instead seen "as compelling proof of the need to keep fighting the 'infamous' smuggling networks that take advantage of the misery of others". Migrant deaths "underline the subhuman nature of treacherous transporters (and sometimes those transported), and serve to mark and reinforce the boundaries between acceptable and unacceptable behavior" (ibid.). Consequently, they legitimise further criminalisation and the use of more extensive forms of control (Carrera et al., 2019). In some official documents, anti-immigration and anti–smuggling/trafficking measures have merged to an extent which makes these policies almost indistinguishable (Segrave et al., 2018). As O'Connell Davidson (2015: 130) observes, "contemporary state efforts to combat 'trafficking' go hand in glove with wider actions against 'illegal' migration". Protection of migrants is, therefore, "not only a policy objective, but also a rhetorical tool for justifying control measures" (Carling and Hernández-Carretero, 2011: 45).

Homines sacri and the power to let die

The discussion reveals the complex terrain in which various notions of migrants (and narratives about migration) shape border policies. Although in legal terms a migrant is an exclusionary category, which relies on a binary "distinction between the citizen and the foreigner, between inside and outside" (Basaran and Guild, 2017: 273), it is in practical terms differentiated according to a number of parameters, which structure the actions of state authorities and others. In policy and in practice, categories of migrants are differentiated according to a moral language which, despite deeply divided views on migration, has a certain consensual force. One of the central distinctions made is that between the human smuggler and trafficker, seen as an epitome of the malign actor, and, on the other hand, the passive migrant as a "genuine refugee" who is his victim. As we shall see below, the notion of migrant victimhood can then be further differentiated in terms of purity, blamelessness, and worthiness of protection, but the distinction between a passive victim and an active perpetrator remains. Such binary, black-and-white categories are not only "designed to make international migration legible to and manageable by states" (Watson, 2015: 48), but also enable a particular border control model which is marked by a combination of control and salvation.

Such connections between the use of penal power and humanitarian concerns are, as Bosworth (2017) observes, both novel and, in their post-colonial context, also familiar. While the evil smugglers and traffickers legitimise the use of increasingly militarised modes of control (Carrera et al., 2019), the passivity of their victims suggests slavery and introduces a discourse of salvation, particularly in the case of children and trafficked women (O'Connell Davidson, 2015). Thus Operation Sophia was named after a Somali baby who was born on board a German frigate operated in the Central Mediterranean as part of the EUNAVFOR MED Task Force, with the objective stated on its website (italics added):

> To honour the lives of the people we are saving, the lives of people we want to protect, and to pass the message to the world that *fighting the smugglers and the criminal networks is a way of protecting human life*. [27]

The passage is a clear example of the intricate (and intimate) discursive and practical connections between military and humanitarian approaches to migration, or what has been termed "military-humanitarianism" (Garelli and Tazzioli, 2018). Sophia was designed as a military mission that was both crime control and humanitarian action. A combination of these elements is replicated in numerous EU documents, which include a mixture of stricter border control measures and concern for loss of life.

However, the moral clarity of the language of state control obscures deep paradoxes and ambiguities on the ground. As mentioned above, the Mediterranean is arguably the most fatal border in the world (IOM, 2017). According to IOM's Missing Migrant Project, 3,139 migrants lost their lives in 2017 and 2,297 in 2018.[28] Immediately after the introduction of Operation Sophia (and the related dismantling of the Italian Mare Nostrum operation) the Mediterranean death toll rose dramatically from 3,782 in 2015 to a peak of 5,143 in 2016. The numbers suggest that fighting the smugglers is *not* a way of protecting human life, which among other things was recognised in a recent House of Lords (2017: para 45) inquiry, which declared:

> We remain of the view that Operation Sophia has not in any meaningful way deterred the flow of migrants, disrupted the smugglers' networks, or impeded the business of people smuggling on the central Mediterranean route. An unintended consequence of Operation Sophia's destruction of vessels has been that the smugglers have adapted, sending migrants to sea in unseaworthy vessels, leading to an increase in deaths.

The report pointed out that the EU's approach, despite its stated aim to the contrary, not only increased migrant mortality but also endangered migrants' lives and human rights in other ways (ibid.: para. 47):

> We are concerned by reports of serious abuses of the human rights of migrants by the Libyan coastguard. We ask the Government to provide us with its assessment of the extent to which the human rights elements of Operation Sophia's training packages are likely to improve the treatment of migrants by the Libyan coastguard.

While dichotomous concepts of migrants as victims and perpetrators may at first glance create a clear and unambiguous moral terrain, the reality on the ground is a complex and deeply paradoxical. Although saving lives is discursively used to reinforce border control, in practical terms the two are deeply at odds with each other. The "saving" can only be carried out if conducted according to state-defined parameters and in accordance with the objectives of border control. This tension is particularly evident in the sustained criticism directed by Frontex and national authorities of some EU member states at NGO search and rescue missions. As Carrera et al. (2019) point out, international legal instruments designed to counter the smuggling of human beings, such as the UN Smuggling Protocol 2000, stipulate that the facilitation of entry and stay for non-profit purposes should be exempted from criminalisation. Nevertheless, the EU Facilitators Package left it optional for EU member states to exempt individuals or civil society groups which provide humanitarian assistance to irregular immigrants from criminal penalties (ibid.). Consequently, authorities of several member states are increasingly choosing the threat of criminal sanctions against search and rescue NGOs.

In a 2017 interview, the head of Frontex accused NGOs operating close to the Libyan coast of interfering with EU migration and crime control objectives by making it difficult to conduct interviews with migrants to check their origins, identify their smuggling routes, and open police investigations.[29] Migrants are, therefore, not simply "subjects at risk", whose lives need to be saved, but also "risky subjects" (Aradau, 2004; Garelli and Tazzioli, 2018), whose origins and identity need to be examined and who are always a potential source of information for criminal investigations. Criminal law and criminalisation, as well as crime control models of action, are therefore increasingly deployed in the context of the governance of migration (Carrera et al., 2019). Such approaches correspond to Jonathan Simon's (2007) concept of governing through crime, where the category of crime is, among others, deployed to "legitimate interventions that have other motivations" (ibid.: 4). They are, despite the discursive importance of saving of lives, increasingly at odds with protecting migrants' vulnerability.

This intricate duality of care and control was one of the main features of the interviews we conducted with officers who had participated in Frontex operations (Aas and Gundhus, 2015). Tasked with interviewing migrants about their journeys, and about their knowledge of smugglers and smuggling routes, officers had to reconcile the policing objectives of their mission with personal humanitarian inclinations. On the one hand, officers saw their mission – and migrants – in terms of policing and crime control. As one officer said:

> We know that asylum is being used to get criminal elements into the country. So there should be more thorough interviews, to put it this way ... Because we know that most of them come without ID papers and all of that. And we don't know what is coming in. And I think we should open up our eyes for that.
>
> *(PU5)*

Others, on the other hand, expressed concern and actively sought to alleviate migrants' suffering. One officer described his experience thus:

> I usually have lots of water in my car when I leave the hotel. There are such big contrasts; you leave a five-star hotel and then come to the border. It is 40 degrees, no sanitation. I took water and some crackers and some bread with me. I bought Paracet [amol] for example, and the cream against mosquitoes and after you are bitten by mosquito. Because there were lots of children who had been bitten by mosquitoes. So, this was to create trust and so on. And you see that there is a child who does not have milk and hasn't had milk in days, and you give milk and so on. It is about the human side of it all. It is not just that you go there, do the screening and then you are finished with it, and go back to the hotel. I have done my job. There is also the human side of it ... Although clearly, you have to screen them at the same time and have to make sure you're not fooled; that you do a proper job, there is that as well.
>
> *(PU7, Frontex screener in Aas and Gundhus, 2015)*

This account – which is by no means atypical – reveals, on the one hand, the desire to alleviate human suffering and, on the other, the fear of "being fooled" and the need to do the policing tasks properly.

This duality challenges the perception that a migrant is simply someone who finds himself or herself outside the sphere of state protection in a position of absolute abjection. The tragic death toll at the border is undoubtedly one of the most visible expressions of the citizen/non-citizen duality. It indicates migrants' exclusion from traditional biopolitical rationalities (Aas and Gundhus, 2015). This has created a strong perception that asylum seekers and irregular migrants at the border find themselves in the position of *homines sacri*, whose lives are marked by precariousness and bareness. This view, popularised by Giorgio Agamben (1998), underlines the essentially violent nature of sovereignty, its ability to inflict death and to exclude life from the sphere of legal protection.

In contrast to Foucauldian biopolitics, such political rationalities have been characterised as *zoëpolitics* (Agamben, 1998; Schinkel, 2009) or by Achille Mbembe's (2003) concept of *necropolitics*. They suggest that the "ultimate expression of sovereignty resides, to a large degree, in the power and the capacity to dictate who may live and who must die" (in De León, 2015: 67). Or, as Jason De León (2015: 68) argues in his analysis of border deaths on the US–Mexico border: "Lacking rights and protections when they illegally cross into sovereign territory, undocumented people are killable in the eyes of the state." According to De León, these deaths are not the unintended consequences of natural events. Rather, the logic of general deterrence at the border is an example of the operationalisation of necropower in which nature does the state's "dirty work" (ibid.).

The migrant does not only come up against differentiated levels of rights. Hierarchies of citizenship also entail differentiated values of life within the emerging global order. Although European law unequivocally states as one of its main principles that "everyone's right to life shall be protected by law" (ECHR, Art. 2.1), in practice, this principle becomes a question of operationalisation and political will. The lack of political will to protect life at the border, regardless of other objectives, is visible in the criticism directed at NGO search and rescue missions by Frontex, and its refusal to offer "a shuttle service" for migrants, as well in the agency's ambivalence about recording migrant mortality. Despite its systematic collection of a great number of border-related statistics, Frontex does not count border deaths. An officer responsible for risk analysis acknowledged this in an interview in March 2013:

> We were thinking some time ago that we should start it [collecting information about casualties], but at that moment it was too early. But especially now that Eurosur is becoming – and one of the

main purposes of Eurosur is to prevent the loss of life – so we thought that we should perhaps establish something more systematic. Of course, Eurosur as such should provide opportunity for that, it is important, of course, and also to a certain extent an issue related to land borders. There are areas which are mountainous and with the circumstances we can see people dying or sometimes there is flooding and all that, so it is important. But we don't do it systematically at this stage, but our intention is to start taking action on that.

(FR3 in Aas and Gundhus, 2015: 10)

While Frontex statistics, as we saw in Chapter 1, offer ample substantiation of the threats that migrants may represent to European borders and member states, migrant mortality remains undocumented by the agency. However, Frontex has begun to refer to mortality in their recent reports, saying: "These, however, are only estimates, which also include the number of missing persons, since there is no system of recording the exact number of those who perish at sea" (ibid.: 32). The job of counting has thus been outsourced to non-state actors such as IOM and various research projects (Last et al., 2017).

Andreas and Greenhill (2010: 1) point out that "to measure something – or at least claim to do so – is to announce its existence and signal its importance and policy relevance". According to Judith Butler (2006), to develop a more inclusive and egalitarian way of recognising precariousness, questions need to be asked about "whose lives are considered valuable, whose lives are mourned, and whose lives are considered ungrievable". By not having their deaths counted by state actors, migrants are not part of the regular, state-sponsored biopolitical reason, which is concerned with EU citizens and their health and security. This would support the Agambeian view that migrant lives belong to the sphere of *zoepolitics* where their victimisation is not properly acknowledged or communicated in the realm of state-sponsored knowledge production. However, this is only part of the picture. In recent years, migrant mortality has been a subject of considerable public debate and emotional engagement, as in the case of Alan Kurdi, mentioned in the opening pages of this book. Although not seen as "proper" security subjects of the state, our investigation has revealed that the loss of migrant lives does seem to be an important factor for those working in Frontex operations. They often define their missions as search and rescue missions. The Norwegian ship *Siem Pilot*, for example, frequently referred to this aspect of their missions in Twitter messages: "Our personnel have saved nearly 14,000 lives so far in 2016." The boat's crew insisted on systematic counting, and the captain publicly expressed that they would continue to collect data so that "If someone comes in 30 years' time and asks about the dead on board *Siem Pilot*, they will get their answers."[30]

Working in humanitarian borderlands: novel assemblages of care and control

Despite its powerful narrative, the *homo sacer* captures only one part of the story. Rather than being completely bare and ungrievable, migrant lives can be seen as belonging to the sphere of minimalist biopolitics, which, as William Walters (2010: 145) describes it, is "Holding together in an uneasy alliance a politics of alienation with a politics of care, and a tactic of abjection and one of reception" (see also Redfield, 2005; Aas and Gundhus, 2015). Although excluded from national humanity, the migrant belongs to the larger sphere of global humanity and is thus deserving of life-saving efforts and of human rights, if often only at a discursive level. This type of political reasoning employs the language of humanity and humanitarian assistance and is usually a feature of the activities of national and international humanitarian actors (Fassin, 2012).

Modes of humanitarian governance give state power a veneer of benevolence. As Didier Fassin suggests (2012: xii): "Humanitarianism has this remarkable capacity: it fugaciously and illusorily bridges the contradictions of our world, and makes the intolerableness of its injustices somewhat bearable. Hence, its consensual force." A growing body of scholarship has pointed out the intricate connections not only between border governance and humanitarianism (Fassin, 2012; Cuttitta, 2014; Pallister-Wilkins, 2018), but also between the exercise of penal power and humanitarianism (Aas and Gundhus, 2015; Bosworth, 2017; Lohne, 2018). Penal humanitarianism "conjoins migration control and criminal justice through humanitarian goals and rhetoric"

(Bosworth, 2017: 57). Although the humanitarianisation of borders seems to some extent to represent a corrective to openly punitive and exclusionary impulses, its critics see it as first and foremost a form of governance whose purpose is to effectively manage disasters so as to maintain the liberal world order (Pallister-Wilkins, 2018). Humanitarianism is marked both by its eminent usefulness as a form of governance and as a form of "care for distant strangers" (ibid.: 1).

Understanding the conundrum of the crimmigrant other, therefore, entails capturing the diversity of often contradictory subjectivities: exclusion and inclusion, care and control, subjects who represents a risk and are themselves at risk. These intertwining rationalities resemble a patchwork that I have (Aas, 2013a) described elsewhere as a form of assemblage. The concept of an assemblage offers a productive insight into the changes taking place at the border and the intertwining of the humanitarian, the penal and the military. Stemming from Deleuze and Guattari's classic *A Thousand Plateaus*, this concept gains its strength from its connotations of instability and difference, and the productive qualities of the two (Marcus and Saka, 2006). It introduces "a radical notion of multiplicity into phenomena which we traditionally approach as being discretely bounded, structured and stable" (Haggerty and Ericson, 2000: 608), which is how national criminal justice systems have traditionally been perceived and conceived. As a concept, an assemblage "makes it easier to think about disparate elements with contingent and emergent roles but which ultimately work together" (Lippert and Pyykkönen, 2012: 1). It can be made use of to pull together disparate forms of control which, although heterogeneous, have varying degrees of "borderliness",[31] punitiveness, or humanitarianism inscribed in them.

How the different elements come to be put together varies; the complexity of existing control practices, populations, and actors involved in them demands concrete empirical investigation. Their juxtaposition can at times raise issues and may even "feel wrong" for the actors involved. In Chapter 3, we saw how assemblages of the "bordered" and the "ordered" – crime control and immigration control – are breaking up long-standing traditions of the exercise of penal power in Scandinavian countries. Such configurations need not imply a process of merging and melting (as the concept of "crimmigration" is at times understood), but does demand an examination of their constitution in different institutional, national, and historical configurations. Analytically, one of the main advantages of the global assemblage is precisely its concreteness, partiality, and situatedness. As Collier and Ong (2005: 12) argue:

> An assemblage is the product of multiple determinations that are not reducible to a single logic. The temporality of an assemblage is emergent. It does not always involve new forms, but forms that are shifting, in formation, or at stake. As a composite concept, the term "global assemblage" suggests inherent tensions: global implies broadly encompassing, seamless, and mobile; assemblage implies heterogeneous, contingent, unstable, partial, and situated.

The humanitarian element testifies to the diversity and complexity of the global assemblages of power that are guiding contemporary migration, and their irreducibility to a single logic of securitisation and exclusion. The diverse and complex nature of the assemblages makes it analytically challenging to map the diverse networks of national and transnational actors, technologies, and rationalities of governance (bio- and zoepolitical, humanitarian, punitive, military, nationalist, etc.). It also makes it difficult to disassemble and disentangle the "punitive" from the "bordered", the sovereign from the regulatory, and the humanitarian from the exclusionary. The diverse nature of the border is also reflected in the varied, often contradictory, nature of its legal regulation: the lawlessness of frontiers and the seeming absence from them of the state contrast with spaces where there is intense state surveillance and almost Kafkaesque bureaucratic regulation.

The dynamics of the law's presence and absence are evident in the growing discursive and symbolic presence of human rights despite their elusiveness and the inability of the majority of migrants to access them (Gammeltoft-Hansen and Vested-Hansen, 2017). We are therefore dealing not only with borders, but also frontiers – the shifting terrain between legality and illegality – the "no-man's lands" (Barker, 2013) of Libya and endless detention that co-exist with an illusion of the strict enforcement of bureaucratic procedure. The exhortation by the French president, Emmanuel Macron, to police officers in Calais that their behaviour should be "exemplary and in absolute respect of professional ethics and absolute respect of the law" – which in practical terms means not "waking people up in the middle of the night, not using teargas during mealtimes" – indicates the paradoxical nature of the border.

The complexity of the assemblages involved is reflected in, and related to, the complexity of perceptions about migrants and their subjectivities. These include, as Garelli and Tazzioli (2018: 695) describe:

> fake migrants who are actually potential terrorists who try to enter Europe, fake refugees who are undocumented economic migrants trying to access the EU labor market, or finally "real" asylum see-kers who, nevertheless, would be a burden for EU member-states and are hence targeted by actions of preventive containment.

It is within this paradoxical terrain, marked by a multiplicity of ration-alities and logics, that the notion of the crimmigrant other gains its meaning and structuring force. It is precisely due to ambiguity and lack of clarity – so characteristic of strangers – that binary distinctions between good and bad, victims and offenders, worthy and unworthy, make particular sense. The power of the notion of the crimmigrant other lies in its ability to create distinctions. In that respect, it is an essential element in the effective governance of migration. As such, it is not primarily a category that provides an understanding of the migrant, but rather one that is vital for effective migration governance. In a field marked by ambiguity, it provides actors with distinctions and enables their initiatives to define their sphere of activity. This is true not only for state agents, but also for various NGOs and humanitarian actors. As we shall see below, perceptions of ideal victimhood, of goodness and badness, right and wrong, are central to defining how those tasked with controlling the border perceive themselves and their work.

The moral discomfort at the border

In scholarly literature about borders, the complex layers of border governance often seamlessly merge and morph into a growing number of configurations and -isms – such as crimmigration or military-huma-nitarianism – but these processes seem incongruous to those tasked with actually performing border control. President Macron's exhortation to police officers to do their work in an "exemplary" manner reveals the deep paradox involved in carrying out border policing. The humanitarian and penal elements may be possible to reconcile at the discursive level, but they are utterly contradictory in practice.

Interviews with Frontex officers revealed how they, on their own initiative, often attempted to reframe their mission in terms of humanitarian assistance by providing migrants with water, clothing, and medicines (Aas and Gundhus, 2015). Unsurprisingly, it was children that – in moral and ethical terms – represented the greatest challenge for them. One officer conveyed his strong feelings:

> People lived on several floors with poor access to water. Yes, they got food and some medical supervision, eventually. It came after we arrived. And I will never forget … there was a father … the cells were dark, there was clothing hanging out to dry in front of the windows and stuff, it was like coming to the Middle Ages. With a two-storey grid in the front. And there was a father with his daughter of maybe three years in his arms. She was wearing one of those small pink jogging suits. Inside there was chaos … crowded with people. And the only thing he says is: "Please, help me". This made an impression on me and … it is still here, that image. Because he was in a way a symbol of what those people wanted from me while we were down there.
>
> *(FRN2, Frontex screener)*

The extensive use of penal measures such as detention and deportation thus becomes particularly problematic when it is directed at children. Their perceived innocence highlights an acute moral and ethical deficit on the side of those executing such measures.

In February 2015, a Norwegian parliamentary committee held hearings on controversial deportations of families with children, many of whom had been living in the country for much of their lives. The deportations were partly a result of intense political pressure to meet high performance targets, mentioned in Chapter 3. The testimonies given revealed how such activities, although seemingly legal, are ethically deeply ambiguous and create a desire for moral clarity. As the representative of the Immigration Police union said during the hearing:

> What I will try to convey is that it is in the employees' interest to know whether what they are doing is, morally and ethically, completely right. It is difficult for them to deport asylum seekers with a [negative] final decision if they are in doubt that this is the right thing to do. This is why we need to know through political processes that this is an agreed policy. We cannot do anything about this, because the ones we deport have, as said, a final decision. So we are doing something that is legal. But the moral and the ethical bit is important for PU [Police Immigration Unit] employees as well …
>
> This is a very difficult job. It is hard for employees. It is hard to deport families with children. It can be hard to deport single adults without children as well. A lot of our employees are concerned about doing things right, so that they can go home with a good conscience, feeling that they have done a good job, and not have a bad conscience, even though many of them probably have.[32]

This testimony reveals how moral judgments are inherent to performing border control and can represent a burden that those performing them try to alleviate in various ways. Bosworth's (2018) study of immigration detention reveals the emotional costs on staff of such facilities. Similarly, Jonas Hansson's (2017) study of Swedish officers carrying out deportations shows that they employ a number of coping mechanisms and cognitive manoeuvres: "somebody has to do it", believing that the responsibility lies with those making deportation decisions, that "repatriation is best for the child", and that "good and kind treatment" of children can make deportation dignified. They create their own definitions of dignity and ways to achieve it. Officers can thus choose to make gestures, such as letting a child pick up a mobile phone before leaving or checking in an extra suitcase for them.

Similar to Sykes and Matza's (1957) techniques of neutralisation, such cognitive manoeuvres aim to place responsibility for morally problematic actions elsewhere. Thomas Ugelvik (2016), also, shows how detention officers, conscious of working in an institution with a legitimacy deficit, ascribe immigration detainees a presumption of choice and ill will, which lessens their own responsibility. By stressing that the police are simply "executing orders" taken higher up in the system,

responsibility is outsourced to others. Another technique for out-
sourcing responsibility is used by Frontex (2017: 33) when arguing that
the rising death toll on EU borders "mainly results from criminal
activities aimed at making a profit through the provision of smuggling
services at any cost". The presence of criminal offending thus serves to
redraw the lines of responsibility in a morally ambiguous terrain.
Hansson's (2017) study points out that police officers, when possible,
prioritise deportations of criminal offenders over those of children. The
Norwegian Police Immigration Unit has similar priorities, as is made
clear by its union representative who stated: "I can say that PIU
employees wish to do a good and professional job and take firm action
against criminals – or those who have become criminals – who have
been given a final decision".[33]

"Do[ing] a good … job" and "taking firm action against criminals"
are closely connected. This should not come as a surprise, since moral
judgments have always had an important role in shaping police culture
(Loftus, 2010). Although in line with such tendencies, the creation of
moral divisions and hierarchies carries a greater urgency in the context
of border control due to a legitimacy deficit that characterises the field
(Bosworth, 2013). Notions of innocence and blameworthiness structure
the field of migration on several levels. As we saw earlier, perceptions
of evil smugglers go hand in hand with notions of innocent women
and children, who are their "ideal victims" (O'Connell Davidson, 2015;
Segrave et al., 2018). This black-and-white landscape also has important
gender dimensions. The figure of the crimmigrant other often involves
what Katherine Pratt Ewing (2008) terms "stigmatised masculinity".
Cast as its opposites are the innocent child and the trafficked victim, an
expression of victimised femininity.

Here the discourse of humanitarianism, particularly as promoted by
various NGOs – guided though it may be by worthy and important
goals – inhabits a terrain which is by no means opposed to othering.
Griffiths (2017: 531–532) thus points out that the growing political and
popular demonisation of immigrants encourages NGOs to "accept the
mythical distinction between Good and Bad Migrants", portraying the
former as "innocent, vulnerable and only reluctantly mobile". Similarly,
Kmak (2015: 89) points out that it is precisely the perception of genuine refugees as "passive and traumatized victims of human rights

violations" that gives states "the power to exclude from protection those aliens tinted by the "apparent pathology of unauthorized arrivals'" (Zagor, in Kmak, 2015).

Conclusion: towards a moral economy of border control

The discussion above highlights the borders that also exist within the humanitarian imaginary. Distinctions between "good" and "bad" migrants, and between victims and offenders, are part of broader distinctions within the sphere of refugee protection between what Cathryn Costello (2018) terms refugees and "other migrants". Appeals for refugee protection coexist with calls to fight the evils of human smuggling. Drawing on Simon's (2007: 4) terminology of governance through crime, we can see that the technologies, discourses and metaphors of crime and criminal justice have become a visible feature of contemporary migration governance and its institutions. The figure of the (male) crimmigrant other thus performs a certain kind of work. He enables categorisations – between what Kmak (2015) terms "the good, the bad and the ugly" – and reinforces divisions in the seemingly universal notion of humanity, where exclusion is possible precisely on humanitarian grounds and justified by appealing to morality.

This chapter has outlined how the EU's external (and internal) borders are not merely securitised, as is commonly assumed, but are also in vital aspects "moralised", or structured according to a particular moral economy (Fassin, 2005). Within this economy, the systematic association of migration and crime, and the construction of distinctions between good and evil, supports and legitimises the production of punitive regimes and interventions. The term "moral economy" was developed by the historian Edward P. Thompson (1971) in his analysis of food rioting in the 18th century, to help understand the dynamics which legitimised rioting in the eyes of the participants. In recent years, the term has been separated from its historic connotations (and its connection to class relations), thus broadening its field of applicability. It has been used to illuminate the workings of contemporary civil society, humanitarianism, and immigration control (Fassin, 2005; Bourgois and Schonberg, 2009; Edelman, 2015; Götz, 2015), particularly within the emerging field of moral anthropology (Fassin, 2015).

Today, Edelman (2015: 59) points out, "moral economy has become a polysemic category with multiple genealogical strands and contemporary interpretations". Thompson (1991) himself was critical of this expansion of the term, suggesting that, if the term was to be divorced from its class connotations and simply equated with values, it would become meaningless.

The concept is, nevertheless, useful for this study because it helps in understanding the construction of altruistic meanings given to certain acts, which might otherwise be interpreted according to other imperatives. If we think of the detention of children in prison-like institutions, waking up families in the middle of the night to deport them, using military measures in the context of a humanitarian emergency, such actions demand intricate bridging exercises and balancing acts. One officer involved in deportation gave the following description of what happens:

> I think that the dynamics are about this victim perspective against the criminal – so these two. And one somehow does not manage to see both … You wish to be efficient and not be too late, so turning up at four o'clock in the morning is perhaps efficient because you know that people will be there. But it is tough for those who are exposed to this. And when it is reported in the media then you have that aspect as well. Is it an unnecessary use of power and unnecessary use of force and so on? So the case is that I think that these things are a bit difficult … Even though we feel perhaps that there is no substance in it [criticism], that we are following the rules, or that we are doing things properly, I think that at least we know that there is also that aspect. Because quite often the focus is the opposite. You get a very negative focus on foreigners and asylum seekers and see them as suspicious. (P10)

The concept of moral economy also makes sense because it is situated within a particular system of production where demands of mass production are at odds with traditional notions of professionalism and craftsmanship. The officer in the quote above talks about the demands for efficiency. Similarly, we saw how in Chapter 3 deportability of migrants is driven by the demands of new public management (see also Gundhus, 2016).

In a field where there is often intense media scrutiny, demands for efficiency, moral ambivalence, and what may appear insurmountable contradictions, talking about victims and offenders, suspicious people and blameless people, gives a particular structuring force. The intense social exclusion taking place on the border is framed in the language of morality: fighting evil perpetrators, protecting innocent life and penalising cheating and lying behaviour. The ethically problematic aspects of migration control thus take on different connotations when seen in relation to the moral depravity of rogue actors, whether it be evil smugglers or migrants themselves. In fact, such a moral framework may even turn the tables. In the heated disagreements between Frontex and NGOs about search and rescue strategies, NGO efforts to save life at sea were discredited on the grounds that they supported organised crime. Frontex (2017: 32) argued:

> Apparently, all parties involved in SAR [search and rescue] operations in the Central Mediterranean unintentionally help criminals achieve their objectives at minimum cost, strengthen their business model by increasing the chances of success. Migrants and refugees – encouraged by the stories of those who had successfully made it in the past – attempt the dangerous crossing since they are aware of and rely on humanitarian assistance to reach the EU.

Frontex thus outsources and externalises practical responsibility for European border control to third countries, and externalises moral responsibility, too. Claiming others are to blame for the high levels of migrant mortality can thus be seen as an attempt to disperse moral discomfort. This dynamic provides an important insight into the psychological work of othering, which satisfies the very human "need to confirm one's humanity while committing inhumane acts" (Coates, 2017: xii). Police officers carrying out deportation, for example, often defined their acts in terms of "good causes", particularly that of protecting the asylum system from fraud.

Migrants call into question Europe's commitment to some of its central and loudly proclaimed values. Amid such deep moral unease, the crimmigrant other does important work. Divisions between "good" and "bad" migrants are vital in enabling social exclusion to take place in societies with a humanitarian and inclusive self-image. The figure of the crimmigrant other justifies the use of force; it even demands it. It makes the need to use force self-evident and thus eases the discomfort that this might create in wider society, as well as at the individual and institutional levels. Europe's humanitarianism is not only a mode of governance defined by specific sentiments (Fassin, 2012), but also includes a new set of actors whose presence within the field of contemporary penal governance is slowly beginning to be addressed (Bosworth, 2017). Campesi (2015: 432) describes, for example, the involvement of humanitarian agencies in Italian pre-removal detention centres, where their "managerial philosophy, which is widely inspired by the model of humanitarian assistance, inevitably conflicts with the features of a detention facility where everything is organized and conceived in terms of security".

While the figure of the crimmigrant other may appear to be at odds with the growing presence of humanitarian actors and sentiments within the field of European migration governance, this is far from the case. The use of force and penal power is an essential element of border control. In essence, contemporary migration is governed through crime: "Crime has now become a significant strategic issue. Across all kinds of institutional settings, people are seen as acting legitimately when they act to prevent crimes or other troubling behaviours that can be closely analogized to crimes" (Simon, 2007: 4).

This means not only that central aspects of migration governance are shaped by strategies of criminalisation and illegalisation (Bosworth and Guild, 2008; Mitsilegas, 2015), but also that the categories of criminal offenders and victims are actively used, politically and in bureaucratic practice, to denote the moral unworthiness and criminal nature of particular migrants, and thus distinguish between "good" and "bad" mobilities (Kmak, 2015). "Migrants", "refugees", "victims of trafficking", "children", and "human smugglers" are not neutral categories. They are intricately connected to connotations of blame-worthiness, innocence, passivity, choice and the agency of individuals. Like other agents of migration control, humanitarian actors use and shape these categorisations in order to define their mission. They are active participants in the moral economy of border control, which ultimately also structures the use of force on the border.

This moral economy should not be separated from the monetary economy (Andersson, 2016). Penal power exercised in the context of migration control is more open to profit generation than are traditional forms of penality, where the presence of private actors, at least in Europe, often arouses controversy: private prisons are an exception, but in the context of immigration detention privatisation is close to a rule. In a field where private actors often perform tasks traditionally conducted by state employees, who have a much clearer sense of purpose, justification, legitimacy, and professional identity, the moral power of categories gains particular salience. For state and non-state actors alike, the innocence of children, the suffering of victims of trafficking, and the evil of human smugglers, offer opportunities for the production of "profit" – in terms of funding, visibility, legitimacy, and the easing of moral discomfort.

Notes

1 www.theguardian.com/world/2018/jan/16/macron-visits-calais-before-migrant-crisis-meeting-with-may
2 The chapter is based on interviews with officers participating in Frontex operations conducted together with Helene Oppen Ingebrigtsen Gundhus (see also Aas and Gundhus, 2015; Gundhus and Franko, 2016).
3 https://frontex.europa.eu/assets/Publications/General/Agency_at_Glance_2018_EN.pdf
4 www.theguardian.com/world/2018/jun/28/future-of-eu-hinges-on-solving-migration-issue-says-merkel
5 www.bbc.com/news/world-europe-44632471
6 www.ein.org.uk/news/european-court-human-rights-rules-pushback-migrants-external-eu-borders-unlawful
7 http://ec.europa.eu/eurostat/statistics-explained/index.php/Statistics_on_enforcement_of_immigration_legislation
8 www.dw.com/en/follow-the-money-what-are-the-eus-migration-policy-priorities/a-42588136
9 http://frontex.europa.eu/partners/third-countries.
10 As of March 2012, Frontex had concluded working arrangements with the authorities of 16 countries and was at various stages of negotiation with the authorities of a further nine countries (http://frontex.europa.eu/partners/third-countries). Several aspects of this co-operation, particularly those

concerning Libya, have been heavily criticised for prioritising border control objectives at the expense of human rights (Aas, 2011).

11 www.consilium.europa.eu/en/press/press-releases/2018/06/29/20180628-euco-conclusions-final/#

12 www.dw.com/en/follow-the-money-what-are-the-eus-migration-policy-priorities/a-42588136

13 https://ec.europa.eu/eurostat/statistics-explained/index.php/Statistics_on_enforcement_of_immigration_legislation#Returns_of_non-EU_citizens

14 Source: www.frontex.europa.eu/assets/Attachments_News/ara_2011_for_public_release.pdf

15 Council Regulation (EC) 2007/2004 (26.10.2004, OJ L 349/25.11.2004).

16 All EU members of the so-called Schengen acquis contribute to the Frontex pool. Norway and Switzerland contribute to the pool as Schengen associate countries, and Ireland and the United Kingdom participate on the basis of case-by-case decisions by the Frontex management board. For an analysis of the origins of Frontex, see Neal (2009) and Fink (2018).

17 https://data.europa.eu/euodp/en/data/storage/f/2016-03-07T113253/Annual%20Risk%20Analysis%202014.pdf

18 Regulation (EU) 2016/1624 of the European Parliament.

19 https://frontex.europa.eu/assets/Publications/Risk_Analysis/Risk_Analysis/Risk_Analysis_for_2018.pdf

20 https://twitter.com/Frontex?ref_src=twsrc%5Etfw%7Ctwcamp%5Eembeddedtimeline%7Ctwterm%5Eprofile%3AFrontex&ref_url=https%3A%2F%2Ffrontex.europa.eu%2F

21 www.express.co.uk/news/politics/822773/Migrant-crisis-Angela-Merkel-EU-people-smugglers-illegality-G20-Italy

22 www.bbc.com/news/world-africa-44408373

23 https://ec.europa.eu/home-affairs/what-we-do/policies/irregular-migration-return-policy/facilitation-irregular-migration_en

24 Documentary. Available at www.imdb.com/title/tt8094178/

25 Several observers have also pointed out that "deviant supply is driven by deviant demand" (Gilman et al., 2011: 16). What Calavita (2005) aptly calls the "economics of *alterité*", has been very beneficial to the economies of certain Southern European countries, but has also reinforced the migrants' otherness, increasing their fragility and deepening their legal and social exclusion.

26 https://ec.europa.eu/home-affairs/what-we-do/policies/irregular-migration-return-policy/facilitation-irregular-migration_en

27 www.operationsophia.eu/about-us/

28 https://missingmigrants.iom.int/

29 www.theguardian.com/world/2017/feb/27/ngo-rescues-off-libya-encourage-traffickers-eu-borders-chief

30 www.aftenposten.no/amagasinet/i/Odw53/Siem-Pilot-registrerer-alle-dode

31 The term "borderliness" (coined by Sarah Green) emerged as a concept during the development of the EastBordNet project. It means "what gives something or somewhere the sense of being a border" and refers to border

as a *quality* rather than as an object, and more as ongoing activity rather than a fixed "thing". See http://wiki.manchester.ac.uk/eastbordnet/index. php/Borderliness

32 Åpen høring i kontroll- og konstitusjonskomiteen 6. feb. 2015 – Høring med politioverbetjent Geir Petter Pettersen, Politiets utlendingsenhet [Open hearing in the Committee for Control and Constitutional Matters, 6 February 2015 – Testimony of Police Sergeant Geir P. Pettersen, Police Immigration Unit]: 73–74.

33 Åpen høring i kontroll- og konstitusjonskomiteen 6. feb. 2015 – Høring med politioverbetjent Geir Petter Pettersen, Politiets utlendingsenhet: 74.

5

JUSTICE AND THE MORAL BOUNDARIES OF THE NATION

The Baldizzis – Adolfo and Rosaria, together with two-year-old Jose-
phine and baby John – moved into 97 Orchard Street in 1928, about
five years after Adolfo, a stowaway from Palermo, landed in New York.
Adolfo was a skilled cabinetmaker, having begun to learn his trade at
the age of 14. In 1935, one of the grimmest years of the Great
Depression, like millions of others, he was "self-employed". In Adolfo's
case, this meant that, toolbox in hand, he walked up and down the
streets of the neighbourhood hoping someone would need a job done.
Rosaria, the youngest of four children in a relatively well-off Palermo
family, married Adolfo when she was sixteen and he was twenty-six.
On what her daughter describes as "doctored papers," Rosaria also came
to America illegally, a year after her husband. Then, to regularise their
situation, the two left for Canada and re-entered the United States
"legally" … Their first apartment in the New World was on Elizabeth
Street, a centre of Sicilian life on the Lower East Side. But, moving
several times before they got to Orchard Street, they behaved like many
poor tenants during the Depression: families "forgot" to pay their September rent, then moved into another building in October after having
secured a month's rent concession from the new landlord.[1]

The story of the Baldizzi family can be found in New York's Lower East
Side Tenement Museum. The story is in many ways unremarkable and

shows the long history of irregular migration and the long-standing and intricate connections between migration and (il)legality. Rosaria and Adolfo's story shows how migrants throughout history have employed survival strategies which make them vulnerable to the use of state penal power. The realities of the migration of poor populations create an ever-extending repertoire of acts that can lead to criminalisation and public condemnation: illegal entry as a stowaway, the use of false documents, illegal re-entry, not paying rent, and unemployment.

Such dynamics have inspired some of the central insights about social processes surrounding criminalisation. As Nils Christie (2004: 3) forcefully argues, crime does not exist as an objective entity:

> Only acts exist, acts often given different meanings within various social frameworks. Acts, and the meaning given them, are our data. Our challenge is to follow the destiny of acts through the universe of meanings. Particularly, what are the social conditions that encourage or prevent giving the acts the meaning of being crime.

This book has shown how, in contemporary Europe, such acts as those of Rosaria and Adolfo Baldizzi are increasingly met with state penal measures and, ultimately, deportation and cancellation of claims to membership. The Lower East Side Tenement Museum, on the other hand, provides a different narrative. It offers an acknowledgment of irregular migration as a possible path to membership and as a legitimate part of national history.

Paths to membership in the nation have always been many and complex. In the case of Norway, as shown in Chapter 3, political and state bureaucratic changes can speed up the production of penal alienage and thus intensify the processes of exclusion from membership. Chapter 4 outlined how the discourses of security, organised crime, and moral threats serve to militarise borders and close off access to territory. This final chapter examines the normative frameworks which underpin such processes and the conceptions of membership inherent in them. It outlines the normative placement of the crimmigrant other outside the moral boundaries of the nation and, thereby, how this makes him or her a central element in the constitution and daily production of these same boundaries. Finally, the chapter examines different conceptions of justice and inclusion, which may offer a glimpse of an alternative normative and ethical landscape.

The power to make distinctions

Chapter 4 showed that, while excluded from the nation state model of security, migrants are, to some extent at least, included in the humanitarian discourse built on notions of compassion, care, and protection of life (Fassin, 2012; Ticktin, 2011; Aas and Gundhus, 2015). However, as Fassin (2012) points out, the humanitarianism does not operate through the universalist language of rights, but is rather structured by the discourse of emotion and morality. The glorification of the innocence, passivity, and victimhood of certain groups of migrants serves to differentiate between good and bad (if only by focusing on the "good", while remaining silent on the "bad" or indeterminate categories). Refugees, as Costello (2018) points out, are "carved out" from "other migrants", thus downplaying the protection needs of the latter. The prevalence of the discourse of victimhood permeates humanitarian action with moral judgements (Sandvik, 2010). A sector caught up in the language of goodness therefore has considerable difficulty in articulating the language of rights, justice, and inclusion for the un-ideal migrant. While civil society initiatives sometimes challenge the use of penal power, the humanitarian discourse has been unable to critically address the notion of the crimmigrant other and the ways in which it structures the politics and practices of migration governance and control.

There are, as Toni Morrison (2017: 19) observes, "major benefits in creating and sustaining an Other". In the context of contemporary migration policies, the crimmigrant other – in its many manifestations – makes it possible to make distinctions: between good and bad mobility, victims and offenders, and deserving and non-deserving migrants. Above all, this figure provides the ability to distinguish between members and non-members. So, then, while Chapter 4 located the "work" performed by the crimmigrant other within the moral economy of border control, this chapter examines its productive nature on a broader level of the constitution of society. Border enforcement practices are not simply about reflecting status – essentially, they are about *producing* it (Anderson, 2013). Borders and boundaries, as Donnan and Wilson (1999) point out, create frameworks for who is considered a legitimate member of a particular community, and determine the common traits of its members. Borders do not simply delineate territorial entities to be policed and protected, but "reach into the heart of political space" (Anderson, 2013: 2).

The processes of social production of the crimmigrant other play a central role in shaping (and destabilising) contemporary notions of belonging. In Chapter 3, we saw how various modalities of bordered penality are employed for the purpose of questioning and cancelling membership. Penal power is used to deny claims to membership and the aspirations of those on the margins of society, such as asylum seekers and the Roma (Barker, 2018). It is also used to cancel the already tenuous membership positions of established Eastern European residents, for example, or of refugees with acknowledged protection claims (Westfeldt, 2008; Aas, 2014). Such acts as the use of "doctored papers" or "forgetting" to pay the rent represent an almost inexhaustible resource for the production of deportability and alienage. Chapter 3 showed how the production of alienage can be strongly influenced by political priorities and internal bureaucratic performance measures. Finally, in contemporary societies, penal power is also used to question and cancel membership of members who are already established as citizens. On a daily basis, the effect of internal border control and frequent stop-and-search practices, for example, is to call into question the full membership of second and third generation immigrants (Bradford and Jackson, 2018). Recent scholarship has also uncovered a growing tendency towards the revocation of citizenship of various categories of suspect citizens (Zedner, 2016). Brekke et al.'s recent study (2019) shows, for example, that Norwegian authorities between March 2017 and December 2018 started proceedings to revoke residence permits and citizenship status of more than 3,000 immigrants, many on the grounds of alleged use of fraudulent information. Several European countries have also either considered or introduced measures to revoke the citizenship of so-called foreign fighters (Zedner, 2016).

As Vanessa Barker (2018) observes, such processes reveal the structuring power of law and penal power. The use of penal power at the border – in its many sites – is essentially connected to issues of citizenship (Bosworth et al., 2018). As a political technique and penal measure, deportation strengthens the value of citizenship, giving it a privileged and exclusive position (Anderson, 2013; Gibney, 2013). This position is real, in terms of access to rights, particularly welfare rights (Barker, 2018), but also symbolic, because it creates a privileged sense of identity for the insiders. The social production of the crimmigrant other, therefore, is not simply a legal or a bureaucratic process, but is at the heart of the dynamics through which a community is imagined. The crimmigrant other is crucially connected to the question of how a "we" is constructed. As Anderson (2013) observes:

> The exclusion of migrants helps define the privileges and the limitations of citizenship, and close attention to the border (physical and metaphorical) reveals much about how we make sense of ourselves ... [rather] than simple competitors for the privileges of membership, citizens and migrants define each other, and [that] they do so through set of relations that shift and are not in straightforward binary opposition.

Similarly, Wendy Brown (2010) points out that borders produce political subjectivity, identity, morality, and goodness – they do not just bound, but *invent* the societies they delimit. In 2012, for example, the former French president Nicolas Sarkozy said that a crackdown by the authorities on radical Islamists "will allow us to expel from our national territory a certain number of people who have no reason to be here".[2] Bordered penality is, therefore, not only about the right to be physically present on the national territory but, ultimately, also about exclusion from the common "we". The practices of bordered penality thus reveal the productive nature of penal power (Foucault, 1977) and are "deeply rooted in collective identifications and the assumption of a common sense of belonging" (Balibar, 2010: 316). These dynamics are essential for understanding the emerging forms of punitive attitudes towards non-members, particularly in otherwise inclusive and non-punitive societies, such as Scandinavian societies (Franko et al., 2019).

The crimmigrant other comes up against the desire to punish those who are different, and the determination to exclude those who do not belong. The reason why expulsion, rather than (domestic) punishment, is often the preferred path is to be found in the intensified struggle over who has the right to belong to the nation – who has a legitimate "reason to be here". The processes involved in producing the crimmigrant other are thus part of a broader trend towards "rebordering" political and territorial space (Brown, 2010). In a rigidly stratified global order, where citizenship is a privilege, crime control is one of the most legitimate reasons for border maintenance and thereby social exclusion. It transforms issues of global privilege and scarcity of resources into questions of morality and the maintenance of moral order. Immigrant criminality thus becomes a means to establish the right to belong in a world marked by ever-greater struggles over citizenship. As Peter Geschiere (2009) suggests, these struggles are increasingly articulated through claims about autochthony, about creating special links with the local or, quite literally, being "born from the soil" (ibid.: 2). While this may be a primordial form of belonging, it is also, as Geschiere points out, a very contemporary and global one that is undergoing a powerful renaissance in many parts of the world.

In what follows, we shall see how these dynamics also affect the nature of justice for non-members. The social production of the crimmigrant other is a result of profound social division, which is also reflected in the standards of justice available to them.

From normal to abnormal justice

In *Scales of Justice*, Nancy Fraser (2008) argues that, in a global age, discourses of justice are gradually moving from a normal to an abnormal frame. Normal justice is imagined and practised territorially, as a domestic relation between fellow citizens where "parties frame their disputes as matters internal to territorial states, thereby equating the 'who of justice' with the citizenry of a bounded polity" (ibid.: 54). There are clear divisions between domestic and international space. Globalisation, however, disturbs this neat Westphalian order of clearly delineated units. It expands the geographical scope of struggles for justice, as well as the question of who is to be counted as the subject of the discourse, and how and where to address disputes about justice. In the emerging forms of abnormal justice, Fraser claims, participants no longer share common assumptions about the "what", the "who", and the "how" of justice.

While the historic stability and neatness of Westphalian sovereignty have been called into question by several observers (Benton, 2010), "abnormal" struggles for justice are now receiving considerable attention in such areas as human rights, international criminal law, humanitarian interventions, and campaigns for environmental justice, to name but a few. In many respects, the migrant is a key figure of the struggle for abnormal justice (Benhabib, 2004; Dembour, 2015). However, the issue has been far less often addressed as regards domestic criminal justice (Aas, 2014). Fraser sees the emerging abnormality as potentially liberating, but, as we shall see, when it comes to criminal justice, it produces a particular set of challenges which are not easily grasped by means of established conceptual, theoretical, and normative frameworks (Bosworth et al., 2018).

In previous chapters, we saw that the crimmigrant other is subjected to a hybrid system of control: he or she encounters administrative measures belonging to the sphere of penal power, without the language of criminal justice having caught up with developments. Deprived of freedom in institutions which resemble prisons, but which belong to the administrative domain, and subjected to measures such as deportation that feels painful and punitive, the crimmigrant other undergoes punishment in all but name. These developments are destabilising the normal framing of domestic criminal justice and criminal law and raising questions such as: "Who is the subject of normative criminal justice discourse and practice?" "What is (just) punishment? What is punitiveness?", and "How and where should the issues be addressed?" (Aas, 2014).

The use of penal power over various populations of non-citizens creates a need for new frames of understanding, and a reconsideration of some central assumptions about justice and penal power which are deeply rooted in established conceptions of "normal penality" (Bosworth et al., 2018). In other words, it requires a change of perspective within studies of penality from the social science of the normal to that of the abnormal (see also Kuhn, 1996; Kuhn, 2008). As pointed out in Chapter 3, conventional measures of punitiveness are not well suited to recognising punitive and exclusionary aspects of Scandinavian societies, precisely because the punitive nature of bordered penality (and of border control measures more generally) is not immediately apparent in the traditional criminal justice frame (see also Barker, 2013). In order to fully recognise its move towards punitiveness, Norway's greater use of imprisonment needs to be seen in conjunction with the steep rise in the use of deportation. The crimmigrant other is subjected to punitive measures that disturb the normal frame of criminal justice by radically transforming the "who" and the "what" of punishment. In the forms of abnormal justice now emerging, the "who" are increasingly non-citizens and, in addition to ordinary penalties, the "what" of punishment also includes deportation and termination of membership.

It is important to note, however, that adjustment to the novel realities of bordered penality and crimmigration control would entail acknowledging the penal nature of such immigration measures as detention and deportation. It would also entail including non-citizens more fully in discourses of justice and giving them rights that are normally given to nationals (Zedner, 2013). Our empirical inquiry in Norway revealed that, when penal power is exercised over individuals without formal membership, it changes its nature, and becomes – even in what is arguably one of the most inclusive and least punitive societies in the world – more openly exclusionary (Aas, 2014). The absence of formal membership is the essential factor which helps shift the aim of penal intervention from reintegration into society to territorial exclusion.

This is not only visible on the political level, where foreign citizens are subjected to what Todd-Kvam (2018) describes as "bordered penal populism". The development is perhaps even more present at the level of practice. It is to be seen in the fact that non-citizens are increasingly being deprived of their freedom in different institutions from citizens: detention centres, special prison wings and prisons (Ugelvik, 2013; Ugelvik and Ugelvik, 2017), as well as being imprisoned on different grounds. At any one time, approximately 50 per cent of Norwegian pre-trial detainees are non-citizens. As is pointed out in a Statistics of Norway report, Norwegian citizens are generally imprisoned following a judicial sentence while non-citizens are largely imprisoned following a judicial order made because of a fear they will abscond. This is a trend that can be seen in many Western EU countries.[3] The courts regularly regard lack of citizenship as a "lack of attachment to the country" which means there is a danger that non-citizens will abscond (Arentzen, 2013). The perceived mobility of non-citizens in these cases constitutes grounds for imprisonment.

After serving their sentence, citizens are released into the community, and the ambition of the inclusionary welfare penalty is that they should be fully re-integrated into society (Smith and Ugelvik, 2017). Non-citizens, on the other hand, are generally deported and thus completely excluded from society. For them, in addition to ordinary penalties, a sentence also leads to the termination of membership. The redemptive aspects of welfare penalty are only available to full members. As one social worker with long experience in the criminal justice system observed: "It is almost as if it is only Norwegians that are allowed to do something wrong." Similarly, Griffiths (2017: 531) suggests that offenders in the UK "are punished harder and denied redemption when they are non-citizens, casting them as more seriously and indelibly criminal than their British counterparts". Also, other academic critics have pointed out that non-members are punished more harshly than members and that the principles of proportionality apply differently to this group (Stumpf, 2006; Legomsky, 2007). While, for a citizen, the penalty of a certain number of months or years in prison is considered proportionate to the offence, a non-citizen has deportation added to their sentence.

The absence of formal citizenship status, therefore, crucially affects the procedural and substantive standards of justice afforded to non-members. The otherness of the crimmigrant other is thus not only a product of an exclusionary populist or nationalist discourse, but also institutionalised in the everyday processes of administration of justice. The differentiation of the citizen from the alien produces two different types of justice: in effect, a two-tier system of justice (Aas, 2014). In Europe, and particularly in Scandinavia, the "normal" one (envisioned primarily as a relationship between citizens), despite periodic popular punitive onslaughts, is wedded to the idea of reintegration into society. The other, globalised "abnormal" form of justice departs from the ordinary – it is bordered, and geared towards exclusion from the national social body and fails to take into account the claims of non-members.

The non-citizens on the receiving end of it often experience such abnormal forms of justice as deeply discriminatory. As Ugelvik and Damsa (2017), point out, the injustice of being subjected to a prison regime that is different from that of citizens can be seen as an additional pain of imprisonment. The sense of not being thought to deserve the same standards of justice and citizenship as nationals was summarised by one deportee, who said: "I think that democracy is just for Norwegian people" (Strømnes, 2013). Similarly, foreign citizens imprisoned for breaches of immigration law interviewed by Slettvåg (2016) expressed disillusionment with the Norwegian justice system, particularly with the speed of proceedings:

> Legal is zero here in Norway, no have power, no have nothing. Because today arrest me, second day, give me ten months. My lawyer no have time for speak, no have time for nothing. For fighting for me. My advocate said, "I'm sorry for you."

Another prisoner spoke in a similar way about being unable to challenge the system and the uselessness of legal aid: "The police tell something, the lawyer tells the same. It's the same, don't help, the lawyer ... the lawyer here is only for... legal you have lawyer. But don't tell you nothing good for me."

These quotes reveal frustration with the quality of legal aid and with the hastiness of the process. Our investigation revealed that the Norwegian authorities employ several strategies to prioritise such cases and speed up deportation. At some point, they also suggested an introduction of a fast-track criminal justice process. A similar trend has also been observed in the US, where expansions of fast-track, rights–infringing systems of exclusion and deportation, as Kanstroom (2018: 1326) points out, "fundamentally challenge the relationship between executive power and law, especially in regard to human and civil rights, and between territorial presence and rights". The speed of proceedings is inevitably detrimental to due process. The fact that the process results in removal from the country also makes it difficult to challenge state decisions, both from a logistical point of view, and because there are few remedies available to those wrongly deported (Kanstroom, 2012).

In the US, excesses of immigration enforcement can be ascribed to the nationalist and exclusionary ideology of the current administration, which is "profoundly uncommitted to the ideas of rights for noncitizens (or their families)" (Kanstroom, 2018: 1326), but developments in Norway also indicate that we may be dealing with some universal phenomena. The field of so-called crimmigration law is for various reasons inductive to creating lower standards of rights: it suffers from a lack of judicial oversight, puts pressure on due process, and gives priority tor efficiency and expediency (Sklansky, 2012; Stumpf, 2006, 2013; Menjívar and Kanstroom, 2014; Kanstroom, 2018). In Norway, as in several other countries, removal involves administrative proceedings which entail fewer rights protections than criminal proceedings in court (Eagly, 2010). There is thus reason to believe that the field suffers from a deficit of rights (Husabø and Suominen, 2011). This also applies to the much-debated situation of children and minors caught in the system (Humlen and Myhre, 2014). Detention and deportation of children and families challenges established notions of the best interests of the child and his or her right to family life (Dembour, 2015).

As a result of the intertwining and interchangeability of criminal law and immigration law at the practical level, non-citizens often do not enjoy the same legal protections as citizens, such as the privilege against self-incrimination and eligibility for legal aid in deportation cases (Husabø and Suominen, 2011; see also Pauw, 2000; Stumpf, 2006; Vazquez, 2012). As we saw in Chapter 3, there are pressures of efficiency, and a considerable degree of police and prosecutorial discretion (Van der Woude and Van der Leun, 2017). The top–down pressure to learn how to change tracks and "think with two hats on" has created a deeply unsystematic, arbitrary and unpredictable use of the law (see also Sklansky, 2012). If the rule of law means that, as Hayek (1994, in Sklansky, 2012) argues, "government in all its actions is bound by rules fixed and announced beforehand – rules that make it possible to foresee with fair certainty how the authority will use its coercive powers in given circumstances", then crimmigration law is clearly deficient. In the everyday application of justice, the crimmigrant other is subjected to extreme uncertainty and is often unable to influence his or her legal standing with regard to state authorities. Brekke et al. (2019), for example, report the negative psychological effects that prolonged state proceedings for cancellation of residence permits and citizenship status have on those subjected to them.

A review of immigration cases conducted by the Norwegian Bar Association (Humlen and Myhre, 2014) revealed that, in 65 per cent of cases between 2007 and 2014, where the Association chose on "pro bono" grounds to challenge legal decisions of the immigration authorities, the challenge was eventually successful. These findings indicate a need for better legal aid and a need to give such cases more judicial oversight (ibid.). The Norwegian government, however, has chosen to go in the opposite direction. Until the 2017 parliamentary change of citizenship law, it was even possible to deprive asylum seekers suspected of providing false information to the immigration authorities of citizenship without judicial oversight.[4] The tendency towards moving decisions from the courts to the administrative domain, and the willingness to dispense with the judicial process altogether, are, therefore, not only characteristics of the current US administration (Kanstroom, 2018), but can be found in one of the most liberal and inclusive European democracies, with expressed commitment to human rights.

While the "abnormal" justice described in this book could be described as exceptional, I choose not to do so for two reasons. In recent scholarship, exceptionalism has been thought to explain why Scandinavian societies are less punitive and have lower prison figures and better prison conditions (Pratt and Eriksson, 2012; Ugelvik and Dullum, 2012). The phenomena outlined in this book, however, demonstrate exceptionalism of a different, punitive kind. I also refrain from using the term "exceptionalism" in order to avoid associations which might naturally be made with the state of exception – the term most notably developed by Giorgio Agamben (2005), which has been taken up by a vast body of work within migration studies (see, inter alia, De Genova and Peutz, 2010). In this context, state of exception is used to denote migrants' extra-legal position and almost total exclusion from legal protection. Several developments described in this book clearly support this thesis, not least the tragic loss of life at sea and the controversial European practices of externalising border control to its neighbours described in Chapter 4.

Shortly after it was opened, the Trandum detention centre (mentioned in Chapter 3) was described by one newspaper as "Norway's

Guantanamo".[5] It was given this dramatic label partly because the facility largely employed private security guards and detained families and children, practices which are unthinkable in the context of "ordinary" Norwegian criminal justice facilities. Most importantly, Trandum was at the time – in legal terms – unregulated. The bureaucratic regulations that usually determine the minutiae of life in Norwegian prisons did not apply to the detention centre. Today, Trandum is far from an unregulated space. The facility, though still operated by the police, has been in practical and legal terms changed into a "proper" prison facility and subjected to regulation and oversight (Sivilomudsmannen, 2015). The living conditions of the men, women, and minors detained there are essentially the same as those of "ordinary" Norwegian inmates – except, of course, for the fact that most of them have not been convicted of a criminal offence and practically all of them will be excluded from society and deported.

The transformation of Trandum offers a good illustration of the developments described in this book. The institution is not exceptional in the sense of being extra-legal, outside the law, or a case of suspension of the law. What we are witnessing is in the main a legally regulated, but differentiated, two-tier system of justice. The question is, then, not whether the crimmigrant other is seen at all as deserving of justice, but whether he or she deserves the *same* standards of (normal) justice as the citizen.

The departure from the ordinary is often exacerbated by the rhetoric of threat. As we saw in Chapter 1, the crimmigrant other is a threatening figure who provides the justification for extraordinary measures. Migration flows are spoken about in the same way as military threats (Gundhus and Jansen, 2019) and as calling for immediate executive action. In 2018, declaring a state of national emergency, US President Donald Trump said: "We're talking about an invasion of our country, with drugs, with human traffickers, with all types of criminals and gangs." In a much more temperate political environment, this line of reasoning was expressed in a recent Norwegian White Paper (Meld. St.10 (2016–2017))[6] as follows:

> The Government will appoint a panel that will consider the establishment of trans-sectoral authorisation within our legislation on preparedness to be applied in extraordinary situations other

> than when the country is at war or when war is imminent or when the country's independence or security are in danger. This can apply, for example, to high numbers of arrivals of asylum seekers, natural catastrophes, accidents, pandemics or breakdowns of infrastructure ...
>
> A [trans-sectoral] authorisation can also make it possible to intervene where necessary to quickly prioritise resources, or where because of the situation there is reason to set aside procedural rules.

Prompted by the 2015 "migration crisis", these provisions clearly connect the arrival of asylum seekers to an expansion of executive powers similar to that which takes place in situations of war. They make it possible to strengthen the executive branch at the expense of procedural rules, judicial oversight, and democratic deliberation. Interestingly, the passage does not mention terrorism, which in many European countries has been an important motor of similar developments (Ashworth and Zedner, 2014). Remarkably, in 2012 Norway delivered "normal justice" in the most serious case of terror, and one of the most extraordinary crimes, in its history. The trial of the Utøya perpetrator indicates that membership status may be equally important as the actual nature of the threat when justice departs from the ordinary.

The morality of nationalism

The deportee's observation, mentioned above, that "democracy is just for Norwegian people" (Strømnes, 2013) expresses the perception that justice presupposes a closed national community (Bosniak, 2006). Despite the fact that those affected by penal power are increasingly non-citizens, the normality of the national frame of understanding is perhaps even more entrenched in criminal law and in criminal justice than in other legal domains. As Zedner (2013) observes, criminal law has traditionally been conceptualised as a social contract between citizens. Criminal law is part of public law, and the public has traditionally been thought of as a national public. This conception of the national as the normal crucially affects penal regimes directed at non-citizens. By definition, the position of the non-citizen, the foreigner, or the alien is bound to be different: he or she falls outside the national frame.

In practice, as we have seen throughout this book, the differential status of the crimmigrant other stems largely from immigration law. In political and legal theory, the justifications for the differential treatment of non-citizens have been debated in terms of the pros and cons of cosmopolitan, national, and communitarian approaches to membership (see, inter alia, Honig, 2001; Duff, 2010; Zedner, 2013). Normal justice is built on what Linda Bosniak (2006: 134) terms normative nationalism: a "prevailing set of baseline premises according to which the territorial nation state is the rightful, if not the total, world of our normative concern". It is taken for granted, and understood as common sense, that "compatriots take priority" (ibid.: 135). As Bosniak observes (ibid.: 7): "Analysts maintain a presumption of national priority without the need for either its acknowledgement or its defense. Their moral nationalism appears not to be a normative choice but a metaphysical given."

Such an understanding, as we saw in Chapter 3, provides the necessary framework for the pursuit of equal/democratic citizenship within the strictly limited boundaries of membership, which results in a two-sided, "hard-on-the-outside, soft-on-the-inside" penal culture that is lenient towards insiders and punitive towards outsiders. Within the normative nationalist frame, the state enjoys the sovereign prerogative to lay down the rules at the border, and to criminalise any infringements of them. Within this framework, infringements of immigration law are endowed with the "metaphysically given" nature of being a crime.

While Bosniak (ibid.: 6) and others (Benhabib, 2004) regard community closure as implausible, empirically untenable, and "normatively unsatisfying premises on which to ground any political theory of justice and governance", in the current political climate their critique is constantly challenged by the growing tide of nationalism. As Benedict Anderson observed (2006: 3): "The reality is quite plain: the 'end of the era of nationalism,' so long prophesied, is not remotely in sight. Indeed, nation-ness is the most universally legitimate value in the political life of our time." In the penal domain, the salience of nationalism finds its expression in Vanessa Barker's (2018) thoughtful analysis of penal nationalism, where penal power is deployed to preserve the benefits of the welfare state for its members. Such "attempts to reserve the benefits of the welfare state for those who really belong" (Ceuppens and Geschiere, 2005: 397) are grounded in an understanding of the world as limited – not only geographically bordered but, more importantly, limited also in terms of wealth and resources (Barker, 2018). "This is a full country" and "The Netherlands is full" were slogans constantly repeated by the Dutch populist politician Pim Fortuyn, who achieved great popularity through his anti-immigration stance.

Various practices of bordered penality described in this book are expressions of a normative ideal – that of the sovereign territory (Cornelisse, 2010: 108) – which mobilises national and international policing efforts towards the "compulsory allocation of subjects to their proper sovereigns" (Walters, 2010: 90). They are based on a conception of citizenship which is fundamentally a global regulatory technique. Citizenship is a privilege which is inherited by birth. As such, as Ayelet Shachar (in Bosniak, 2006: 136) observes, it serves to "sustain global inequality". Through the centrality of citizenship, domestic penality becomes part of a particular global mobility regime (Guild, 2009; Dauvergne, 2008; Aas, 2013a), and is inscribed with unequal global geopolitical relations. In Chapter 4, we saw how such unequal geopolitical relations (with clear neo-colonial undertones) shape relations between the EU and its neighbours. While the intersections of punishment and social inequality are a perennial source of interest in criminological and sociological studies, in the case of bordered penality this inequality is primarily a matter of what might be termed geographical privilege. The border, defended by the joint forces of immigration law and criminal law, daily reinstates the centrality of territory and territorial membership, and reinforces geographical distance. It is thus one of the mechanisms regulating access to personal and economic security and maintaining the present, rigidly stratified, global order.

However, this seemingly self-evident framework of the "hard-on-the-outside, soft-on-the-inside" conception of citizenship is built on social division between the inside and the outside which is proving increasingly difficult to sustain: "Border and the interior are in fact inevitably interpenetrated – nowhere more clearly than in the case of alienage" (Bosniak, 2006: 16). The porosity of borders, multiplicity of identities and belongings, and lack of clarity about which sovereign an individual actually belongs to make the task of distinguishing between insiders and outsiders far more difficult, and ultimately the distinction becomes arbitrary. Citizenship and nationalism are exclusionary. Admissions to membership are made on the basis of shared history, language, and traditions. The scholarly task at hand, therefore, is to understand the nature of such distinctions. As Benedict Anderson (2006) points out:

> nation-ness, as well as nationalism, are cultural artefacts of a particular kind. To understand them properly we need to consider carefully how they have come into historical being, in what ways their meanings have changed over time, and why, today, they command such profound emotional legitimacy.

Although taken for granted, and commanding emotional legitimacy, the exclusionary nature of nationalism and citizenship can be experienced as "nasty" and arbitrary even by insiders (Goodin, 1997). For, even though normative nationalism may seem a self-evident ethical framework for discussing membership and its boundaries in contemporary societies, it is also intrinsically (and increasingly) problematic. Distinguishing between citizens and aliens, and according to the latter lower levels of rights, less favourable treatment, and even using force against them, may seem problematic and discriminatory. From a legal perspective, differential treatment on the basis of nationality, as Dembour (2015: 503) suggests, can be seen as a "form of institutionalized racism or at least discrimination". How can the state in deportation decisions justify denying an alien child the right to family life on the grounds that he or she is an alien, while it otherwise makes the rights of children one of its utmost concerns? Similarly, in liberal democracies, depriving entire families of their liberty is an act that is unthinkable for citizens and is beset with ethical difficulties.

Because access to citizenship may appear fundamentally arbitrary – as we saw, an accident of birth – Bridget Anderson suggests (2013: 2) that modern states portray themselves not simply as:

> arbitrary collections of people hung together by a common legal status but as a *community of value*, composed of people who share

common ideals and (exemplary) patterns of behavior expressed through ethnicity, religion, culture, or language – that is, its members have shared values.

The conception of membership as being part of a community of value introduces a certain rationale into the arbitrariness. Rather than being understood as a privilege inherited by birth, citizenship is "fundamentally about status in the sense of worth and honour" (Anderson, 2013: 4). And it is precisely here that the figure of the crimmigrant other becomes particularly significant. It introduces reason, even urgency, into seemingly arbitrary and problematic distinctions between the alien and the citizen. It makes social exclusion – which might otherwise appear to be based on race, poverty, and religion – seem reasonable and legitimate. At the level of political discourse, Cathrine Thorleifsson's (2019: 8–9) comparative ethnographic study of European populist radical right parties shows that, although operating in different geographical and political contexts, they all deploy dystopian imaginaries of criminal migrants to reinforce the boundaries of the nation. The figure of the graphically portrayed "Ivan S., violeur et bientôt Suisse?" (translated as "Ivan S., rapist and soon to become Swiss?") played a major role in the 2010 Swiss federal initiative "For the Expulsion of Criminal Foreigners" initiated by the right-wing SVP party (Garufo and Maire, 2019). As one SVP party publicist explained:

> Ivan is the bad guy. He has the muscles, the t-shirt, he's not shaved. Does a man convicted for rape have the right to stay in Switzerland? This is a tough question. But you see Ivan for one or two seconds and you can instinctively feel the answer: No.
>
> *(Faure, 2010, in Garufo and Maire, 2019)*

The exclusionary nature of nationalism is founded not only on the view that migrants represent a drain on the resources of the welfare state (Barker, 2018), but also on the notion of their otherness in terms of values and morality.

However, the cultural artefacts that distinguish nations and ethnic groups from one another do not primarily refer to qualities inherent in them. Drawing on Fredrik Barth's seminal work, Eriksen and Jakoubek

(2019: 3) point out that "[e]thnicity is essentially an aspect of a relationship, not a property of a group." Nations and ethnic groups do not exist in isolation. A definition of "us" is therefore always created in relation to others. Within such processes, the crimmigrant other plays a constitutive role in defining the moral boundaries of the nation. His or her existence makes the privilege of citizenship (and the use of penal power inherent in its defence) justified and less arbitrary and morally ambiguous. By making crime a marker of cultural otherness and non-belonging, the punitive and the bordered begin to mesh and complement each other.

While the normative nationalism outlined by Bosniak offers an abstract philosophical framework (without passing explicit moral judgments on those excluded from it), the populist discourse does the opposite: it builds on deeply emotive and morally charged othering of the migrant (Thorleifsson, 2019). Although markedly different in terms of style, the two approaches meet in the bureaucratic practices of bordered penality. Without showing apparent signs of heated political debates, everyday bureaucratic practices that produce crimmigrant others reassert the normative nationalist framework. Public debates often frame the control practices of the police and border agents as discriminatory or even driven by prejudice. This is certainly a valid perspective, but it overlooks the extent to which distinctions between (native) citizens and aliens are systematically built into the daily operation of the law. In Chapter 1, we saw how bureaucratic practices of knowledge production focus on distinguishing between the immigrant and the native population in terms of recorded crime rates, while failing to record migrant mortality at the border. More importantly, the normative nationalist framework supports a state infrastructure that enables – through the joint forces of immigration and criminal law – the extensive use of penal power at the border (Aas and Bosworth, 2013; Aliverti, 2013; Mitsilegas, 2015; Barker, 2018). The Northern state is able to turn social exclusion based on inequality into a question of illegality. In this process, the normative nationalist framework provides a number of "metaphysical givens": that it is the state's prerogative to control borders by all necessary means; and that infringements of this prerogative should be penalised. Within this "national order of things" (Malkki, 1995) the concept of the nation state is, as Kmak (2015: 90) points out, "inherently based on effective control of the population inhabiting a particular territory". And, in the case of non-citizens, the state exercises its right over its territory without limitations (ibid.). From this premise follows another "metaphysical given": that those responsible for infringements of the state's prerogative should be permanently excluded from society. Non-native offenders are to be excluded, even though far greater offences committed by native offenders are, at least in the European context, generally followed by a possibility of redemption and attempts to reintegrate them.

Although refugees through the international human rights regimes represent, as Kmak (2015: 91) points out, a disquieting element in this national order of things, European states are doing their utmost to challenge their position and ascribe to them labels of bogusness and economic fortune hunting. The exclusion of the crimmigrant other from the nation is thus the result of several layers of othering that support each other. Exclusions grounded in bureaucratic classifications and the daily operation of criminal and immigration law are added to by the normative philosophical frameworks and the othering of political and media discourse. This includes not only blatant examples, such as "Ivan S., the rapist", but also the discourse of humanitarian actors. Although more temperate, the latter is nevertheless deeply permeated by moral sentiments and actively employ notions of innocence and evil. As we saw in Chapter 4, the European system of border control draws heavily on the discourse of combating evil smugglers to establish its own legitimacy. Similarly, Costello (2018: 6) points out that one of the most important recent political and legal documents on the regulation of international migration, the Global Compact for Safe, Orderly and Regular Migration, "has an entire section on smuggling, also based on the assumption that it is simply a wrong to be suppressed". The project of crime control carries broad consensual force in an area that is otherwise deeply divided about how to deal with issues connected with the mobility of the global poor. Here, too, the need to combat dangerous criminal offenders becomes a "metaphysical given", paving the way for the exclusionary use of force at the border.

The "value" of the crimmigrant other lies in the fact that he or she is not designated as simply a transgressor of rules but as an offender, and thus defined by criminality in a profound and existential way. Classical sociological and criminological insights about how "deviant forms of behavior are often a valuable resource in society" (Erikson, 1966) are particularly useful in this context. In his seminal historical analysis *Punishment and Welfare*, David Garland (1985/2018: 100) describes how, at the end of the 19th century, the use of penal power was greatly marked by class bias "which failed to disguise the grave economic and social inequalities which the law reproduced". This legitimacy deficit, Garland suggests, was remedied by the gradual development of a discourse which characterised the problem of crime in a way that radically divorced it from social and political processes. By making crime into "an inevitable outcome of a particular kind of character or constitution", the law was able to turn attention away from questions of social inequality and direct it to issues of personality (ibid.):

> The existence of a class which was constantly criminalised – indeed the very existence of an impoverished sector of the population – could now be explained by reference to the natural, constitutional propensities of these individuals, thereby excluding all reference to the character of the law, of politics or of social relations.

While the constitution of criminal character described above was established on the basis of scientific discourse about abnormality, contemporary discourses draw more on notions of cultural otherness. In both cases, though, attention is turned away from the operations of the law itself and firmly directed at questions about the character of individuals and particular groups.

Because citizenship is multifaceted and not simply a legal status, the use of penal power to achieve exclusion from citizenship also means designating the excluded as non-members not just in terms of their formal identity but of their social identity, moral constitution, and value to the community. The moral narrative about the nation is an important aspect of contemporary normative nationalism. The primary interest of this book has been to examine how these lines of reasoning shape not only political discourse, but also the everyday practices of the law and actions of those carrying out the tasks of border control. In Chapter 4, we saw how the crimmigrant other plays a central role in the intricate moral economy at the border. Our interviews also revealed that the idea of protecting the nation from those seen as intruders and a drain on limited resources can be used to make acceptable actions that would otherwise be intolerable. For example, several Norwegian police officers participating in Frontex operations expressed condemnation of the way Greek police officers at times treated migrants in "a bit of a rough way", disregarding human rights (see also Franko and Gundhus, 2015). One officer, however, explained why such actions could be understandable:

> Because you have to, at least in operations of this kind, understand the culture and be interested in asking why things are as they are instead of being, hm … I remember in the beginning I thought: "Why are they not more like Norway?" We are really good about safeguarding human rights and do everything right … I am talking about internal culture in the Greek police … Well, they give and give and give, and at the end feel that there is no end to it. And now there is nothing more to give. And this is something that they have given privately. They have, Greek police have always had low salaries, and in addition they are in a way giving from their own pockets to those they feel are invading their country. Yes, you had a very comfortable job in a village outside of Athens, then suddenly you are in the countryside, far away from everything you know. It is not about justifying what is going on, but about understanding it.
>
> *(FRN2)*

The statement illustrates how penal nationalism, as Vanessa Barker (2018) observes, turns solidarity away from distant others and places it firmly within the nation. One's compatriots take priority.

The difficult child

However, at times, such exclusionary acts can be problematic for the state agents involved. This is the case not only in the explicit breaches of rules of conduct described in the example above, but also in more mundane acts of border control. Despite the normative importance of nationalism, exclusionary practices of border control can, as we saw in Chapter 4, in practice create deep moral discomfort. The use of penal power at the border often lacks traditional forms of legitimacy (Bosworth, 2013). In such contexts, those performing the task of border control rely on narratives about crimmigrant others to frame their actions within a "good cause". In our interviews, border control officers framed their work as protection of the nation, and often as protection of the asylum system itself from hyper-criminal asylum seekers. As two officers from Oslo explained:

> A: We actually had examples of people who had been expelled and expelled and deported like five, six times. Many tens of offences on them. Many of those have mass criminality, not just drugs, but also thefts, petty thefts, threats, violence against police officers and such, all kinds of things. These are criminals. They are criminals who use asylum. They are not asylum seekers in a sense that they deserve protection. These are criminals.

> B: When we established the first [initiative] – with these asylum seekers, criminals – it was so that they would not stigmatise our entire asylum system. Those who really needed asylum, they should not – these criminals – should not be allowed to ruin things for everyone else.

Such stories were not uncommon. The official discourse in Norway also tends to frame its eagerness to fight transgressions of immigration law as a way of protecting the asylum system. Such narratives firmly attach notions of asylum to offending and misuse and, importantly, also to the need for protection. The notion of a crimmigrant other allows border control to tap into the repertoire of meanings, narratives, and justifications that are traditionally available to punishment and criminal justice: notions of victims and offenders and narratives of protection from hyper-criminals who are not governable by ordinary control measures. In such circumstances, the use of force becomes not only a necessity, but the right thing to do.

This moral world, populated by the blameworthy and the innocent is not without its complications. As we saw in Chapter 4, the extensive use of penal measures such as detention and deportation can be seen as problematic, particularly when it comes to children. Exemplified by the moving images of Alan Kurdi, the migrant child personifies innocence, victimhood, the need for protection and humanitarian compassion. The vulnerability of children is commonly used to define the worthiness of humanitarian efforts, whether those of NGOs or state authorities. The ideal victimhood of the child stands in stark contrast to the figure of the crimmigrant other and creates a powerful appeal for the extension of solidarity beyond the boundaries of citizenship. Cases of children with long-standing connections to a country often arouse controversy and public support. In Norway, such cases have resulted in a number of vocal support groups in local communities and led to the 2016 Parliamentary inquiry into state deportation practices.

The use of penal power at the border is particularly incongruous when used on children. The arbitrariness of nationalism becomes problematic when it comes up against the needs of children and their right to be included in the normative concerns of the nation. Unlike the crimmigrant other, the child's blamelessness throws into relief the injustice and lack of legitimacy in the use of force at the border. In late 2017, the UN Committee on the Rights of the Child (CRC) joined the Committee on Migrant Workers (CMW) to issue a "Joint General Comment" providing authoritative guidance on the treatment of child migrants:

> Offences concerning irregular entry or stay cannot under any circumstances have consequences similar to those derived from the commission of a crime. Therefore, the possibility of detaining children as a measure of last resort, which may apply in other contexts such as juvenile criminal justice, is not applicable in immigration proceedings as it would conflict with the principle of the best interests of the child and the right to development.
>
> *(CRC-CMW "Joint General Comment", 2017)*[7]

Similarly, we saw earlier that the Norwegian Parliamentary Ombudsman defined the Trandum detention centre – an institution that strongly resembles a prison – as a place "not suitable for children". In recent years, the detention of children in the borderlands of Europe, particularly in Greece, has aroused considerable concern among human rights observers, academic researchers, and NGOs. Médecins sans Frontières (MSF; Doctors Without Borders) recently described the situation in the Moria detention centre in Lesvos as follows:

The policy of containing asylum seekers on Greek islands has led to more than 9,000 people, a third of whom are children, being stuck indefinitely in the Moria camp, which has a maximum capacity of 3,100 people. MSF teams are seeing multiple cases each week of teenagers who have attempted to commit suicide or have self-harmed. Teams are also responding to numerous critical incidents as a result of violence, child self-harm and the lack of access to urgent medical care, highlighting significant gaps in the protection of children and other vulnerable people.[8]

Other aspects of border control, especially deportation, also have serious effects on the wellbeing of children and families. In December 2018, the Norwegian police authorities openly acknowledged for the first time that deporting children can have damaging effects on them. Their spokesperson said: "We see that there is a high risk of inflicting damaging stress and trauma on children when we arrest and deport them." The police authorities therefore decided that they would no longer wake up families with children in the middle of the night to deport them.[9]

We also saw in Chapter 4 that officers involved in deporting children may use various neutralisation techniques in order to ease their moral discomfort (see also Ugelvik, 2016). In their accounts, some Norwegian officers tried to minimise the damaging effects of deportation on minors; they also raised doubts about their status as children. Thus, one officer involved in deportation missions on behalf of the Police Immigration Unit said:

And they have all those [support groups] at home shouting about how bad it is. But when they are sitting on a plane and we are approaching Kabul, then suddenly they stop being children and turn 25 and are doing just fine.

A conversation with two senior officers from Oslo police district reveals the intricate negotiations about the identities of children and minors:

A: When a person comes in with a beard and – you – he claims he is 15 – then you can say, "Listen now, you. You are lying! I can see that you are not 15." We have some photos over there, we don't need any background ... The reason why I am so sceptical is because they are criminals. And when they are doing crime, I do not accept anything they say.

On the other hand, his colleague, a prosecution lawyer from the same district, pointed out that, although there are legal possibilities for refusing to treat individuals as minors in cases of doubt, the risks of doing so could be grave.

> B: The problem is that you don't want to take a chance and end up being wrong. Then, in reality, it is better to treat an adult as a child than the other way around. So this is a bit of a dilemma, I think. It is not easy. There are many challenges, but then there are also many possibilities.

Persistent doubts about whether young people actually are children are also made clear by the development of a plethora of technologies, such as skeletal and dental tests, for use by the authorities to determine a minor's age (Gundhus, 2020). Such practices show how the crimmigrant other casts a shadow over children and minors, by raising the possibility of fraudulence and thus setting limits on their rights and reducing compassion for them. Similarly, Marie-Bénédicte Dembour's analysis (2015: 464) of the European Court of Human Rights points out that, in contemporary European case law, states tend to see children as representing a "risk of exploitation", meaning that parents might exploit the birth of a child to secure a residence permit for themselves and their family. Thus, the best interests of children and their right to family life often have to take second place to state immigration policy considerations.

Migrant children are liminal figures inhabiting a space between innocence and potential blameworthiness. Even when their status as minors is acknowledged, as Gundhus and Egge (2013) point out, many young migrants find themselves excluded from welfare provision available to citizens of a similar age. After all, the Norwegian state's explicit intention is to deport all those without a valid residence permit when they reach the age of 18. The state is also investing considerable resources in finding possible caregivers for unaccompanied minors in their country of origin, so as to make it easier to expel them. One minister described the government's policy as follows:

> If we establish care centres in Afghanistan, more unaccompanied minors will be able to receive a negative decision, so that we can send more back. This will be the case for those who currently get a residence permit because they do not have access to adequate care in Afghanistan. Those are the very people who will get adequate care at the centre, if we succeed.
>
> *(Listhaug, in Vårt Land, 2016)*[10]

Here, too, the understanding of "adequate care" differs greatly between citizen and non-citizen minors.

Conclusion: carrying the burden of history

The position of children clearly shows the primacy of the nationalist normative framework. Despite frequent displays of empathy and compassion towards minors, at root, notions of justice are connected to membership. Philosophers and legal scholars have argued the need to articulate a language of membership and justice that transcends the nationalist outlook and opens the way to aliens and irregular migrants having a "right to have rights" (Benhabib, 2004; Dembour and Kelly, 2011). Such forms of justice would inevitably require a move from a territorial understanding of citizenship to one that acknowledges paths to membership based on mobility and alienage (Bosniak, 2006). They would, as Basaran and Guild (2017: 276) suggest, "destabilise statist views on legal status of subjects" and would, by implication, also question securitisation based upon legal status "by rendering legal status and other legal constructions inherently unstable".

However, in the current social and political order such understandings of justice and membership seem remote. As Dembour (2015) points out, even in the eyes of the European Court of Human Rights – the symbolic and institutional embodiment of European justice – migrants are still primarily defined by their status as aliens. She observes (2015: 504) that:

> For most people it does not appear objectionable that the European Court approaches the migrant, first as an alien (if she is one) who is subject to the control of the state, even though this means that human rights strangely take second place to the sovereignty principle.

Although important progress has been made on several issues, Dembour (2015: 503) suggests that much of migrants' suffering is left out of account by the court – it is considered illegitimate and outside its area of concern.

Nevertheless, this book has also shown evidence of moral concern for suffering at the border, which is not only found in predictable contexts such as the humanitarian sector (Fassin, 2012). Chapter 4 gave examples of compassion and the wish to help arising from direct encounters between migrants and those tasked with border control (Aas and Gundhus, 2015). Such encounters should be distinguished from the performative aspects of humanitarianism visible particularly in political discourse and policy documents, though there are links between the two (Franko and Gundhus, 2019). Our empirical evidence revealed that the wish to help and alleviate suffering was not only directed at children but also arose from close personal encounters with migrants more generally. As one officer said, "you see the hopelessness of it. I have in a way understood it for several years, but now I can see the reality of what they are talking about" (PU4). Such experiences were often connected to physical closeness to suffering, as in the ethical appeal arising from "the living presence" of the Other described by Emmanuel Levinas (1969/1991). This presence is experienced and is different from, and not reducible to, words and ideas. While the bureaucratic apparatus is geared towards finding flaws and evidence of "cheating" and "bogusness" in migrant stories, such meetings open up a space for a different kind of understanding based on close encounters and physical proximity.

Such feelings of compassion also gave rise to a sense of moral discomfort. This discomfort was dealt with quite differently by those carrying out border control and is felt by some more acutely than others. Nevertheless, moral discomfort, amplified by intense public criticism, seems to be an inherent part of doing border control. Mary Bosworth's (2018: 1) study of immigration detention in the UK points to the "affective nature of wielding power at the border". While the study reveals that officers "turn away (deny) and switch off (emotionally withdraw) from those before them in order to do their job" (ibid.), our study discovered that the unease in some cases lead to outright resistance. In Chapter 3, we saw how the Norwegian union of senior police officers openly challenged high deportation performance targets as detrimental to their relations with local communities. In our interviews with police officers, references to the Second World War were not uncommon. Officers compared migrants' living conditions in Greece to "concentration camps" (Aas and Gundhus, 2015), and likened the moral and ethical challenges they encountered to those of the war. This is how one Frontex officer described his experiences:

> The most challenging part for me was what I talked about earlier. Well, it was so bad that my thoughts went to the dark sides of our European history. I started to think about – these are very personal thoughts – but I thought about those who collaborated under Nazism, who were involved, were they thinking the same as I am now? Did they try to find a way to justify it? Did they understand that what they were doing was wrong? Is it wrong? Should we be involved in this? Should we not be involved? I have a very large apparatus guarding my back, which in a way reassures me that this is good, but then you see, at least I see, that nothing happens. What's the point? Many such things. This part has been a challenge and we talked quite a bit about it down there, not exactly taking the same perspective, but about whether it was right for us to be involved. Are we contributing to something good or are we just helping Greece to do something wrong? ...
>
> I hope that my children and grandchildren can look back on what their father and grandfather did as something that was right, that he did something good – that this will not be a shadow in European history that I have contributed to. I really hope so.
>
> *(FRN2, Frontex screener in Aas and Gundhus, 2015)*

Although unexpected for us as researchers, the references to the Second World War revealed the morally charged nature of the situation. The Holocaust has, as Jeffrey Alexander observes (2009: 3), been "transformed into a generalized symbol of human suffering and moral evil". It symbolises the ultimate moral failure, an abyss. For the officers, the moral ambiguity of their actions, at its most acute, was expressed as a fear of repeating mistakes made in the past. One experienced officer working in the Oslo Police Department questioned the practices involved in searching for documents:

> A policeman who has never read about the war. That is not good. Right? ... Because the Norwegian police made serious mistakes during the war years. It is a shameful side of our history. It's not right for the police to start hunting down groups and minorities, which are not committing crime. Just because they are from one group of people. Well, this is wrong ... It is not like we wish to have 70-year-old grannies from Pakistan in police custody cells. What's the point, really?
>
> *(OPD)*

The statement reveals the moral doubt that frequently surrounds the exercise of penal power over migrants. Having 70-year-old grannies from Pakistan in police custody simply feels wrong. Wielding power at the border, as Bosworth (2018: 1) observes, comes at a cost. The excessive use of penal power often lacks a clear basis of moral legitimacy and can be "painful and corrosive, for staff and for detainees" (ibid.).

The narratives above do not offer alternative conceptions of justice and inclusion, but do reveal the limits to the othering of migrants that may emerge in face-to-face encounters. They open a window into a universe in which moral meaning is ascribed to individual acts and where simple words such as "decency", "good", and "wrong" represent an important perspective for understanding human actions. While European states are doing their utmost to limit their legal obligations towards unwanted strangers (Gammeltoft-Hansen and Vedsted-Hansen, 2017), the sense of moral obligation seems to be more difficult to disperse.

Notes

1 www.thirteen.org/tenement/baldap.html
2 http://m.bbc.co.uk/news/world-europe-17607155

3 See   http://wp.unil.ch/space/files/2018/03/SPACE-I-2016-Final-Rep
   ort-180315.pdf
4 www.stortinget.no/no/Saker-og-publikasjoner/Saker/Sak/?p=67575
5 Source: www.nytid.no/tortur_pa_norsk/
6 Risiko i et trygt samfunn — Samfunnssikkerhet [Risk in a safe society –
   Societal security] 13.9.3 Sektorovergripende fullmakts-bestemmelser
7 https://idcoalition.org/news/authoritative-guidance-immigration-detentio
   n-is-a-violation-of-childrens-rights/
8 www.msf.org/child-refugees-lesbos-are-increasingly-self-harming-and-a
   ttempting-suicide
9 www.nrk.no/norge/pu-vil-gjore-det-mer-skansomt-a-uttransportere-ba
   rn-1.14319280
10 www.vl.no/nyhet/flere-barn-skal-til-afghanistan-1.722666?paywall=true

CONCLUSION

The power of a metanarrative

> Pinned at the top of President Trump's Twitter feed Wednesday was a
> video. The man on the screen has a shaved head and a mustache and
> long chin hair. Smiling, he announces, "I killed f----- cops." The man
> is Luis Bracamontes, a twice-deported Mexican immigrant who was
> given the death penalty in April for killing two California law enforce-
> ment officers in 2014. At the time of the shootings, Bracamontes was in
> the United States illegally – and now, with the midterm election
> approaching, he's the star of the GOP's latest campaign ad. "Illegal
> immigrant, Luis Bracamontes, killed our people!" reads text on the 53-
> second video, which is filled with audible expletives. "Democrats let
> him into our country ... Democrats let him stay."
>
> (Washington Post, 2018)[1]

For many observers, the Luis Bracamontes video held an uncomfortable
resemblance to the infamous "Willie Horton" ads aired during the
1988 US presidential race (ibid.). The latter cemented the political
importance of the US "tough on crime" racial policies. The case cast a
long shadow and marked the "emergence of a populist punitive bipar-
tisan consensus" in US and UK politics (Newburn and Jones, 2005:
74). Penal populism and symbolic politics rely on the use of myths and
symbols about crime and offending to convey key political messages

about fear and social solidarity (Garland, 2001; Newburn and Jones, 2005; Pratt, 2007). "Toughness" became the key symbolic message to be adopted by politicians of all colours. It replaced more inclusive welfare-oriented policies and paved the way for massive expansion of the US prison complex.

The Bracamontes video is in many ways a paradigmatic example of populist symbolic messaging and of the political usage of the crimmigrant other. However, earlier lessons from penal populism have shown that the impact of symbolic politics on actual policy should not be overestimated and that there are considerable national variations (Newburn and Jones, 2005). Even though symbolic messages and discourses may travel from one national context to another and appear to have a global pattern, what practical impact they have is often difficult to predict. As Newburn and Sparks (2004: 11) point out, "we cannot and should not take for granted that surface similarities necessarily imply deeper convergencies". Punishment is deeply embedded in the national/cultural specificity of the environment which produces it (Melossi, 2004: 84). Also, when it comes to contemporary crimmigration policies, they change their character depending on their cultural settings (Van der Woude et al., 2017). Patterns of bordered penality exhibit considerable national differences. For example, while the UK and Greece excessively rely on the use of detention, Norway is quite restrictive in this respect. The country, on the other hand, relies heavily on deportation compared to many of its European counterparts (Van Houte and Leerkes, 2019). Even aspects that may appear as genuinely transnational, such as EU's migration-related databases SIS and Eurodac, show considerable national variation in their usage and implementation (Weber et al., 2019).

Moreover, the processes described in this book have not primarily focused on the populist political discourse, which is the most visible and frequently addressed aspect of the othering of migrants. Instead, the focus has been on the considerably quieter and "cooler", yet no less forceful, processes of bureaucratic production and constitution of migrants as particular penal subjects. Such processes were examined in one particular national context, as well as within the framework of the EU's external border governance. A challenge in understanding the social processes surrounding the crimmigrant other is to grasp aspects of both universality and cultural specificity, as well as to capture the processes that have long historic roots and those that are distinctly contemporary.

The crimmigrant other is, in many ways, an archaic figure; a reconfiguration of the stranger that becomes particularly pronounced in a time perceived as a time of crisis and social turmoil. One of the arguments of this book has been that he or she should not be understood simply as a perceived security threat to the nation state, but should be instead situated within a particular moral economy surrounding migration and border control. As Mary Douglas (1995: 90) succinctly observes, stereotyped belief in insidious damage of specific groups at a time of crisis "enables the community to restructure itself on previous lines by absolution from certain specified moral obligations". In the contemporary European context, these moral obligations are Europe's long-standing commitments to human rights. They are an ideal that is increasingly difficult to meet (Dembour, 2015; Gammeltoft-Hansen and Vedsted-Hansen, 2017), in a similar vein as the ideal of welfare and social inclusion of "everyone" that has become unattainable in Scandinavian societies (Barker, 2018).

The universal aspects of the crimmigrant other, as a stranger of our time, can perhaps be usefully understood as a form of a metanarrative. Although the contemporary condition is commonly seen as one that is essentially sceptical of metanarratives (Lyotard, 1984), several observers have found indication of their persistent salience. In their illuminating study of children's literature, Stephens and McCallum (1998) point out that stories are often told and retold according to some consistent cultural patterns. Such metanarratives offer "a global or totalizing cultural narrative schema which orders and explains knowledge and experience" (ibid.: 6). This does not mean that a story is same everywhere, but rather one that is instantly recognisable, yet with distinct cultural, historically specific, and local connotations. A metanarrative "expresses significant and universal human experiences, interlinks 'truth' and cultural heritage" and, importantly for the purpose of our discussion, it is informed by legitimising stances and "rests moral judgements within an ethical dimension" (ibid.: 7).

While not directly applicable, Stephens and McCallum's analysis may offer a fruitful perspective for understanding the figure of the crimmigrant other. As in children's literature, also when it comes to crime and deviance, stories can be told and retold in different versions, yet involving the *same* character (ibid.: ix). They engage mythologies that are built on particular social assumptions and are immediately recognisable to their audience (Presser and Sandberg, 2015). Although not offering a distinct narrative, the figure of the crimmigrant other is immediately recognisable and refers to long-standing patterns of social behaviour. It offers clarity at a time when this seems to be a social scarcity. Most importantly, its value lies in creating a universal imprint for legitimate and morally justified social exclusion.

The exclusion of the crimmigrant other – embodied in criminal and fraudulent asylum seekers, evil human smugglers, and violent Muslim men from the suburbs – has the power to invoke popular mythology and the potential to create unity across the ever more divided political spectrum. It seems self-evident and can transcend social divisions. Although shaped by bureaucratic and legal processes that give it concrete substance and anchorage, the figure of the crimmigrant other is also marked by vagueness and possesses almost mythical and haunting qualities. As an imprint for legitimate social exclusion, the figure involves "recycling" of particular frames for ethical social action that are deeply imprinted in our cultural understanding of a good society (Stephens and McCallum, 1998: xi). Just as walls and borders, as Wendy Brown (2010) observes, represent cultural objects of desire, harbouring fantasies of containment, impermeability, security, innocence, and goodness, so does the exclusion of the treacherous stranger recreate a universal fantasy about purity and the power of social boundaries. Seen in this perspective, contemporary European responses to migration do not call for analytical perspectives that reiterate the importance of the novel and the unprecedented, but rather show the relevance of classical sociological, criminological, and anthropological insights.

Any community, as Douglas (1995: 99) observes, is liable to try to control its boundary by engaging in blaming behaviour, such as "accusing the fringes of harbouring infection or limiting the influx of poverty-stricken strangers by a theory of imported disease". Such dynamics are shaping the boundary constitution of any society. Similarly, ever since Durkheim, studies of punishment's role in society have pointed at the importance of penal power for the maintenance of social boundaries. This line of thought has shown that the use of penal power should not only be understood instrumentally, defined by the objectives of social control, but also as a moral institution (Smith, 2008; Garland, 2013a). Through the control of the crimmigrant other, contemporary modalities of penal power are a central mechanism for guarding the boundaries of citizenship. They mobilise notions of innocence, goodness, right, and wrong in the processes of the making and unmaking of contemporary membership and belonging.

The growing use of penal power at the border speaks of the increasingly contentious and privileged nature of Northern citizenship and residence rights in a deeply unequal global order. This book's contribution lies in pointing out that the use of force at the border is not simply a question of practical implementation of more exclusionary, even militarised, border policies but, crucially, also a question of assigning blame and (re)imagining the national in moral terms. Questions of who should be let in across the borders, what kind of treatment and what rights they deserve are about who "we" are as a community. While essentially an issue of allocation of resources and access to welfare, the crimmigrant immigrant becomes a mode of transforming questions of global privilege into a question of criminality and an issue of maintenance of the moral order. He or she becomes a symbolic representation of justified social exclusion.

The findings point not only to the limits of seeing contemporary use of penal measures at the border simply as a question of securitisation, power, and efficiency, but also to the value of cultural understandings of penality. As Philip Smith (2008: 170–171) points out:

> Punishment is not simply about regulating the politically dangerous or economically costly nor even maintaining the "social order" and ensuring system stability … Rather it is about eliminating the disgusting and the unruly, effecting the decontamination of the spiritually and morally offensive, banishing evil, and enforcing cultural classifications and boundaries by shutting down liminal possibilities.

The book presented an argument that hierarchies of global mobility, shaped by long-standing colonial and racial legacies, are being transformed into moral hierarchies of migrants. Distinctions between deserving and non-deserving, "the Good, the Bad and the Ugly" (Kmak, 2015), the victims and the offenders, refugees and "other migrants" (Costello, 2018), in central ways shape the exercise of penal power at the border. This power, I have argued, is wielded within an intricate moral economy (see also Fassin, 2005). European borders can be at several levels described as humanitarian borderlands (Aas and Gundhus, 2015) and are marked by constantly shifting boundaries of law, as well as its absences. Such activities, although seemingly legal, are – for those tasked with performing them on the ground – ethically deeply ambiguous and create a desire for moral clarity. This book has shown that doubt and moral discomfort is visible in the use of analogies with the situation during the Second World War and may at times result in open critique.

Ambivalence, as Zygmunt Bauman (1998) reminds us, may in itself not be a problem. On the contrary, it is morality's "natural habitat and signals a state of health. Ambivalence is the only soil in which morality can grow and the only territory in which the moral self can act on its responsibility" (ibid.: 22). The figure of the crimmigrant other may ease some of the moral discomfort produced by exclusionary border policies by turning the focus towards illegality and the combating of various evils, such as terrorism, human smuggling, and trafficking. In that respect, as earlier criminological studies have shown, deviance can be a "valuable resource" in a society (Erikson, 1966). Yet, maybe here lies the most corrosive aspect of the work done by the crimmigrant other: the numbing of moral unease and neutralisation of guilt at a time when society is faced with an acute ethical challenge. By placing the blame for migrant mortality at the border on the unscrupulous smuggling networks, the processes of construction of the crimmigrant other are fundamentally reshaping the nature of European societies. As Douglas (1999: 100) points out, through the processes of allocation of blame, "community constitutes itself also in a struggle for power between its members". Just as the Willie Horton case was emblematic of a profound penological and social change that reshaped the entire political landscape, on the left and right, so too a question may be asked about the long-term social consequences of the current developments. What are the long-term prospects of Scandinavian societies as inclusionary and exceptional, or the European Union as a continent committed to human rights?

Note

1 www.washingtonpost.com/nation/2018/11/01/democrats-let-him-into-our-country-trumps-new-ad-links-opponents-illegal-immigrant-killer-its-far-worse-than-infamous-willie-horton-ad-say-critics/?utm_term=.4a1588517721

REFERENCES

Aas, K.F. (2006) "'The Body Does Not Lie': Identity, Risk and Trust in Technoculture". *Crime, Media, Culture*, 2(2): 143–158.

Aas, K.F. (2011) "Crimmigrant Bodies and Bona Fide Travellers: Surveillance, Citizenship and Global Governance". *Theoretical Criminology*, 15(3): 331–346.

Aas, K.F. (2013a) "The Ordered and the Bordered Society: Migration Control, Citizenship and the Northern Penal State". In K.F. Aas and M. Bosworth (eds.), *Migration and Punishment: Citizenship, Crime Control, and Social Exclusion*. Oxford: Oxford University Press.

Aas, K.F. (2013b) *Globalization and Crime*. London: Sage.

Aas, K.F. (2014). "Bordered Penality: Precarious Membership and Abnormal Justice". *Punishment & Society*, 16(5): 520–541.

Aas, K.F. and Bosworth, M. (eds.) (2013) *The Borders of Punishment: Migration, Citizenship, and Social Exclusion*. Oxford: Oxford University Press.

Aas, K.F. and Gundhus, H.I. (2015). "Policing Humanitarian Borderlands: Frontex, Human Rights and the Precariousness of Life". *British Journal of Criminology*, 55(1):1–18.

Abraham, I. and van Schendel, W. (2005) "Introduction: The making of illicitness", in I. Abraham and W. van Schendel (eds.), *Illicit Flows and Criminal Things: States, Borders, and the Other Side of Globalization*. Bloomington and Indianapolis: Indiana University Press.

Adler-Nissen, R. and Gammeltoft-Hansen, T. (eds.) (2008) *Instrumentalizing State Sovereignty in Europe and Beyond*. Basingstoke: Palgrave Macmillan.

Aebi, M.F., Berger-Kolopp, L., Burkhardt, C., Chopin, J., Hashimoto, Y.Z. and Tiago, M.M. (2019) *Foreign Offenders in Prison and Probation in Europe: Trends from 2005 to 2015 (Inmates) and Situation in 2015 (Inmates and Probationers)*. Strasbourg: Council of Europe.

Agamben, G. (1998) *Homo Sacer: Sovereign Power and Bare Life*. Stanford, California: Stanford University Press.

Agamben, G. (2004) "Bodies Without Words: Against the Biopolitical Tattoo". *German Law Journal*, 5(2): 168–169.

Agamben, G. (2005) *State of Exception*. Chicago: University of Chicago Press.

Ahmed, S. (2000) *Strange Encounters: Embodied Others in Post-Coloniality*. London and New York: Routledge.

Alexander, J. (2009) "The Social Construction of Moral Universals". In J. Alexander (ed.), *Remembering the Holocaust: A Debate*. Oxford: Oxford University Press.

Aliverti, A. (2012) "Making People Criminal: The Role of the Criminal Law in Immigration Enforcement". *Theoretical Criminology*, 16(4): 417–434.

Aliverti, A. (2013) *Crimes of Mobility*. Abingdon: Routledge.

Andersen, S.N., Holtsmark, B. and Mohn, S.B. (2017) *Kriminalitet blant innvandrere og norskfødte med innvandrerforeldre: En analyse av registerdata for perioden 1992–2015*. Oslo: Statistics Norway.

Anderson, B. (2006) *Imagined Communities: Reflections on the Origin and Spread of Nationalism*. London: Verso.

Anderson, B. (2013) *Us and Them? The Dangerous Politics of Immigration Controls*. Oxford: Oxford University Press.

Anderson, C. (2016) "Transnational Histories of Penal Transportation: Punishment, Labour and Governance in the British Imperial World, 1788–1939" in *Australian Historical Studies*, vol. 37 (3): 381–397.

Andersson, R. (2014) *Illegality, Inc.: Clandestine Migration and the Business of Bordering Europe*. Oakland, California: University of California Press.

Andersson, R. (2016) "Europe's Failed 'Fight' Against Irregular Migration: Ethnographic Notes on a Counterproductive Industry". *Journal of Ethnic and Migration Studies*, 42(7): 1055–1075.

Andreas, P. (2000) *Border Games: Policing the US–Mexico Divide*. Ithaca and London: Cornell University Press.

Andreas, P. (2013) *Smuggler Nation: How Illicit Trade Made America*. Oxford: Oxford University Press.

Andreas, P. and Greenhill, K.M. (eds.) (2010) *Sex, Drugs and Body Counts: The Politics of Numbers in Global Crime and Conflict*. New York: Cornell University Press.

Andreas, P. and Nadelmann, E. (2006) *Policing the Globe: Criminalization and Crime Control in International Relations*. Oxford: Oxford University Press.

Andreas, P. and Price, R. (2001) "From War Fighting to Crime Fighting: Transforming the American National Security State". *International Studies Review*, 3(3): 31–52.

Aradau, K. (2004) "The Perverse Politics of Four-Letter Words: Risk and Pity in the Securitisation of Human Trafficking". *Millennium: Journal of International Studies*, 33(2): 251–278.

Arentzen, S.B. (2013) *Velbegrunnet varetekt? En studie av førstegangsfengslinger fra Oslo tingrett, med særlig henblikk på betydningen av den siktedes statsborgerskap ved rettens begrunnelse for bruk av varetektsfengsel*. Oslo: Faculty of Law, University of Oslo.

Armenta, A. (2017) *Protect, Serve and Deprt: The Rise of Policing as Immigration Enforcement*. Oakland: University of California Press.

Ashworth, A. and Zedner, L. (2014) *Preventive Justice*. Oxford: Oxford University Press.

Balibar, E. (2010) "At the Borders of Citizenship: A Democracy in Transition?" *European Journal of Social Theory*, 13(3): 315–322.

Barker, V. (2013) "Nordic Exceptionalism Revisited: Explaining the Paradox of a Janus-Faced Penal Regime". *Theoretical Criminology*, 17(1): 5–25.

Barker, V. (2017) "Nordic Vagabonds: The Roma and the Logic of Benevolent Violence in the Swedish Welfare State". *European Journal of Criminology*, 14(1): 120–139.

Barker, V. (2018) *Nordic Nationalism and Penal Order: Walling the Welfare State*. Abingdon: Routledge.

Basaran, T. and Guild, E. (2017) "Mobilities, Ruptures, Transitions". In T. Basaran, D. Bigo, E.-P. Guittet and R.B.J. Walker (eds.), *International Political Sociology: Transversal Lines*. Abingdon: Routledge.

Bauman, Z. (1992) "Soil, Blood and Identity". *Sociological Review*, 40(4): 675–701.

Bauman, Z. (1998) "What Prospects of Morality in Times of Uncertainty?" *Theory, Culture & Society*, 15(1): 11–22.

Becker, H.S. (1963) Outsiders: Studies in the Sociology of Deviance. New York: Free Press.

Bendixen, S. and Wyller, T. (2019b) *Contested Hospitalities in a Time of Migration: Religious and Secular Counterspaces in the Nordic Region*. Abingdon: Routledge.

Benhabib, S. (2004) *The Rights of Others: Aliens, Residents and Citizens*. Cambridge: Cambridge University Press.

Benton, L. (2010) A Search for Sovereignty: Law and Geography in European Empires, 1400–1900, New York: Cambridge University Press.

Bergkvist, J. (2008) "En Haard og Dyr Tid" – Fattigdom, tigging og løsgjengerii Christiania 1790–1802". Master's thesis. Oslo: University of Oslo.

Bhui, H.S. (2016) "The Place of 'Race' in Understanding Immigration Control and the Detention of Foreign Nationals". *Criminology & Criminal Justice*, 16(3): 267–285.

Bigo, D. (2006) "Security, Exception, Ban and Surveillance" in D. Lyon (ed.) *Theorizing Surveillance: The Panopticon and Beyond*. Cullompton: Willan Publishing.

Bigo, D., Carrera, S. and Guild, E. (eds.) (2013) *Foreigners, Refugees or Minorities? Rethinking People in the Context of Border Controls and Visas*. Burlington, VT: Ashgate Publishing.

Bosniak, L. (2006) *The Citizen and the Alien: Dilemmas of Contemporary Membership*. Princeton, NJ: Princeton University Press.

Bosworth, M. (2012) "Subjectivity and Identity in Detention: Punishment and Society in a Global Age". *Theoretical Criminology*, 16(2): 123–140.

Bosworth, M. (2013) "Can Immigration Detention Centres be Legitimate? Understanding Confinement in a Global World". In K.F. Aas and M. Bosworth (eds.), *The Borders of Punishment Migration, Citizenship, and Social Exclusion*. Oxford: Oxford University Press.

Bosworth, M. (2014) *Inside Immigration Detention*. Oxford: Oxford University Press.

Bosworth, M. (2017) "Penal Humanitarianism? Sovereign Power in an Era of Mass Migration". *New Criminal Law Review*, 20(1): 39–65.

Bosworth, M. (2018) "Affect and Authority in Immigration Detention". *Punishment & Society*. Published online 18 October. doi:10.177/1462474518803321

Bosworth, M. and Flavin, J. (eds.) (2007) *Race, Gender and Punishment: From Colonialism to the War on Terror*. New Brunswick, NJ: Rutgers University Press.

Bosworth, M. and Guild, M. (2008) "Governing Through Migration Control: Security and Citizenship in Britain". *British Journal of Criminology*, 48(6): 703–719.

Bosworth, M. and Kaufman, E. (2011) "Foreigners in a Carceral Age: Immigration and Imprisonment in the US". *Stanford Law & Policy Review*, 22(1): 429–456.

Bosworth, M., Parmar, A. and Vazquez, Y. (2017) *Race, Criminal Justice, and Migration Control: Enforcing the Boundaries of Belonging*. Oxford: Oxford University Press.

Bosworth, M., Franko, K. and Pickering, S. (2018) "Punishment, Globalization and Migration Control: 'Get Them the Hell out of Here'". *Punishment & Society*, 20(1): 34–53.

Bourgois, P. and Schonberg, J. (2009) *Righteous Dopefiend*. Berkeley: University of California Press.

Bowling, B. and Westenra, S. (2018). "'A Really Hostile Environment': Adiaphorization, Global Policing and the Crimmigration Control System". *Theoretical Criminology Journal*: 1–21. doi:10.2139/ssrn.3145786.

Brachet, J. (2018) "Manufacturing Smugglers: From Irregular to Clandestine Mobility in the Sahara". *ANNALS of the American Academy of Political and Social Science*, 676(1): 16–35.

Bradford, B. and Jackson, J. (2018) "Police Legitimacy Among Immigrants in Europe: Institutional Frames and Group Position". *European Journal of Criminology*, 15(5): 567–588.

Bradford, B. and Loader, I. (2016) "Police, Crime and Order: The Case of Stop and Search". In B. Bradford, B. Jauregui and I. Loader and J. Steinberg (eds.), *The SAGE Handbook of Global Policing*. London: Sage.

Brekke, J.-P., Birkvad, S.R. and Erdal, M.B. (2019) *Losing the Right to Stay: Revocation of immigrant residence permits and citizenship in Norway – Experiences and Effects*. Oslo: Institute for Social Research/Institutt for Samfunnsforskning.

Broeders, D. and Hampshire, J. (2013) "Dreaming of Seamless Borders: ICTs and the Pre-emptive Governance of Mobility in Europe". *Journal of Ethnic and Migration Studies*, 39(8): 1201–1218.

Brotherton, D.C. and Barrios, L. (2009) "Displacement and Stigma: The Social-Psychological Crisis of the Deportee". *Crime, Media, Culture*, 5(1): 29–55.

Brouwer, J. (2019) "Detection, Detention, Deportation: Criminal Justice and Migration Control Through the Lens of Crimmigration". PhD thesis, Leiden University.

Brouwer, J., Van der Woude, M. and Van der Leun, J. (2017). "Framing Migration and the Process of Crimmigration: A Systematic Analysis of the Media Representation of Unauthorized Immigrants in the Netherlands". *European Journal of Criminology*, 14(1): 100–119.

Brouwer, J., Van der Woude, M.A.H. and Van der Leun, J.P. (2018). "Border Policing, Procedural Justice and Belonging. The Legitimacy of (Cr)immigration Controls in Border Areas". *British Journal of Criminology*, 58(3): 624–642.

Brown, W. (2010) *Walled States, Waning Sovereignty*. New York: Zone Books.

Butler, J. (2006) *Precarious Life: The Power of Mourning and Violence*. London and New York: Verso.

Calavita, K. (2005) *Immigrants at the Margins: Law, Race, and Exclusion in Southern Europe*. Cambridge: Cambridge University Press.

Caldwell, B. (2012) "Banished for Life: Deportation of Juvenile Offenders as Cruel and Unusual Punishment". *Cardoso Law Review*, 34: 2261–2311.

Campesi, G. (2015) "Hindering the Deportation Machine: An Ethnography of Power and Resistance in Immigration Detention". *Punishment & Society*, 17(4): 427–445.

Canveren, Ö. and Akgül Durakcay, F. (2017) "The Analysis of the Hungarian Government's Discourse towards the Migrant Crisis: A Combination of Securitization and Euroscepticism". *YÖNETİM VE EKONOMİ* vol 24 (3): 857-876.

Caplan, J. and Torpey, J. (2001) *Documenting Individual Identity: The Development of State Practices in the Modern World*. Princeton, NJ: Princeton University Press.

Carens, J.H. (2015) *The Ethics of Immigration*. Oxford: Oxford University Press.

Carling, J. and Hernández-Carretero, M. (2011) "Protecting Europe and Protecting Migrants? Strategies for Managing Unauthorised Migration from Africa". *British Journal of Politics and International Relations*, 13(1): 42–58.

Carrera, S. and Cortinovis, R. (2019) *Search and Rescue, Disembarkation and Relocation Arrangements in the Mediterranean: Sailing Away from Responsibility?* Brussels: Centre for European Policy Studies. Available at www.ceps.eu/cep s-publications/search-and-rescue-disembarkation-and-relocation-arrangem ents-in-the-mediterranean/

Carrera, S., Mitsilegas, V., Allsopp, J. and Vosyliüté, L. (2019) *Policing Humanitarianism: EU Policies Against Human Smuggling and Their Impact on Civil Society*. Oxford: Hart Publishing/Bloomsbury.

Casella Colombeau, S. (2017) "Policing the Internal Schengen Borders – Managing the Double Bind Between Free Movement and Migration Control". *Policing and Society*, 14(1): 63–77.

Cavadino, M. and Dignan, J. (2006) *Penal Systems: A Comparative Approach*. London: Sage.

Ceuppens, B. and Geschiere, P. (2005) "Autochthony: Local or Global? New Modes in the Struggle over Citizenship and Belonging in Africa and Europe". *Annual Review of Anthropology*, 34: 385–407.

Cheliotis, L. (guest ed.) (2013) Special Section: Immigration Detention Around Europe. *European Journal of Criminology*, 10(6): 690–759.

Christie, N. (1981) *Limits to Pain*. Oslo: Universitetsforlaget.

Christie, N. (2004) *A Suitable Amount of Crime*. London: Routledge.

Christie, N. (2009) *Små ord for store spørsmål*. Oslo: Universitetsforlaget.

Christie, N. and Bruun, K. (1985). *Den Gode Fiende* [The Suitable Enemy]. Oslo: Universitetsforlaget.

Coates, T.-N. (2017) "Foreword". In T. Morrison, *The Origin of Others (The Charles Eliot Norton Lectures)*, Harvard, MA: Harvard University Press.

Cohen, S. (1972/2002) *Folk Devils and Moral Panics*. London: Routledge.

Collier, P. (2013) *Exodus: How Migration is Changing Our World*. Oxford: Oxford University Press.

Collier, S.J. and Ong, A. (2005) "Global Assemblages, Anthropological Problems". In A. Ong and S.J. Collier (eds.), *Global Assemblages: Technology, Politics and Ethics as Anthropological Problems*. Oxford: Blackwell Publishing.

Comaroff, J.L. and Comaroff, J. (2006) "Law and Disorder in the Postcolony: An Introduction". In J. Comaroff and J.L. Comaroff (eds.), *Law and Disorder in the Postcolony*. Chicago: University of Chicago Press.

Cornelisse, G. (2010) *Immigration Detention and Human Rights: Rethinking Territorial Sovereignty*. Leiden and Boston: Martinus Nijhof.

Costello, C. (2018) "Refugees and (Other) Migrants: Will the Global Compacts Ensure Safe Flight and Onward Mobility for Refugees?" *International Journal of Refugee Law*, 30(4): 643–649.

Council of Europe (2006) "Resolution 1509 (2006): Human Rights of Irregular Migrants". Strasbourg: Council of Europe.

Coutin, S.B. (2005) "Contesting Criminality: Illegal Immigration and the Spatialization of Legality". *Theoretical Criminology*, 9(1): 5–33.

Coutin, S.B. (2007) *Nations of Emigrants: Shifting Boundaries of Citizenship in El Salvador and the United States*. Ithaca, NY: Cornell University Press.

Coutin, S.B. (2010) "Exiled by Law: Deportation and the Inviability of Life". In N. De Genova and N. Peutz (eds.), *The Deportation Regime: Sovereignty, Space, and the Freedom of Movement*, Durham, NC: Duke University Press.

Coutin, S.B. (2015) "Deportation Studies: Origins, Themes and Directions". *Journal of Ethnic and Migration Studies*, 41(4): 671–681.

Daems, T., van Zyl Smit, D. and Snacken, S. (eds.) (2013) *European Penology?* Oxford and Portland, OR: Hart Publishing.

Dauvergne, C. (2008) *Making People Illegal*. Cambridge: Cambridge University Press.

Debord, G. (1994) *Society of the Spectacle*. London: Rebel Press.

De Genova, N. (2002) "Migrant 'Illegality' and Deportability in Everyday Life". *Annual Review of Anthropology*, 31: 419–447.

De Genova, N. (2013) "Spectacles of Migrant 'Illegality': The Scene of Exclusion, the Obscene of Inclusion". *Ethnic and Racial Studies*, 36(7): 1180–1198.

De Genova, N. (2018) "The 'Migrant Crisis' as Racial Crisis: Do Black Lives Matter in Europe?" *Ethnic and Racial Studies*, 41(10): 1765–1782.

De Genova, N. and Peutz, N.M. (eds.) (2010) *The Deportation Regime: Sovereignty, Space, and the Freedom of Movement*. Durham, NC: Duke University Press.

De Giorgi, A. (2013) "Punishment and Political Economy". In J. Simon and R. Sparks (eds.), *The SAGE Handbook of Punishment and Society*. London: Sage.

De León, J. (2015) *The Land of Open Graves: Living and Dying on the Migrant Trail*. Oakland: University of California Press.

De Vito, C.G. (2018) "Punitive Entanglements: Connected Histories of Penal Transportation, Deportation, and Incarceration in the Spanish Empire (1830s–1898)". *International Review of Social History*, 63: 169–189.

Dembour, M.-B. (2015) *When Humans Become Migrants: Study of the European Court of Human Rights with an Inter-American Counterpoint*. Oxford: Oxford University Press.

Dembour, M.-B. and Kelly, T. (2011) *Are Human Rights for Migrants? Critical Reflections on the Status of Irregular Migrants in Europe and the United States*. Abingdon: Routledge.

Donnan, H. and Wilson, T.M. (1999) *Borders: Frontiers of Identity, Nation and State*. Oxford: Berg.

Douglas, M. (1995) *Purity and Danger: An Analysis of the Concepts of Pollution and Taboo*. London: Routledge.

Duff, A. (2010) "A Criminal Law for Citizens". *Theoretical Criminology*, 14(3): 293–309.

Eagly, I.V. (2010) "Prosecuting Immigration". *Northwestern University Law Review*, 104: 1281–1359.

Edelman, M. (2015) "E.P. Thompson and Moral Economies". In D. Fassin (ed.), *A Companion to Moral Anthropology*. Oxford: Wiley Blackwell.

Engebrigtsen, A. (2012) *Tiggerbander og kriminelle bakmenn eller fattige EU-borgere? Myter og realiteter om utelandske tiggere i Oslo*. Oslo: NOVA.

Eriksen, T.H. and Jakoubek, M. (2019) "Introduction: Ethnic Groups, Boundaries and Beyond". In T.H. Eriksen and M. Jakoubek (eds.), *Ethnic Groups and Boundaries Today: A Legacy of Fifty Years*. Abingdon and New York: Routledge.

Erikson, K.T. (1966) *Wayward Puritans: A Study in the Sociology of Deviance*. New York: Macmillan.

EULISA (2018) "SIS II – 2017 Statistics". Available at www.eulisa.europa.eu/Publications/Reports/2017%20SIS%20II%20Statistics.pdf

Ewing, K.P. (2008) *Stolen Honor: Stigmatizing Muslim Men in Berlin*. Stanford, CA: Stanford University Press.

Fangen, K. and Kjærre, H.A. (2013) "Ekskludert av staten, inkludert i hva?: opplevelser av inkludering og ekskludering blant illegaliserte migranter i Norge". In N.B. Johansen, T. Ugelvik and K.F. Aas (eds.), *Krimmigrasjon? Den nye kontrollen av de fremmede*. Oslo: Universitetsforlaget.

Fassin, D. (2005) "Compassion and Repression: The Moral Economy of Immigration Policies in France". *Cultural Anthropology*, 20(3): 362–387.

Fassin, D. (2012) *Humanitarian Reason: A Moral History of the Present*. Berkeley: University of California Press.

Fassin, D. (2013) *Enforcing Order: An Ethnography of Urban Policing*. Cambridge: Polity Press.

Fassin, D. (ed.) (2015) *A Companion to Moral Anthropology*. Oxford: Wiley Blackwell.

Feeley, M. M. (2002) "Entrepreneurs of Punishment: The Legacy of Privatization". *Punishment & Society*, 4(3): 321–344.

Fink, M. (2018) *Frontex and Human Rights: Responsibility in "Multi-Actor Situations" Under the ECHR and EU Public Liability Law*. Oxford: Oxford University Press.

Flaatten, S. (2017) *Høyesterett, straffen og tyveriene: Straffeutmålingsbegrunnelser i etterkrigstiden*. Oslo: Universitetsforlaget.

Foucault, M. (1977) *Discipline and Punish: The Birth of the Prison*, trans. A. Sheridan. New York: Vintage Books.

Franko, K. and Gundhus, H.O.I. (2015) "A Divided Fraternity. Transnational Police Cultures, Proximity, and Loyalty". *European Journal of Policing Studies*, 3(2): 162–183.

Franko, K. and Gundhus, H.O.I. (2019) "Moral Discomfort at the Border: Understanding Penal Humanitarianism in Practice". Available at www.law.ox.ac.uk/research-subject-groups/centre-criminology/centreborder-criminologies/blog/2019/03/moral-discomfort

Franko, K. and Mohn, S.B. (2015) "Utvising som straff?" *Tidsskrift for strafferett*, 2: 153–176.

Franko, K., Van der Woude, M. and Barker, V. (2019) "Beacons of Tolerance Dimmed? Migration, Criminalization, and Inhospitality in Welfare States". In S. Bendixen and T. Wyller (eds.), *Contested Hospitalities in a Time of Migration: Religious and Secular Counterspaces in the Nordic Region*. London: Routledge.

Fraser, N. (2008) *Scales of Justice*. Cambridge: Polity Press.

Frontex (2010) *Beyond the Frontiers. Frontex: The First Five Years*. Warsaw: Frontex.

Frontex (2017) *Risk Analysis for 2017*. Available at https://frontex.europa.eu/assets/Publications/Risk_Analysis/Annual_Risk_Analysis_2017.pdf

Frontex (2018) *Risk Analysis for 2018*. Available at https://frontex.europa.eu/publications/risk-analysis-for-2018-aJ5nJu

Galvin, T.M. (2015) "'We Deport Them but They Keep Coming Back': The Normalcy of Deportation in the Daily Life of 'Undocumented' Zimbabwean Migrant Workers in Botswana". *Journal of Ethnic and Migration Studies*, 41(4): 617–634.

Gammeltoft-Hansen, T. (2011) *Access to Asylum: International Refugee Law and the Globalization of Migration Control*. Cambridge: Cambridge University Press.

Gammeltoft-Hansen, T. (2017) "Refugee Policy as 'Negative Nation Branding': The Case of Denmark and the Nordics". *Danish Foreign Policy Yearbook*: 99–125.

Gammeltoft-Hansen, T. (2018) "International Cooperation on Migration Control: Towards a Research Agenda for Refugee Law". *European Journal of Migration and Law*, 20(4): 373–395.

Gammeltoft-Hansen, T. and Vested-Hansen, J. (eds.) (2017) *Human Rights and the Dark Side of Globalisation: Transnational Law Enforcement and Migration Control*. Abingdon: Routledge.

García Hernández, C.C. (2015) *Crimmigration Law*. Chicago: American Bar Association.

Garelli, G. and Tazzioli, M. (2018) "The Humanitarian War Against Migrant Smugglers at Sea". *Antipode*, 50(3): 685–703.

Garland, D. (1985/1918) *Punishment and Welfare: A History of Penal Strategies*, 2nd edition. New Orleans, MO: Quid Pro Books.

Garland, D. (1990) *Punishment and Modern Society*. Oxford: Clarendon Press.

Garland, D. (2001) *The Culture of Control: Crime and Social Order in Contemporary Society*. Oxford: Oxford University Press.

Garland, D. (2013a) "Punishment and Social Solidarity". In J. Simon and R. Sparks (eds.), *The SAGE Handbook of Punishment and Society*. London: Sage.

Garland, D. (2013b) "Penality and the Penal State". *Criminology*, 51(3): 475–517.

Garner, S. (2015) "Crimmigration: When Criminology (Nearly) Met the Sociology of Race and Ethnicity". *Sociology of Race and Ethnicity*, vol. 1 (1): 198–203.

Garufo, F. and Maire, C. (2019) "Culturalisation of Gender: When Ivan Meets Maria". In B. Lüthi and D. Skenderovic (eds.), *Switzerland and Migration*. Basingstoke: Palgrave Macmillan.

Geddes, A. and Scholten, P. (2016) *The Politics of Migration and Immigration in Europe*. London: Sage.

Geschiere, P. (2009) *The Perils of Belonging: Autochtony, Citizenship and Exclusion in Africa and Europe*. Chicago: University of Chicago Press.

Gibney, M. J. (2013) "Deportation, Crime, and the Changing Character of Membership in the United Kingdom". In K.F. Aas and M. Bosworth (eds.), *The Borders of Punishment Migration, Citizenship, and Social Exclusion*. Oxford: Oxford University Press.

Gilman, N., Goldhammer, J. and Weber, S. (2011) *Deviant Globalization: Black Market Economy in the 21st Century*. New York and London: Continuum.

Goodin, R.E. (1997) "Conventions and Conversions, or, Why is Nationalism Sometimes so Nasty?" In R. McKim and J. McMahan (eds.), *The Morality of Nationalism*. Oxford: Oxford University Press.

Götz, N. (2015) "'Moral Economy': Its Conceptual History and Analytical Prospects". *Journal of Global Ethics*, 11(2): 147–162.

Green, D.A. (2008) *When Children Kill Children: Penal Populism and Political Culture*. Oxford: Oxford University Press.

Griffiths, M. (2017) "Foreign, Criminal: A Doubly Damned Modern British Folk-Devil". *Citizenship Studies*, 21(5): 527–546.

Guia, M.J., Van Der Woude, M. and Van Der Leun, J. (2013) *Social Control and Justice: Crimmigration in the Age of Fear*. The Hague: Eleven International Publishing.

Guild, E. (2009) *Security and Migration in the 21st Century*. Cambridge: Polity Press.

Gundhus, H.O.I. (2016) "Å målstyre skjønnsutøvelse: Profesjonalisering av politiets utlendingskontroll". *Sosiologi i dag*, 46(1): 54–79.

Gundhus, H.O.I. (2020) "Sorting Out Welfare: Crimmigration Practices and Abnormal Justice in Norway". In R. Koulish and M. Van der Woude (eds.), *Crimmigrant Nations: Resurgent Nationalism and the Closing of Borders*. New York: Fordham University Press.

Gundhus, H.O.I. and Egge, M. (2013) "Grenser for forebygging? 'De unge fremmede og kriminalitetsforebyggende politiarbeid'". In N.B. Johansen, T. Ugelvik and K.F. Aas (eds.), *Krimmigrasjon? Den nye kontrollen av de fremmede*. Oslo: Universitetsforlaget.

Gundhus, H.O.I. and Franko, K. (2016) "Global Policing and Mobility: Identity, Territory, Sovereignty". In B. Bradford, B. Jauregui, I. Loader and J. Steinberg (eds.), *SAGE Handbook of Global Policing*. London: Sage.

Gundhus, H.O.I. and Jansen, P. (2019) "Policing Migrants as Pre-Crime: Antici-patory Action and Management of Concerns". *Theoretical Criminology*. Available at https://journals.sagepub.com/doi/full/10.1177/1362480619873347

Haggerty, K.D. and Ericson, R.V. (2000) "The Surveillant Assemblage". *British Journal of Sociology*, 51(4): 605–622.

Hansson, J. (2017) "Mind the Blues: Swedish Police Officers' Mental Health and Forced Deportation of Unaccompanied Refugee Children". PhD thesis, Umeå University.

Hart, H.L.A. (2008) *Punishment and Responsibility: Essays in the Philosophy of Law*, 2nd edition. Oxford: Oxford University Press.

Hasselberg, I. (2016) *Enduring Uncertainty: Deportation, Punishment and Everyday Life*. New York and Oxford: Berghahn Books.

Heinemann, T., Helén, I., Lemke, T., Naue, U. and Weiss, M.G. (eds.) (2016) *Suspect Families: DNA Analysis, Family Reunification and Immigration Policies*. Abingdon: Routledge.

Himmelfarb, G. (1991) *Poverty and Compassion: The Moral Imagination of the Late Victorians*. New York: Alfred A. Knopf.

Hobbs, D. and Dunnighan, C. (1998) "Glocal Organized Crime: Context and Pretext". In V. Ruggiero*et al.* (eds.), *The New European Criminology: Crime and Social Order*. London: Routledge.

Holmberg, L. (2000) "Discretionary Leniency and Typological Guilt: Results from a Danish Study of Police Discretion". *Journal of Scandinavian Studies in Criminology and Crime Prevention*, 1(2): 179–194.

Holzberg, B., Kolbe, K. and Zaborowski, R. (2018) "Figures of Crisis: The Deli-neation of (Un)Deserving Refugees in the German Media". *Sociology*, 52(3): 534–550.

Honig, B. (2001) *Democracy and the Foreigner*. Princeton, NJ: Princeton Uni-versity Press.

House of Lords (2017) *European Union Committee, 2nd Report of Session 2017–19: Operation Sophia: A Failed Mission*. Available at https://publications.pa rliament.uk/pa/ld201719/ldselect/ldeucom/5/5.pdf

Humlen, A. and Myhre, J.W. (2014) *Advokatforeningens aksjonsog prosedyregruppe i utlendingsrett 2007–2014: Rapport fra virksomheten og forslag til regelendringer*. Oslo: Den Norske Advokatforening.

Husabø, J.E. and Suominen, A. (2011) *Forholdet mellom straffeprosesslovens og utlen-dingslovens regler om fengsling og andre tvangsmidler: En utredning avgitt til Justisde-partementet* [The Relationship Between Criminal Procedure Rules and Immigration Law Rules Regarding Imprisonment and Other Use of Force: A Report Delivered to the Ministry of Justice]. Bergen: University of Bergen.

Huysmans, J. (2006) *The Politics of Insecurity: Fear, Migration and Asylum in the EU*. London and New York: Routledge.

Iliadou, E. (2019) "Safe Havens and Prison Islands: The Politics of Protection and Deterrence of Border Crossers on Lesvos Island". *Graduate Journal of Social Science*. 15(1): 1–31.

IOM (2017) *Fatal Journeys Volume 3 Part 1: Improving Data on Missing Migrants.* Available at https://publications.iom.int/books/fatal-journeys-volume-3-part-1-improving-data-missing-migrants

Jahnsen, S. and Skilbrei, M.-L. (2018) "Leaving No Stone Unturned: The Borders and Orders of Transnational Prostitution". *British Journal of Criminology*, 58: 255–272.

Jakobi, A. (2013) *Common Goods and Evils? The Formation of Global Crime Governance.* Oxford: Oxford University Press.

Janmyr, M. (2016) "The Effectiveness of Norway's Readmission Agreements with Iraq and Ethiopia". *International Migration*, 54(4): 5–17.

Johansen, N.B. (2013) "Governing the Funnel of Expulsion: Agamben, the Dynamics of Force, and Minimalist Biopolitics". In K.F. Aas and M. Bosworth (eds.), *The Borders of Punishment: Migration, Citizenship, and Social Exclusion.* Oxford: Oxford University Press.

Johansen, N.B. (2016) "Controlling Roma in Norway: Governing Through the Administration of Social Distance". In A. Ericsson (ed.), *Punishing the Other: The Social Production of Immorality Revisited.* Abingdon: Routledge.

Johansen, N.B., Ugelvik, T. and Aas, K.F. (eds.) (2013) *Krimmigrasjon? Den nye kontrollen av de fremmede.* Oslo: Universitetsforlaget.

Kanstroom, D. (2007) *Deportation Nation: Outsiders in American History.* Cambridge, MA: Harvard University Press.

Kanstroom, D. (2010) "The Right to Deportation Counsel in *Padilla v. Kentucky*: The Challenging Construction of the Fifth-and-a-Half Amendment". *UCLA Law Review*, 58 (2011): 1461–1514.

Kanstroom, D. (2012) *Aftermath: Deportation Law and the New American Diaspora.* Oxford: Oxford University Press.

Kanstroom, D. (2018) "Expedited Removal and Due Process: 'A Testing Crucible of Basic Principle' in the Time of Trump". *Washington and Lee Law Review*, 75(3). Available at https://scholarlycommons.law.wlu.edu/wlulr/vol75/iss3/5

Kaufman, E. (2015) *Punish & Expel: Border Control, Nationalism and the New Purpose of the Prison.* Oxford: Oxford University Press.

Khosravi, S. (2010) *"Illegal" Traveller: An Auto-Ethnography of Borders.* Basingstoke: Palgrave Macmillan.

Kmak, M. (2015) "'The Ugly' of EU Migration Policy: The Role of the Recast Reception Directive in Fragmentation of the Refugee Subject". In D. Gozdecka and M. Kmak (eds.), *Europe at the Edge of Pluralism* (Ius Commune Europaeum, 134). Cambridge, UK: Intersentia.

Knepper, P. (2010) *The Invention of International Crime: A Global Issue in the Making, 1881–1914.* Basingstoke: Palgrave Macmillan.

Kriminalomsorgen (2018) "Kriminalomsorgens årsstatistikk – 2018" [Norwegian Correctional Service Statistics], Available at: www.kriminalomsorgen. no/statistikk-og-noekkeltall.237902.no.html

Kubal, A. (2013) "Conceptualizing Semi-Legality in Migration Research". *Law & Society Review*, 47(3): 555–587.

Kuhn, T.S. (1996) *The Structure of Scientific Revolutions*, 3rd edition. Chicago: University of Chicago Press.

Lazarus, L., Goold, B. and Goss, C. (2013) "Control Without Punishment: Understanding Coercion". In J. Simon and R. Sparks (eds.), *The SAGE Handbook of Punishment and Society*. London: Sage.

Legomsky, S.H. (2007) "The New Path of Immigration Law: Asymmetric Incorporation of Criminal Justice Norms". *Washington & Lee Law Review*, 64 (2/3): 469–528.

Last, T.K., Mirto, G., Ulusoy, O., Urquijo, I.*et al.* (2017) "Deaths at the Borders Database: Evidence of Deceased Migrants' Bodies Found Along the Southern External Borders of the European Union". *Journal of Ethnic and Migration Studies*, 43: 693–712.

Levinas, E. (1969/1991) *Totality and Infinity*. Dordrecht: Kluwer Academic Publishers.

Lippert, R. and Pyykkönen, M. (2012) "Introduction: Immigration, Governmentality, and Integration Assemblages". *Nordic Journal of Migration Research*, 2(1): 1–5.

Loader, I. and Sparks, R. (2011) *Public Criminology?* London: Routledge.

Loftus, B. (2010) "Police Occupational Culture: Classic Themes, Altered Times". *Policing and Society*, 20(1): 1–20.

Lohne, K. (2018) "Penal Humanitarianism Beyond the Nation State: An Analysis of International Criminal Justice". *Theoretical Criminology*: 1–18. Published online 20 October. doi:10.1177/1362480618806917

Lyon, D. (2009) *Identifying Citizens: ID Cards as Surveillance*. Cambridge: Polity Press.

Lyotard, J.-F. (1984) *The Postmodern Condition: A Report on Knowledge*, trans. G. Bennington and G. Massumi. Minneapolis: University of Minnesota Press.

McLeod, A.M. (2012) "The US Criminal–Immigration Convergence and its Possible Undoing". *American Criminal Law Review*, 49: 105–178.

Maher, S. (2018) "Out of West Africa: Human Smuggling as a Social Enterprise". *Annals of the American Academy of Political and Social Science*, 676: 36–56.

Malkki, L.H. (1995) "Refugees and Exile: From 'Refuge Studies' to the National Order of Things". *Annual Review of Anthropology*, 24: 495–523.

Marcus, G.E. and E. Saka (2006) "Assemblage". *Theory, Culture & Society*, 23 (2/3): 101.

Mbembe, A. (2003) "Necropolitics". *Public Culture*, 15(1): 11–40.

Melossi, D. (2003) "'In a Peaceful Life': Migration and the Crime of Modernity in Europe/Italy". *Punishment & Society*, 5(4): 371–397.

Melossi, D. (2004) "The Cultural Embeddedness of Social Control". In T. Newburn and R. Sparks (eds.), *Criminal Justice and Political Cultures: National and International Dimensions of Crime Control*. Cullompton: Willan Publishing.

Melossi, D. (2013a) "People on the Move: From the Countryside to the Factory/Prison". In K.F. Aas and M. Bosworth (eds.), *The Borders of Punishment: Migration, Citizenship, and Social Exclusion*. Oxford: Oxford University Press.

Melossi, D. (2013b) "Punishment and Migration Between Europe and the USA: A Transnational 'Less Eligibility'?" In J. Simon and R. Sparks (eds.), *The SAGE Handbook of Punishment and Society*. London: Sage.

Melossi, D. (2015) *Crime, Punishment and Migration*. London: Sage.

Melossi, D., Sozzo, M. and Brandariz García, J.A. (eds.) (2017) *The Political Economy of Punishment Today: Visions, Debates and Challenges*. Abingdon: Routledge.

Menjívar, C. (2006) "Liminal Legality: Salvadoran and Guatemalan Immigrants' Lives in the United States". *American Journal of Sociology*, 111(4): 999–1037.

Menjívar, C. and Kanstroom, D. (2014) "Introduction – Immigrant 'Illegality': Constructions and Critiques". In C. Menjívar and D. Kanstroom (eds.), *Constructing Immigrant "Illegality": Critiques, Experiences, and Responses*. Cambridge: Cambridge University Press.

Milivojevic, S. (2019) *Border Policing and Security Technologies: Mobility and Proliferation of Borders in the Western Balkans*. Abingdon: Routledge.

Miller, D. (2016) *Strangers in our Midst: The Political Philosophy of Immigration*. Cambridge, MA: Harvard University Press.

Mitsilegas, V. (2010) "Extraterritorial Immigration in the 21st Century: The Individual and the State Transformed". In B. Ryan and V. Mitsilegas (eds.), *Extraterritorial Immigration Control: Legal Challenges*. Leiden: Nijhoff.

Mitsilegas, V. (2015) *The Criminalisation of Migration in Europe: Challenges for Human Rights and the Rule of Law*. Cham, Switzerland: Springer.

Moffette, D. (2018) "The Jurisdictional Games of Immigration Policing: Barcelona's Fight Against Unauthorized Street Vending". *Theoretical Criminology*: 1–18. Published online 4 November. doi:10.1177.1362480618811693.

Mohn, S.B. (2013) "Passet påskrevet: Utlendinger og kontroll i kriminalstatistikkens grenseland". In N.B. Johansen, T.Ugelvik and K.F. Aas (eds.), *Krimmigrasjon? Den nye kontrollen av de fremmede*, Oslo: Universitetsforlaget.

Mohn, S.B. (forthcoming) "Politiet i deportasjonsmaskinen" [Police in a deportation maskin], PhD thesis. Oslo: University of Oslo.

Morrison, T. (2017) *The Origin of Others*. Harvard, MA: Harvard University Press.

Neal, A.W. (2009) "Securitization and Risk at the EU Border: The Origins of FRONTEX". *Journal of Common Market Studies*, 47(2): 333–356.

Neumann, I.B. (1999) *Uses of the Other: "The East" in European Identity Forma-tion*. Manchester: Manchester University Press.

Newburn, T. and Jones, T. (2005) "Symbolic Politics and Penal Populism: The Long Shadow of Willie Horton". *Crime, Media, Culture*, 1(1): 72–87.

Newburn, T. and Sparks, R. (eds.) (2004) *Criminal Justice and Political Cultures: National and International Dimensions of Crime Control*. Cullompton: Willan Publishing.

Norsk Politi (2013) "Kunnskapspolitiet er i Støtet". *Norsk Politi*, 2: 14–16.

O'Brasill-Kulfan, K. (2019) *Vagrants and Vagabonds: Poverty and Mobility in the Early American Republic*. New York: New York University Press.

O'Connell Davidson, J. (2015) *Modern Slavery: The Margins of Freedom*. New York: Palgrave Macmillan.

Pallister-Wilkins, P. (2018) "Hotspots and the Geographies of Humanitarian-ism". *Environment and Planning D: Society & Space*: 1–18. Published online 25 January. doi:10.11770263775818754884

Parmar, A. (2011) "Stop and Search in London: Counter-terrorist or Counter-productive?" *Policing & Society*, 21(4): 369–382.

Parmar, A. (2019) "Arresting (Non)Citizenship: The Policing Migration Nexus of Nationality, Race and Criminalization". *Theoretical Criminology*: 1–19. Published online 27 May. doi:10.1177/1362480619850800

Pastore, F. (ed.) (2017) *Beyond the Migration and Asylum Crisis*. Rome: Aspen Institute.

Pauw, R. (2000) "A New Look at Deportation as Punishment: Why at Least Some of the Constitution's Criminal Procedure Protections Must Apply". *Administrative Law Review*, 52: 305–345.

Philippopoulos-Mihalopoulos, A. (2010) "Law's Spatial Turn: Geography, Justice and a Certain Fear of Space". *Law, Culture and the Humanities*, 7(2): 187–202.

Pickering, S. and Weber, L. (2013) "Policing Transversal Borders". In K.F. Aas and M. Bosworth (eds.), *The Borders of Punishment: Migration, Citizenship, and Social Exclusion*. Oxford: Oxford University Press.

Pijenburg, A., Gammeltoft-Hansen, T. and Rijken, C. (2018) "Controlling Migration Through International Cooperation". *European Journal of Migration and Law*, 20(4): 365–371.

Piquero, A.R., Bersani, B.E., Loughran, T.A. and Fagan, J. (2016) "Long-itudinal Patterns of Legal Socialization in First-Generation Immigrants, Second-Generation Immigrants, and Native-Born Serious Youthful Offen-ders". *Crime & Delinquency*, 62(11): 1403–1425.

Politidirektoratet (2010) *Utlendinger og kriminalitet. Kontroll, metode og sanksjoner – veileder*. Oslo: Politidirektoratet.

Pratt, A. and Valverde, M. (2018) "From Deserving Victims to 'Masters of Confusion': Redefining Refugees in the 1990s". *Canadian Journal of Sociology*, 27(2): 135–161.

Pratt, J. (2007) *Penal Populism*. London: Routledge.

Pratt, J. (2008) "Scandinavian Exceptionalism in an Era of Penal Excess". *British Journal of Criminology*, 48: 119–137.

Pratt, J. and Eriksson, A. (2012). *Contrasts in Punishment: An Explanation of Anglophone Excess and Nordic Exceptionalism*. London: Routledge.

Presser, L. and Sandberg, S. (eds.) (2015) *Narrative Criminology: Understanding Stories of Crime*. New York and London: New York University Press.

Prop. 181 L (2012–2013) "Endringer i utlendingsloven mv. (heving av strafferammen ved brudd på innreiseforbud)" [Changes in Immigration Act (Raising of Penalties for Breaches of an Entry Ban)]. Available at www.regjeringen.no/no/dokumenter/prop-181-l-20122013/id730821/sec1

Redfield, P. (2005) "Doctors, Borders, and Life in Crisis". *Cultural Anthropology*, 20: 328–361.

Reiter, K. and Coutin, S.B. (2017) "Crossing Borders and Criminalizing Identity: The Disintegrated Subjects of Administrative Sanctions". *Law & Society Review*, 51(3): 567–601.

Rose, N. (2010) "Screen and Intervene – Governing Risky Brains". *History of the Human Sciences*, 23(1): 79–105.

Ryan, B. and Mitsilegas, V. (2010) *Extraterritorial Immigration Control: Legal Challenges*. Leiden: Nijhoff.

Sætnan, A.R., Lomell, H.M. and Hammer, S. (2011) "By the Very Act of Counting – The Mutual Construction of Statistics and Society". In A.R Sætnan, H.M. Lomell and S. Hammer (eds.), *The Mutual Construction of Statistics and Society*. Abingdon: Routledge.

Sampson, R.J. (2008) "Rethinking Crime and Immigration". *Contexts*, 7(1): 28–33.

Sanchez, G. (2017) "Critical Perspectives on Clandestine Migration Facilitation: An Overview of Migrant Smuggling Research". *Journal on Migration and Human Security*, 5(1): 9–27.

Sanchez, G. (2018) "Five Misconceptions About Migrant Smuggling". Policy brief, European University Institute. Available at http://cadmus.eui.eu/bit stream/handle/1814/54964/RSCAS_PB_2018_07.pdf?sequence=1

Sandvik, K.B. (2010) "Unpacking World Refugee Day: Humanitarian Governance and Human Rights Practice?" *Journal of Human Rights Practice*, 2(2): 287–298.

Sausdal, D. (2018) *The Last Policeman: Local Police Concerns in a Global World*. Department of Criminology, Stockholm University: Stockholm University/ Akademitryck AB.

Schinkel, W. (2009) "'Illegal Aliens' and the State, or: Bare Bodies vs the Zombie". *International Sociology*, 24(6): 779–806.

Schrover, M.J., Leun, V., Lucassen, L. and Quispel, C. (2008) "Introduction: Illegal migration and gender in a historical perspective". In M.J. Schrover, V.

Leun, L. Lucassen and C. Quispel (eds.), *Illegal Migration and Gender in a Global and Historical Perspective*. Amsterdam: Amsterdam University Press.

Scott, J.C. (1998) *Seeing Like a State: How Certain Schemes to Improve the Human Condition have Failed*. Yale University Press.

Segrave, M., Milivojevic, S. and Pickering, S. (2018) *Sex Trafficking and Modern Slavery: The Absence of Evidence*. Abingdon: Routledge.

Simmel, G. (1964) *The Sociology of Georg Simmel*, trans., ed. and intro. by K. H. Wolff. New York: The Free Press.

Simon, J. (2007) *Governing Through Crime: How the War on Crime Transformed American Democracy and Created a Culture of Fear*. Oxford: Oxford University Press.

Simon, J. (2013) "Punishment and the Political Technologies of the Body". In J. Simon and R. Sparks (eds.), *The SAGE Handbook of Punishment and Society*. London: Sage.

Sivilombudsmannen (2015) *Besøksrapport: Politiets utlendingsinternat på Trandum 19.–21. mai 2015*. Available at www.sivilombudsmannen.no/wp-content/up loads/2017/04/Trandum-besøksrapport-2015.pdf

Skardhamar, T., Aaltonen, M. and Lehti, M. (2014). "Immigrant Crime in Norway and Finland". *Journal of Scandinavian Studies in Criminology and Crime Prevention*, 15(2): 107–127.

Skilbrei, M.-L. (2019) "The 'Normal' and the 'Other' Woman of Prostitution Policy Debates: New Concerns and Solutions". In M.-L. Skilbrei and M. Spanger (eds.), *Understanding Sex for Sale: Meanings and Moralities of Sexual Commerce*. Abingdon: Routledge.

Sklansky, D.A. (2012). "Crime, Immigration, and Ad Hoc Instrumentalism." *New Criminal Law Review*, 15(2): 157–223.

Slettvåg, K.K. (2016) "Å straffe ikke – borgere: En studie av brudd på innreiseforbud ". Master's thesis, Department of Criminology and Sociology of Law, University of Oslo.

Smith, P. (2008) *Punishment and Culture*. Chicago: University of Chicago Press.

Smith, P.S. and Ugelvik, T. (2017) *Scandinavian Penal History, Culture and Prison Practice: Embraced by the Welfare State?* London: Palgrave Macmillan.

Squire, V. (2011) *The Contested Politics of Mobility*. Abingdon: Routledge.

Stambøl, E.M. (2019) *The EU's Fight Against Transnational Crime in the Sahel*. Institute for European Studies Policy Brief, 2019/04.

Stephens, J. and McCallum, R. (1998) *Retelling Stories, Framing Culture: Traditional Story and Metanarratives in Children's Literature*. New York and London: Garland Publishing Inc.

Stone-Cadena, V. and Alvarez-Velasco, S. (2018) "Coyoterismo in the Indigenous Ecuadorian Migration Industry". *Annals of the American Academy of Political and Social Science*, 676: 194–211.

Strømnes, K.R. (2013) "'Jeg tror at demokratiet bare er for norske folk': utvisning og opplevelser av eksklusjon" ["I think democracy is just for

Norwegians": Deportations and experiences of social exclusion]. Master's thesis, University of Oslo.

Stumpf, J.P. (2006) "The Crimmigration Crisis: Immigrants, Crime, and Sovereign Power". *American University Law Review*, 56(2): 367–420.

Stumpf, J. (2013) "The Process is the Punishment in Crimmigration Law". In K.F. Aas and M. Bosworth (eds.), *The Borders of Punishment: Migration, Citizenship, and Social Exclusion*. Oxford: Oxford University Press.

Sykes, G.M. and Matza, D. (1957) "Techniques of Neutralization: A Theory of Delinquency". *American Sociological Review*, 22: 664–670.

Thompson, E.P. (1971) "The Moral Economy of the English Crowd in the Eighteenth Century". *Past & Present*, 50: 76–136.

Thompson, E.P. (1991) "The Moral Economy Reviewed". In E.P. Thompson (ed.), *Customs in Common*. London: Merlin Press.

Thorbjønsrud, K. (2015) "Framing Irregular Immigration in Western Media". *American Behavioral Scientist*, 59(7): 771–782.

Thorleifsson, C. (2019) *Nationalist Responses to the Crisis in Europe: Old and New Hatreds*. Abingdon: Routledge.

Ticktin, M. (2007) "Medical Humanitarianism in and Beyond France: Breaking Down or Patrolling Borders?" In A. Basford (ed.), *Medicine at the Border*. Basingstoke: Palgrave Macmillan.

Ticktin, M. (2011) *Casualities of Care*. Berkeley and Los Angeles: University of California Press.

Tinti, P. and Reitano, T. (2018) *Migrant, Refugee, Smuggler, Saviour*. London: Hurst.

Todd-Kvam, J. (2018) "Bordered Penal Populism: When Populism and Scandinavian Exceptionalism Meet". *Punishment & Society*, 21. doi:10.1177/1462474518757093

Torpey, J. (2000) *The Invention of the Passport: Surveillance, Citizenship and the State*. Cambridge: Cambridge University Press.

Travis, J. (2002) "Invisible Punishment: An Instrument of Social Exclusion". In M. Mauer and M. Chesney-Lind (eds.), *Invisible Punishment: The Collateral Consequences of Mass Imprisonment*, New York: The New Press.

Turnbull, S. (2017) "Immigration Detention and Punishment". *Criminology and Criminal Justice*, Oxford Research Encyclopedias. Available at http://criminology.oxfordre.com/view/10.1093/acrefore/9780190264079.001.0001/acrefore-9780190264079-e-231#acrefore-9780190264079-e-231-bibItem-0108

Turnbull, S. and Hasselberg, I. (2017) "From Prison to Detention: The Carceral Trajectories of Foreign-National Prisoners in the United Kingdom". *Punishment & Society*, 19(2): 135–154.

Ugelvik, S. and Ugelvik, T. (2013) "Immigration Control in Ultima Thule: Detention and Exclusion, Norwegian Style". *European Journal of Criminology*, 10(6): 709–724.

Ugelvik, T. (2012) "Imprisoned on the Border: Subjects and Objects of the State in Two Norwegian Prisons". In B. Hudson and S. Ugelvik (eds.), *Justice and Security in the 21st Century*. Abingdon: Routledge.

Ugelvik, T. (2013) "Seeing Like a Welfare State: Immigration Control, Statecraft, and a Prison with Double Vision". In K.F. Aas and M. Bosworth (eds.), *Borders of Punishment: Citizenship, Crime Control, and Social Exclusion*. Oxford: Oxford University Press.

Ugelvik, T. (2016) "Techniques of Legitimation: The Narrative Construction of Legitimacy Among Immigration Detention Officers". *Crime, Media, Culture*, 12(2): 215–232.

Ugelvik, T. (2017) "The Incarceration of Foreigners in European Prisons". In S. Pickering (ed.), *The Routledge Handbook on Crime and International Migration*. Abingdon and New York: Routledge.

Ugelvik, T. and Damsa, D. (2017) "The Pains of Crimmigration Imprisonment: Perspectives from a Norwegian All-Foreign Prison". *British Journal of Criminology*, 58(5): 1025–1043.

Ugelvik, T. and Dullum, J. (2012) *Penal Exceptionalism: Nordic Prison Policy and Practice*. London: Routledge.

Valier, C. (2003) "Foreigners, Crime and Changing Mobilities". *British Journal of Criminology*, 43(1): 1–21.

van der Ploeg, I. (1999) "The Illegal Body: 'Eurodac' and the Politics of Biometric Identification". *Ethics and Information Technology*, 1: 295–302.

Van der Woude, M.A.H., Barker, V. and Van der Leun, J.P. (2017). "Crimmigration in Europe". *European Journal of Criminology, 14*(1): 3–6.

Van der Woude, M. and Brouwer, J. (2017) "Searching for 'Illegal' Junk in the Trunk: Underlying Intentions of (Cr)immigration Controls in Schengen's Internal Border Areas". *New Criminal Law Review*, 20(1): 157–179.

Van der Woude, M. and Van der Leun, J. (2017) "Crimmigration Checks in the Internal Border Areas of the EU: Finding the Discretion That Matters". *European Journal of Criminology*, Vol. 14(1) 27–45.

Van der Woude, M.A.H., Van der Leun, J.P. and Nijland, J.A. (2014) "Crimmigration in the Netherlands". *Law & Social Inquiry*, 39(3): 560–579.

Van Houte, M. and Leerkes, A. (2019) "Dealing with (Non-)Deportability: A Comparative Policy Analysis of the Post-Entry Migration Enforcement Regimes of Western European Countries. Unu-Merit". Available at www. merit.unu.edu/to-return-or-not-to-return-how-various-european-states-dea l-with-deportation/

van Kalmthout, A.M., Hofstee-van der Meulen, F.B.A.M. and Dünkel, F. (eds.) (2007) *Foreigners in European Prisons*, vols 1 and 2. Nijmegen: Wolf Legal Publishers.

van Zyl Smit, D. and Snacken, S. (2009) *Principles of European Prison Law and Policy: Penology and Human Rights*. Oxford: Oxford University Press.

Vaughan-Williams, N. (2015) *Europe's Border Crisis: Biopolitical Security and Beyond*. Oxford: Oxford University Press.

Vazquez, Y. (2012) "Where Do We Go from Here? Advising Noncitizen Defendants on the Immigration Consequences of a Criminal Conviction After Padilla". *Fordham Urban Law Journal*, 38: 169.

Vecchio, F. (2015) *Asylum Seeking and the Global City*. Abingdon: Routledge.

Vigh, H. (2016) "Life's a Trampoline: On Nullification and Cocaine Migration in Bissau". In J. Cole and C. Groes (eds.), *Affective Circuits: African Migrations to Europe and the Pursuit of Social Regeneration*. Chicago and London: University of Chicago Press.

Vigneswaran, D. (2013) "Making Mobility a Problem: How South Africal Officials Criminalize Migration" in K.F. Aas and M. Bosworth (eds.), *The Borders of Punishment Migration, Citizenship, and Social Exclusion*. Oxford: Oxford University Press.

Villadsen, K. (2019) "Emergency Care Between State and Civil Society: The Open Clinic for Irregular Migrants". In S. Bendixen and T. Wyller (eds.), *Contested Hospitalities in a Time of Migration: Religious and Secular Counterspaces in the Nordic Region*. Abingdon: Routledge.

Von Hirsch, A. (1996) *Censure and Sanctions*. Oxford: Oxford University Press.

Vukov, T. (2003) "Imagining Communities Through Immigration Policies: Governmental Regulation, Media Spectacles and the Affective Politics of National Borders". *International Journal of Cultural Studies*, 6(3): 335–353.

Wacquant, L. (2009) *Punishing the Poor: The Neoliberal Government of Social Insecurity*. Durham, NC: Duke University Press.

Walker, N. (2003) "The Pattern of Transnational Policing". In T. Newburn (ed.), *Handbook of Policing*. Cullompton: Willan.

Walters, W. (2008) "Putting the Migration-Security Complex in Its Place". In L. Amoore and M. de Goede (eds.), *Risk and the War on Terror*. London and New York: Routledge.

Walters, W. (2010) "Deportation, Exclusion, and the International Police of Aliens". In N. De Genova and N. Peutz (eds.), *The Deportation Regime: Sovereignty, Space, and the Freedom of Movement*. Durham, NC: Duke University Press.

Watson, S. (2015) "The Criminalization of Human and Humanitarian Smuggling". *Migration, Mobility, & Displacement*, 1(1): 39–53.

Weber, L. (2013) *Policing Non-Citizens*. Abingdon: Routledge.

Weber, L. and Bowling, B. (2008) "Valiant Beggars and Global Vagabonds". *Theoretical Criminology*, 12(3): 355–375.

Weber, L. and Bowling, B. (2012) *Stop and Search: Police Power in Global Context*. Abingdon: Routledge.

Weber, L., Mohn, S.B., Vecchio, F. and Fili, A. (2019) "Beyond Deportation: Researching the Control of Outward Mobility Using a Space of Flows Logic". Published online 20 January. *Global Networks*. doi:10.1111/glob.12226

Weber, L. and Pickering, S. (2011) *Globalization and Borders: Death at the Global Frontier.* London: Palgrave Macmillan.

Westfeldt, L. (2008) *Migration som straff? Utvisning på grund av brott 1973–2003 med fokus på flyktningskydd.* Stockholm: Stockholm University.

Yıldız, C. and De Genova, N. (2018) "Un/free Mobility: Roma Migrants in the European Union". *Social Identities*, 24(4): 425–441.

Zedner, L. (2013) "Is the Criminal Law Only for Citizens? A Problem at the Borders of Punishment". In K.F. Aas and M. Bosworth (eds.), *The Borders of Punishment Migration, Citizenship, and Social Exclusion.* Oxford: Oxford University Press.

Zedner, L. (2016) "Citizenship Reprivation, Security and Human Rights". *European Journal of Migration and Law*, 18(2): 222–242.

Zureik, E. and Salter, M. (eds.) (2005) *Global Surveillance and Policing: Borders, Security, Identity.* Cullompton: Willan Publishing.

INDEX

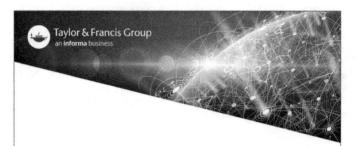

CPSIA information can be obtained
at www.ICGtesting.com
Printed in the USA
LVHW021823090921
697458LV00016B/1713

9 781138 545977